Black Women Affirmations and Emotional Self Care:

2 Powerful Books in 1 Boost Your Confidence & Mental Health in 90 Days. Daily Affirmations to Hack Your Mind to Positivity, Confidence, Health & Money.

999 Powerful Affirmations for Black Women:

Daily Affirmations to Hack your Mind to Positivity, Confidence, Health, Money, Success & Motivation. Learn to Overcome Anxiety and Depression in Modern World.

By reading this document, the reader agrees that under no circumstances is the author responsible for any losses, direct or indirect, which are incurred as a result of the use of information contained within this document, including, but not limited to, — errors, omissions, or inaccuracies.

Table of Content

About The Book

Have you ever imagined what your life would look like if you didn't entertain any form of negative talk around you? It would be really beautiful. In fact, it is one of the most beautiful things ever. You might raise your eyebrows in surprise and ask me if I am not aware that negative talking and self-sabotaging are inherent behaviours among people. I am very much aware of this, but you can work on eliminating all of that in your own space. You shouldn't let the norms and the things everyone else does dictate how you should live your life. You can reprogram your mind and create the life you want for yourself. It is no stroll in the park, but it is possible and I know that you can do it. Yes, you can do it even if you have no knowledge on how to go about it. You know, experts were once novices. This book exists to teach you just how to reprogram your life into the life that you desire. Read on and watch me unravel it all to you.

It is not unusual to find people who talk down on themselves simply because things are not going as they should for them. This behavior can make such people become blind to the magic in themselves. Each and everyone of us has our own magic and wonder. But you tell me, how can you see the magic in you when you blind yourself with negative talk and self-pity? How do you expect to get that job when all you do is rant on and on about how much you don't deserve it? What makes you think you are less qualified because you are a black woman? Why do you think you're not beautiful enough because you are not the standard the world is used to?

You may not realize the power of the words you speak to yourself until you sit and carefully analyze how much negativity has cost you and how powerful a single word could be. If you've been living a life of negativity to this point, I'm going to help you stop. Negativity is no thriving ground. Believe me, it is one of the worst places to be in. You should know this one truth; negativity has no advantage. Rather, it diminishes you continuously until you become one of the things you have always dreaded and hoped not to become. I know you don't want to walk that road at all. So, I'll help you attain great heights by exploring positivity and affirmations step by step.

999 Powerful Affirmations for Black Women will help you take all the big steps you need and help you live and create your ideal life through powerful words and speaking all that you want into your life. This book also has key points for every section. These key points are a summary of the section. Even if you're too busy to read the book word by word, you can go directly to the key points and get value from them. This book is written to serve you to the fullest. Get this book today and begin your journey into reprogramming your mind and becoming the badass Queen that you are meant to be. It is time to explore all of your magic. Shall we begin?

INTRODUCTION

It's the repetition of affirmations that leads to beliefs. And once that belief becomes a deep conviction, things begin to happen. —Muhammad Ali.

The first time I saw the quote above, it didn't make any sense to me. I wondered how things would begin to happen just because someone repeated a string of positive words. No matter how I tried to make sense out of it, it still sounded crazy to me. It was absurd. I only began to understand affirmations better when I began to associate with them deeply. Affirmations are way beyond saying 'today is a good day when you get up from bed in the morning. It is a thing of the heart and soul. It requires that you pour yourself into it without holding back anything at all. Affirmation is a lot of soul and inner energy and belief. That's why it requires consistency too.

I know you're getting curious here. Questions are brewing in your mind already, aren't they? Come along with me. I'll take you through what you need to know about affirmations. So, the first question is; what is an affirmation? It's a very simple answer. An affirmation is simply a positive, encouraging, strengthening and powerful statement that one makes to eliminate negative thoughts and fear. It's simply amazing, right? Yes, this simplicity is so powerful that it can turn your life around forever. It is a gradual but steady process.

First, you must understand that affirmation is not magic. You don't begin an affirmation today and expect it to work the very next moment. It is a process. There is no set time frame within which affirmations work. Rather, they work on their own volition. But I have come to learn that the greater my belief in my affirmations, the faster they all manifest. You gradually become the things you affirm. You have the rare ability to become anything that you speak into your being. Be it positivity or negativity. So, you make the choice. Would you choose negative talk or positive talk? The choice lies on you, but I encourage you to choose positivity. That's what this book is all about!

I remember calling affirmations bluff because I couldn't just fathom the working principles behind them. I mean, how could things become better because I said they would? I kept on doubting the power of affirmations until I came across an affirmation theory by Claude Steele which made me understand that affirmations work first by reworking the mind. It would take a negative mind a lot of work to actually experience the power of affirmations. This is because negativity has a way of blinding a person to the good things. Do you remember that one person who always made you feel like you were not doing enough no matter how much you tried? You'd feel as though you were the worst person on earth. You'd feel yourself crumbling from the inside. It is a very terrible way to feel. I know this first hand because I have had my own share of it in the past. If negative talk can get into one so much and make one feel very terrible, don't you think positive talk can also get to one and reshape things? I believe you get the drift now! This is how it works.

Descartes the philosopher wasn't joking at all when he said 'I think, therefore I am'. When you think of yourself as something and affirm that thing to yourself very often, it stays in your subconscious. At that level, your whole being would be convinced of that thing. You'll begin to manifest that thing.

I'll give you an example. I used to have this potted plant that I used in designing my home. When the gardener brought in this plant, it was very green and beautiful. It looked very tender and frail too. I appreciated the beauty of the plant and asked the gardener if the plant would last considering the fact that it looked really tender. You know what he told me?
He said 'it'll last as long as you nurture it'. His answer amazed me for a while. I wondered what he really meant by that answer. Every morning, I'd grumble while watering the plant because I expected it to die soon. I'd say 'Hey pretty one, I'll water you anyway. But I know you'll die soon...'
Then, the plant began to wither and die. This happened within a very short time! When I noticed it, I concluded that my prediction was right after all. I was like, 'I saw it coming all along! I knew you wouldn't make it far'. I called my gardener to let him know about the plant and he told me I fed the plant a lot of negativity. That it was only manifesting what I wished for. Boy, did that amuse me! A plant would die just because I said so! Tell me another tale, please.

I decided to 'nurture' the plant back to life by speaking good things to it while I watered every morning. I'd water and say 'my beautiful plant, look how you dazzled me today. See how green you are. So full of life and color. I love you, my plant...' this sounds weird to you, doesn't it? I'd have found it weird too if I didn't have this experience. After some time, my plant began to bounce back to life. It was like magic. It surprises me to this day. It was as though the plant could hear every single affirmation I made in its favour every morning. It was then I realized the power of positive affirmations and how they could affect everything around me in a good way.

Does my little encounter with my plant amaze you? You'll get further amazements in this book which is written for your gorgeous and amazing self. I understand the struggles black women go through each day in their quest to better their worlds and leave their own marks in the world. It's overwhelming sometimes, very much overwhelming. So I won't let you go through all of the stressful journeys alone. This affirmation book is written for you to strengthen you on days you feel like giving it all up, to speak peace and love and positivity into your life on days the fights within self threaten to overpower you, to share in your joys, to make you have more and more control over your life. You are the boss babe. Boss babes are in control of everything that concerns them.

Some people find it difficult to be consistent with making affirmations. If you are this kind of person, you don't have to be worried one bit. I have solutions for you. First of all, you must understand that every single thing is a process. It's just like the growth of children. Today, you see them crawling. Tomorrow you see them trying to stand on their own. Of course, they go through so many falls while at it. But that doesn't stop them from attaining balance because they'd eventually learn how to walk and run and even jump! That, my friend, is the beauty of the process. You walk despite the falls.

So, gorgeous black woman, believe me when I say it's okay that you don't know exactly how to go about this affirmation thingy. I've been in that place before. Now, I literally can't live without affirmations. I can't imagine starting my day without speaking positivity, power and strength into it first. Isn't this very surprising for someone who once said affirmations were empty talks? So, come with me. We'll go through your affirmation journey together. I am holding your hand through these pages on every step. There's no need to fret about a thing. I've got you! With this book, you'll get to know the power of affirmations in all its forms. You'll also enjoy the luxury of creating the kind of life that you have always dreamed of by speaking it into your life. Don't you think it is high time you let go of all the negativity that society, environment, toxic people and others once made you embrace? It is high time you shaped your space into your kind of life. Queens like you don't thrive in toxic spaces. I'll walk with you as you step out of those toxic spaces with self-affirmations. It's not a very easy journey, but trust me, it will be worth the while. Let us begin. But before we begin, I'd first answer that one question that many people have asked and still wonder about. When is the best time to say affirmations?

When Is The Best Time To Say Affirmations?

A lot of people have made different rules about the best time to say affirmations. The truth is; there are no rules to it. You can speak power into yourself and your whole existence at any time of the day and you would still get brilliant results.

Some people argue that morning is the best time for it. You know, the first thing you do after waking up from sleep. Making so many rules for affirmations could make it boring and difficult for you. So, it all lies on you to choose the most suitable time for you and stick to it. You could do it in the morning when you wake up, you could also do it in between the day while you go about your activities. Either of these are fine. But we advise you to try saying your affirmations in the morning before you get engrossed in the activities of the day. You know, once that happens, you may not get the time and concentration you need to say your affirmations the way you want to say them. Concentration is very vital in the making of good affirmations. Remember this always.

Now all you have to do is proceed with me to the next chapter as I welcome you into the world of life changing, powerful and beautiful affirmations.

The Beginning Before The Chapters.

Everyday's a chance to begin again. Don't focus on the failures of yesterday, start today with positive thoughts and expectations.
—Catherine Pulsifer

The title of this part of the book sounds really crazy, right? Well, a little fun would do a black woman no harm. So, this part of the book is some sort of mini section before the main chapters. Say, it is a sort of preamble to what you would get in the book.

I am dedicating this section to you and your day. The beginning of your days especially. You know, the beginning of a thing is the most important and most delicate part of it. It is for this reason that I'm writing this section sweetly and delicately just for you. There's something that I have noticed about myself. I don't know if it's that way with other people. How I begin my day plays a very crucial role in how it turns out. For instance, if I begin my day with a lot of negative energy and the acceptance of things that I do not want, it tends to affect the rest of my day. When I realized that, I began to take the beginnings much more seriously. Instead of gloating over my bulky workload first thing in the morning, I'd rather speak power and strength into my day. I'd speak these heart-felt and beautiful words of affirmation, bless my day and decree it a blessing.

I've been doing this for so long now that it has become an essential part of my routine. It is not just routine now, it is a habit. A very powerful one at that. I know you want to experience this kind of power too. I am ready and beyond willing to lead you into it. It is for this reason that I'll begin these affirmations. Now, hold my hand and journey with me through some delicate, warm and power-filled affirmations curated specially for the beginnings.

Affirmations for The Beginning

1. I declare my day a blessing.
2. Today, I choose joy and laughter. I'll laugh loudly and be joyful until the end.
3. I excel beyond doubts today.
4. I am in control of my day.
5. I'll not let anything steal my joy nor rob me of my peace.
6. I shine brilliantly like the sun.
7. Today is my day of rising, and I'll rise with so much elegance that the sun would become jealous of me.
8. I thrive in all areas of my life.
9. My day is full of excellence and unparalleled success.
10. I thrive everywhere.
11. I blossom like the morning sun.
12. I step away from every distraction that would ruin my day.

13. I perform beyond my expectations today.

14. Today, I choose myself.

15. I am a very beautiful work in progress.

16. I attract positivity today.

17. I know no bleakness today.

18. I am courageous enough to move away from the things
that no longer serve me.

19. I start my day with joy and end with joy.

20. I connect with people who are instrumental to the
achievement of my goals.

21. I dream big dreams today and they come to pass.

22. I do not struggle today.

23. I stand out with ease and elegance.

24. I live my biggest dreams.

25. I sing my best songs in the most sonorous of voices.

26. I am loved fully.

27. I am not overwhelmed by the activities of the day.

28. I have enough strength to help me get through my day.

29. I rid my day of stagnation.

30. I move forward in ease.

31. I reach my destinations safely.

32. I do not get into embarrassing situations.

33. I work with my head held high.

34. I do not cower to defeat.

35. I rise above obstacles.

36. I thrive in every place.

37. I am blessed in big measures.

38. I take advantage of opportunities.

39. I create my happiness.

40. I am aware of myself and the power I possess.

41. I give no one the power to toss me about.

42. I am fully in control of my life and that concerts me.

43. I am aware that I am more than enough.

44. I show myself as much care as I need.

45. I am independent and whole.

46. I do not stay in places that shrink me.

47. I have value to offer.

48. I'm so valuable that mediocrity hides at the sight of me.

49. I speak boldly and wisely.

50. I stand up for myself when the need arises.

51. I do not keep mum in uncomfortable situations.

52. My mental health is safe and healthy.

53. I am a big body of blessings.

54. My life is full of ease.

55. I know no difficulty.

56. I shine effortlessly.

57. I believe so much in myself.

58. I am no home to failure.

59. I am the Queen of my territory, and I am a Queen with pride.

60. I win.

61. I am better than I was yesterday.

62. I have all that I need to have a perfect day.

63. Today is a blessing.

64. Today is full of productivity.

65. I am happy to be alive.

66. I'll smile big smiles today.

67. I am open to learning new things.

68. I am the most wonderful person there is.

69. I know my worth.

70. I do not allow myself to be trampled upon.

71. I am in control.

72. Nothing can stop me from smashing today's goals.

73. I smash my goals with ease.

74. I am ready for today's success.

75. Today is a wonderful day.

76. I am positive about today.

77. I'll grow in new dimensions today.

78. I am elegance in human form.

79. I am full of peace.

80. Nothing can stop me.

81. I cheer myself into excellence.

82. I am full of intelligence and brilliant ideas.

83. I am super strong.

84. I am deserving of greatness.

85. I do not live in regrets.

86. I step into this day with new energy and warmth.

87. I do not focus on yesterday's failures.

88. Today is the best day of my life.

89. Today is a great day to try again.

90. I am strengthened enough to face today.

91. I will have a fulfilling day.

92. I live this day with power and strength.

93. I find joy in the small things.

Key Points

Do you feel these affirmations in your bones? Yes, I want you to feel them all. You have all it takes to have a day as beautiful as you desire. Today, step into the goodness of the day with these affirmations. I have curated the key points that you should remember often. Read them below!

- The beauty of your day is dependent on you.
- You have all it takes to have a wonderful day.
- Call your day blessed, and it will manifest that blessing.
- You are full of strength, remember this.
- You excel in great measures when you take all responsibility for yourself and your day.

Now that we are done with this beginning, let us saunter into a chapter that is set out to empower you as much as you desire. Shall we begin?

Chapter One

Affirmations for The Empowerment of The Black Woman

The empowerment of black women constitutes the empowerment of our entire community.
-Kimberle Williams Crenshaw

When I say black women empowerment is a necessity for the growth of society, I do not mean any jokes. It is one truth that we all must embrace. It is saddening that some parts of our world are yet to embrace the magic that is black women empowerment. I'm writing the first chapter of this book for black women empowerment and for all the struggles that black women have had to face in their quest to create a better society.

Once, I met a black woman crying on a bus. She looked so pained and troubled. I tried to get close to her when we both alighted. There was something about her that kept on pulling me to her. She smiled at me and wiped off the tears after I calmed her down. Then she told me her story. She said she was being oppressed at work by her superior colleagues just because she refused to bow to their crazy rules and tough working conditions at a low pay. In her words, 'they made me understand that I was asking for too much. That I wasn't worth all that...' she broke into tears before she could finish up what she was saying. Even with all that pain and anger, the young woman wouldn't bow to a thing that like that. I found it really beautiful. I left her with a hug and some words of encouragement.

I know there are lots of women like the one I encountered on the bus. Women going through stress and getting disrespected while at it. Women shrinking themselves for small people. Women dimming their lights to entertain people with small minds. It it is for these women that I write these black women empowerment affirmations in this chapter. For the women in business and the corporate world, the women in quest of success and the women just starting out in business. This chapter is all yours! Come with me as I take you through affirmations just for you.

Business Affirmation

1. Today, I excel in my work spaces.
2. I attract wonderful contracts with good pay.
3. I am large enough to contain all of the things I seek.
4. I have an active brain that can conjure up the best business ideas.
5. I am an overflowing well of intelligence.
6. I do not falter in my pursuit for business excellence.
7. My black excellence precedes me and no workspace can steal that from me.
8. I welcome good jobs and offers into my life.
9. Toxic workspaces would flee at the sight of me.
10. I am too big to accommodate small minds.
11. My business blooms despite all hurdles and discouragement.
12. I am the queen in my kingdom and nothing on earth can bring me down.
13. I am in control of my businesses.
14. The market conditions would tilt towards helping me fulfil my goals.
15. I am made for so much more.
16. I am a breathing body of excellence.
17. I am worthy of the best working conditions.
18. I wine and dine with the best people in my industry.
19. I seal the best business deals with grace and ease.

20. I'll not be broken by my quest for better opportunities.

21. I don't write business applications in vain.

22. I am ready to take over my industry with my intelligence and business sense.

23. My best is more than enough.

24. I do not labour to be left empty in the end.

25. I invite ease into my workspace

26. There is no room for toxicity in my business.

27. My customers will come back to me because I offer the best kind of value.

28. I grow everyday and I excel in the newest things.

29. I open my business to the best grants and developments.

30. My business works in sync with the emancipation of other black women from bad jobs.

31. I bounce back much greater from falls and setbacks.

32. I don't lose my business to fear.

33. My zeal grows.

34. I am not shallow minded.

35. My business acumen opens great doors for me.

36. My workspace is rid of every oppression.

37. I welcome great team members into my space.

38. I don't struggle to shine.

39. I am so much of an asset to be ignored.

40. No amount of work pressure has the power to end me.

41. I give no power to any boss who desires to make me shrink into myself.

42. I lead in the workspace.

43. Being a woman is no limitation for me.

44. History would write my name in bold prints for the good work I do.

45. I take charge of my business today. I leave nothing to chance.

46. Good jobs will find me with ease.

47. I do excellent work. There is no space for mediocre things in me.

48. I am ready to learn new skills and implement the knowledge into the betterment of my businesses.

49. The losses I record do not define the future of my business.

50. My mistakes are not the only things there are to me. I am so much more.

51. I am uniquely creative.

52. I'll utilize my skills and talents in my journey towards excellence.

53. I have all the courage I need to do what I want.

54. I will take advantage of every opportunity to learn and improve on myself.

55. I am ever willing to do the needed work to achieve my goals.

56. I am deserving of security in my finances.

57. I am never going to live from hand to mouth.

58. I manifest the life of my dreams.

59. I welcome financial abundance into my life.

60. My destiny lies in my own hands.

61. I create my own success.

62. All of my dreams are achievable.

63. I have value to offer.

64. I market my skills and not self-pity.

65. My hard work pays off in a hundred folds.

66. I have all it takes to reach the heights I desire.

Key Points

There are essential points that you must note in this session. I understand that you may not be able to memorize all of these affirmations in a single read. This is why I'm making the major affirmations you need to remind yourself of everyday into beautiful and lucid key points that your mind can recall with ease. Whenever your workplace begins to cause you pain or when the empowerment of self becomes difficult, say this to yourself with all the boldness in the world and forge ahead like the Queen that you are.

- You have all it takes to be fully empowered.
- You too can thrive amidst all the hurdles, negativity and stress.
- You have the power to change your life for the best.
- The emancipation of the black woman is true freedom.
- You are powerful enough to create the life of your dreams.
- Your creativity flows in abundance.

Do you feel like an underachiever sometimes? It's not a foreign feeling to me at all. I'd look around me and find everyone excelling at something, but I'm not. The thing is this; other people would see the things I do and call them success. But they don't even impress me in any way. That is the thing with black women. They are high fliers and lovers of success. They love to make huge impacts in their respective fields. Be it business or entrepreneurship. The corporate space is not left out too. Black women go all out for excellence or nothing. You know the popular phrase saying 'go big or go home?' Black women heard it, and they listened. And they took it literally.

But if we keep on overlooking how far we have come and focusing only on the things we want at the moment, it could ruin us in many ways. Don't you think so? For instance, you want a job at a big firm so much that you put all of your energy into getting the job. Your hard work pays off and you get this job. Two years later, you see a much bigger firm that you are interested in. You try to get into the firm on your first attempt, but you don't. Instead of getting depressed over the rejection, why not try a different approach?

Commend yourself for trying, then you look out for the mistakes you made and things you didn't do well. Then you restrategize and try again. Doing this would get you the job faster because you won't make the same mistakes ever again. This is way better than gloating. This, my dear, is the right approach to success. Your determination, hard work and faith in yourself is all that matters. And never forget how far you have come.

There is no force equal to a woman determined to rise-W.E.B Dubois.

Remember this quote often and let it reaffirm your belief in yourself. You are a force. A very great one. When you set out to achieve a thing, there's nothing that can stop you unless you give it the permission to do so. Yes, you are that powerful. We will affirm success into the whole of our beings in this section. So, let's dive into some success affirmations in style.

Success Affirmations

1. Success knows me by my name.
2. My failure is not the end of the road for me.
3. I rise into my greatness like the morning sun.
4. I succeed in every aspect of my life.

5. I am a force that can never bend to failure.

6. I do not quit, I try again, and I win.

7. I have all it takes to be successful in this life.

8. I disengage myself and all that is mine from failure.

9. I succeed in my finances.

10. I succeed in my relationships.

11. I open myself to relationships that would lead me to my success.

12. Success is my destiny.

13. I am not fated to be a failure.

14. I am a winner, and I'll do what winners do. Win.

15. I succeed even in places where people struggle.

16. I step into my greatness with so much elegance.

17. I am smart.

18. I dictate all that goes on in my life.

19. I make good decisions.

20. I stand up to my fears.

21. I stand up to everything working against my success.

22. I shut out every self-sabotaging thought from my mind.

23. I cleanse my heart of negative thoughts.

24. I have the strength I need to get my heart desires.

25. I am invincible.

26. Nothing on earth has the power to break me.

27. I utilize my potential to the fullest.

28. I give my all to good causes

29. I step out of the norm.

30. I am not made for small things.

31. I am large enough to accommodate big things.

32. I work hard at my goals and aspirations.

33. I will not be found sleeping when I should be working.

34. I am my own competition.

35. I draw strength from all the times that I have had to try again.

36. My success is not measured by that of others.

37. No one has the power to bring me down.

38. I give myself the permission to stretch my creativity as much as I desire.

39. I am worthy of greatness.

40. I am worthy of all the good things I worked for.

41. Mediocrity has no place in my life.

42. I am the standard.

43. I am becoming the successful black woman I have always dreamed of.

44. I embrace my strengths and I work on my weaknesses.

45. I accept my weaknesses. They don't define me.

46. I am the most intelligent woman in the room.

47. My determination pays off in grand styles.

48. My big dreams are coming to fruition.

49. My dreams are valid and that is what matters.

50. I flourish on every side.

51. I bloom on the roughest grounds.

52. I am not consumed by fear.

53. I will climb all the high places I want to be in with no fear.

54. Success clings to me.

55. My success is not a one time thing. It is my lifestyle.

56. I take advantage of opportunities.

57. I breathe excellence.

58. I am growing on every side.

59. I accommodate no sub-standard things.

60. I am originality in all its forms.

61. I have an active brain.

62. I create the opportunities.

63. My success doesn't rest on anyone but me.

64. No one can pull me down.

65. Everything works in my favor.

66. I am sought after because of my greatness.

67. I am the best in my field.

68. I excel much more than I dreamt of.

69. I am living my biggest dream.

70. No one can belittle me.

71. I have a functional head on my shoulders. I am not shallow nor empty.

I bet you love these success affirmations. They are all yours, make sure to use them to the fullest. When obstacles threaten to hinder your success, affirm these and watch everything play out in your favor. Below are the key points for this section.

- You possess all that you need to become successful.
- You excel the most when you embrace your strengths and weaknesses
- You have the ability to stretch yourself as much as you want.
- Your brain is a reservoir of success, you only have to use it optimally.
- Success knows you by your name.

Affirmations For The Black Woman Who Is Just Starting Out In Business

A big business starts small.
—*Richard Branson*

A lot of black women shy away from starting their own businesses because of fear. You know, fear is so powerful that it can make the best women doubt their own intelligence. But, fear won't overpower you unless you give it the permission to do so. I understand that you are afraid to start because you are afraid it would flop. I understand that there is a lot of competition in the business space. I understand that you want to have a big structure first. I understand that you want nothing short of perfection. But, you must understand that none of these can even happen if you don't begin at all. Business is a lot of risk, but the risk is worth taking, trust me. You might decide to shut away your business dreams by working for someone else. But this won't lead to the actualization of your own dream, would it? It's either you build your own dream or you build someone else's. That's how it works. I'm pretty sure it is your own dream that you desire to build and not someone else's.

Your fears are valid, but you can overcome them by going into business prepared. How can this preparation be done? Take your time and study about business, take courses, learn from the experts and study the market. Mind you, doing all these doesn't guarantee that you'd make no losses. Rather, it reduces the occurrence of the losses and helps you manage them better when they happen. Business is a game of profits and losses. Let this stick to your mind.

In this section, I'll take you through powerful affirmations that'll strengthen you as you begin your start up. Yes, you can excel well in business too. Or, don't you remember that anything black is synonymous with excellence? Now, come with me as I affirm the most positive affirmations for your new business!

1. My business is full of ease.
2. I succeed with grace.
3. Everyday, I get closer to my biggest dream.
4. My small business is preparing me for my big business.
5. I start small and end big.

6. My business is the best there is.

7. I attract supportive people.

8. I'll record more and more profits.

9. I believe in my vision.

10. I can achieve anything I put my mind to.

11. My business will know no hurdles.

12. I celebrate my growth and how far I have come.

13. I did not come this far to end here.

14. I have the ability to transform obstacles into opportunities.

15. There are no limitations to how far I can go.

16. My plans come to pass with ease.

17. I love and enjoy my business.

18. I am on the path that leads to fulfillment.

19. I am on the path that leads to the actualization of purpose.

20. Stumbling stones are stepping stones to me.

21. I am not consumed by the challenges that new businesses face.

22. I am found in the places that I need to be.

23. My business opens great doors for me.

24. I am at the place I am supposed to be.

25. Negativity has no place in me.

26. All the work I put in is coming back to me with great results.

27. I excel a lot more than my former self.

28. I reach my zenith with great ease.

29. I leverage on my strengths and work on my weak points.

30. I build my own dreams and not someone else's.

31. I have enough strength and zeal to do what it takes for the betterment of my business.

32. I attract the perfect customers.

33. I am confident in my abilities to excel.

34. I create the best name for myself in my business.

35. I dissociate myself and my business from all negative energies.

36. I do not struggle to be seen. I am as visible as the sun.

37. I am grateful for how far I have come and for the places I am reaching.

38. I manifest my financial goals.

39. I take advantage of every opportunity.

40. I am strengthened by all the times I have had to try again.

41. I derive joy and peace from my business.

42. My clients love what I do.

43. I make great investments.

44. I am not broken by market fluctuations.

45. Impossibility is non-existent in my space.

46. I manage my business on my own terms.

47. I make the best decisions for my business.

48. I attract hardworking people.

49. I am blessed with enough resources.

50. I am driven by passion.

51. I am unyielding to weakness and hopelessness.

52. I attract loyal and responsible customers.

53. I retain customers with ease.

54. I am a passionate and reliable business person.

55. I meet my business targets before the deadlines.

56. I accomplish difficult tasks with smiles on my face.

57. I am enthusiastic about achieving my goals.

58. I break new records every day.

59. Money flows into my business from every corner.

60. I open my business to abundance and huge profits.

61. I am financially secure.

62. All my dreams are coming true.

63. I don't try too hard before I win.

64. Excellence is by lifestyle.

65. I have all the emotional intelligence I need to interact well with my clients.

66. I have all I need to expand my business as much as I want to.

67. My vision is my drive.

68. My name is mentioned when the greats are mentioned.

69. No one does it better than me.

70. My strategies are more than efficient to help me in the actualization of my dreams.

Key Points

This section is all about the black woman starting out in business. I know these affirmations will strengthen you as much as you let it. Below are the key points for this session.

- You'll excel more in business if you prepare before going into It.
- Businesses are risks worth taking.
- You have all it takes to be successful in business.
- It is okay to be afraid of venturing into business.
- Small businesses grow to become big businesses.
- You are the captain of your business.
- There are no limitations to how far you can go.

Now that we are done with the first chapter of this book, hold my hand and let us proceed to the second together. This time, it's not about empowerment, not business. It's about the core of our very existence, self-love. Let's dig in!

Chapter Two

I am The Absolute Love of My Own Life; Self-Love And The Black Woman

To fall in love with yourself is the first secret to happiness.
—Robert Morley

How you love yourself is how you teach others to love you.
—Rupi Kaur.

When I talk about self-love, I remember people who think making fancy posts on social media with the caption 'self-love' is all there is to actually loving one's self. No darling, it is way deeper than that. Loving yourself is beyond making posts on it on social media or just muttering you love yourself.

So, what does self-love really entail? Self-love is all about taking care of yourself in all areas. Taking care of your physical body, your mental health and your emotional health. Self-love makes you realize that you come first in your own life. Yes, not even your partner nor your career nor love should come first. That spot is reserved for you and you alone. It is self-love that nudges you to step out of places that shrink you and depreciate you. It is the amount of love that you have for yourself that would show people how to treat you. You don't have to sacrifice your well being for anyone just because you want to make the person comfortable or happy. I remind you again, you come first in your life.

Also, self-love is one of the greatest recipes for true happiness. Robert Morley reaffirms this. He says to fall in love with yourself is the first secret to happiness. Are you unhappy? Could it be that you are yet to fall truly in love with yourself? Yes, it is actually possible not to love one's self. When you neglect your well being and go after things that diminish you, it is a sign that you don't love yourself. And, self-love goes hand in hand with happiness. So, you must first love yourself. It is the first and most important step you need to take in your pursuit of happiness.

One more thing. Self-love doesn't rob you of empathy. You can love yourself and still love other people too. You only have to show yourself a greater amount of love. You know, you can't really love other people well if you don't know how to love yourself. Crazy, right? But it is the one truth. It takes a great amount of self-love to be able to love others. And for this reason, you must love you first. This chapter will be all about self-love and care because I care deeply about your well being. I'll hold you gently in this chapter and guide you as you fall in love with yourself all over again. Let's go!

I Come First In My Own Life.

1. I love myself endlessly.
2. I am the most important person in my life and I treat myself as such.
3. I do not shrink myself to make people feel good.
4. I am not consumed by the negative energies of other people.
5. My well being is my priority.
6. I love myself with all that is in me and all that I am.
7. I am not trampled upon.
8. I am deserving of my own affection and care.
9. I fall endlessly in love with myself.
10. I love myself wholly so I can love others.
11. I choose myself.
12. I allow no one to make me feel guilty for choosing myself.

13. I matter greatly.

14. I am the number one in my own life.

15. I am exceedingly great and important.

16. I care for myself with grace and ease.

17. I glow with love.

18. I invest in myself because I am my greatest asset.

19. I am so full of love and warmth.

20. I love myself fully and I hold back nothing.

21. I am generous with self-care.

22. I take breaks when necessary.

23. I take a rest when I get tired. I will not quit.

24. I am the best cheerleader I could ever have.

25. I embrace myself with elegance.

26. I am more than enough.

27. I am the truest love of my life.

28. I grow into the best version of myself.

29. I love myself more everyday.

30. I am the most gorgeous person on earth.

31. I am beautifully unique.

32. I am surrounded by pure love.

33. Loving myself is easy for me.

34. I am worthy of love.

35. I love myself with no reservations.

36. I do not struggle to accept myself.

37. I am the best thing that can happen to me.

38. I am a body of beauty and perfection.

39. I am deserving of all the care that I get.

40. I am my topmost priority.

41. I am the best there is.

42. I am the brightest star there is.

43. I do not soil myself with hate and toxicity.

44. I love myself enough to walk out of negative spaces.

45. I love myself enough to walk away from people who do not love me.

46. I am the greatest validation I could ever seek.

47. I am the perfection I crave.

48. I care for my mental health with ease.

49. I love myself no matter what happens.

50. I am so full of love to accommodate any strand of hate.

51. My love for myself flows like a river.

Key Points

This section is written to remind you that you come first in your own life. Yes, you are the loveliest love of your own life. Never let anyone tell you otherwise. I have made this section into brief and concise points that you should recall and dwell in as often as you can.

- You come first in your own life.
- People can only love you as much as you love yourself.
- You are deserving of love and affection.
- You become happier when you learn to love yourself with no reservations.
- You are the greatest validation you could ever seek.
- You should never shrink yourself to make people happy at your own expense.
- You are worth it. You are more than enough.

Loving Myself Again After A Terrible Experience.

In order to love who you are, you cannot hate the experiences that shaped you.
—Andrea Dykstra.

Have you ever hated yourself, dear black woman? Do you hate yourself? Asking these questions feels weird, right? When people are asked if they hate themselves, the most popular reaction is a cursory look and some wonderment. I mean, why would you hate yourself? Does this imply that there are people who do not hate themselves?

Just as there are people who love themselves with all of their beings, there are also people who hate themselves deeply. I know you're getting more interested here. People hate themselves for different reasons. For some, self-hate could be sponsored by illnesses like depression and the likes. For some, the hate stems from a feeling of worthlessness. You know, feeling like you aren't worth a thing. Feeling at the bottom of the world. Feeling like you belong to the decrepit. And for some, the hate stems from bad experiences and not so good choices.

This section is going to be focused only on this last category of people. People who hate themselves for the choices and mistakes they made. Mistakes and regrets make a fine and strong pair because the latter comes after the former. But, you must understand that both of them are parts of our existence. We can't eliminate them totally, but we surely can avoid them and we also have the power not to let them decide our lives for us. Yes, I'm powerful like that. You too are powerful. Much more than you know.

Like Andrea Dykstra made us know in the beginning of this section, you cannot love yourself if you go about detesting the experiences that shaped you. You cannot experience the full impact of love for self if you keep on gloating about your mistakes. You have to embrace them as a part of your life. Then you forge ahead and love yourself. This, my dear, is how it all works. So, let's go on another self-love and acceptance trip. Shall we?

Affirmations On Loving Myself Again After All of My Mistakes and Bad Choices

1. My mistakes and terrible choices do not define my whole life.
2. I see my mistakes as stepping stones that led me to the actualization of my truest self.
3. I love myself despite my errors and flaws.
4. I love and accept myself wholly.
5. I learn from my mistakes.
6. I accept all of the things that shaped me.
7. I am the best version of myself.
8. I cherish myself greatly.
9. I do not repeat my mistakes.
10. I am grateful for the learning experience my bad choices offered me.
11. I am not consumed by my mistakes.
12. My heart is healed of all the pains my mistakes caused me.
13. I refuse to wallow in pain and self-pity.
14. I am exceedingly kind to myself.
15. I am so full of love.
16. My life is beautiful.
17. I find joy in living.
18. My heart overflows with peace.
19. I am very proud of who I am becoming.

20. I have the unique ability to create the love I need and dwell in it.

21. I have made peace with my past self.

22. I do not wallow in the past for I do not belong there anymore.

23. I do not judge myself for the mistakes I have made.

24. I embrace joy in abundance.

25. I am unapologetically myself and that is enough.

26. I choose myself everyday.

27. I have inner peace and nothing can take it away from me.

28. I do not give my past the power to steal my joy.

29. There is so much love inside me.

30. I am the best of my kind.

31. I am powerful.

32. I meet my expectations with ease.

33. My mistakes do not reduce my worth.

34. I am not ashamed to seek help.

35. I pay great attention to my body and its needs

36. I trust in all of my abilities.

37. I do not go back to the things that broke me.

38. I love the woman I see in the mirror everyday.

39. I bear so much in me and I will shine brilliantly for all the world to see.

40. I throw away all the negative baggage that delays my journey.

41. I am full of strength.

42. I love myself and all that I am fiercely.

43. I protect myself from all forms of toxicity.

44. My soul is home to a lot of beauty.

45. I bloom with so much grace.

46. I thrive everywhere.

47. I write my story with joy.

48. I am gentle and loving to myself.

49. I sing my best songs and live my best days.

50. I attract kindness and love.

We have come to the end of this chapter. I hope you enjoyed our journey through it. Before we begin another trip of affirmations in the next chapter, I'll leave you with key points for this section. Dig in!

Key Points

- Your mistakes and bad choices do not define you.
- You can rise again from the most terrible events.
- Happiness begins the moment you embrace all of the events that shaped you into your present self.
- You are more than enough.
- Seeking help is no weakness.
- Tell your story with pride. Own it.

Chapter Three

Anxiety And Its Throes

Worrying doesn't empty tomorrow of its sorrow, it empties today of its strength.
—Corrie Ten Boom.

Everyone of us has experienced anxiety in our lives one way or the other. You know, it is our nature to panic, worry and get troubled over things that bother us. We love solutions and not problems. Before I go on and on about anxiety and its throes, it'll be beautiful if I explain what anxiety means in very lucid terms, right? I'll do just that.

Anxiety is a disorder that's characterized by excessive worrying, panic attacks, fright, abnormal sweating and lots of other factors. Anxiety arises when we try to meet up with expectations, do stuff right, meet deadlines. All these and every other thing that has the tendency to bother you and steal your peace can lead to anxiety. A lot of black women often wonder if anxiety can set in independently. This is almost impossible because anxiety must have a trigger.

Your own thoughts and imaginations can trigger anxiety in you. Other people can make you anxious too.

When I was younger, I used to have this crush who made me feel butterflies. I never confessed to the crush because I feared getting rejected so much. I'd tell my friends all about what I felt but I never told the crush. I felt a lot of anxiety. Maybe I'd have not felt all that anxiety if I ever confessed to the crush. Who knows? My friends would always egg me on to confess to the crush. I'd get sweaty palms and itchy armpits because of anxiety. What am I driving that? I'm letting you know that emotions also have the ability to trigger anxiety. In fact, emotions are one of the most powerful things ever. Tell me, have you ever broken a resolve because your emotions came into play? See? Emotions are very powerful, and they can overwhelm you easily if you do not learn how to tame them. Anxiety can mess up your mental health if you give it the chance to do it.

You can overcome anxiety by dealing with that one thing that triggers it. If you try to stop the anxiety without first dealing with the triggers, you might as well be fighting a losing battle. So, gorgeous soul, you have to first deal with the causes of your anxiety. Funny thing is some of these triggers are not things that can be easily eliminated. Say work deadlines for example, they would always be there. In cases like that, try to remind yourself of the power and mastery that you possess. Why worry about a deadline that you'd meet in the end? No reason at all! Worrying only robs you of strength and joy, try your possible best not to indulge it every time.

The good news is that you don't have to bear the burdens of anxiety all alone. I'll help you overcome it and become the relaxed and graceful Queen that you are through affirmations written just for you. Hold my hand and let's begin!

Affirmations for Strength Against Anxiety.

1. I am much stronger and powerful than my anxiety.
2. I meet my deadlines with ease and grace.
3. I do not stutter while presenting my incredible ideas.
4. Everything works in my favor.
5. Nothing is out to hunt me down.
6. I am safe, nobody is after my life.
7. My past experiences have no power over my success.
8. I am relaxed.
9. I have the power to restore calmness to my life.
10. I am calm and hopeful.

11. I refuse to panic.

12. There is no fear in my veins but courage and strength.

13. I can overcome anything in the world.

14. I am set out for victory.

15. I create paths in blocked places.

16. I have survived a lot of bad days. I'll survive this one too.

17. Stress has no power nor control over my life.

18. I do not palpitate when all I need to do is think.

19. I breathe with ease.

20. There is so much happiness in my life.

21. I can handle this one too.

22. Success knows my name and it calls me in a loud voice.

23. I am in control of my life.

24. I am in control of the situation.

25. I am beautiful and I am deeply loved.

26. I distance myself from panic and fear.

27. I am patient enough to handle the most difficult situations.

28. I breathe out all the fear holding me back.

29. I take up difficult tasks without breaking a sweat.

30. I can sail above anxiety.

31. I eliminate all that triggers my anxiety with elegant ease.

32. I have so much talent and I put it into use by doing good work.

33. I am a badass.

34. I'm indefatigable. Nothing can break me.

35. I am too defiant to be broken by anxiety.

36. I pay no heed to the lies that anxiety tells me.

37. I shut out all the negative voices in my head.

38. I guard my sanity with all my might.

39. I control my breaths as much as I want to.

40. I do good work without getting broken.

41. I have no doubts about the value I offer.

42. I get great jobs because I am amazing at what I do.

43. I talk about my brand with all the courage in the world.

44. The faith I have in myself is enough.

45. Negative thoughts do not belong with me.

46. I am larger than my anxiety.

47. I do not give in to irrational fear.

48. I give my best to my job and I do not flop at it.

49. My best is enough.

50. I grow my brand with zeal and joy.

Key Points

My dear, I believe this section has strengthened you against anxiety and its troubles. You can overcome anxiety when you acknowledge the power you possess. With this power, kill anxiety and live your life with ease. I have curated a few salient points that you should recall often. Find them below!

- You are bigger than your anxiety.
- You have all it takes to end your anxiety.
- Anxiety does nothing positive for you. Rather, it robs you of your peace and hinders your productivity.
- Anxiety is inevitable sometimes, but you have the power to shut it out.
- The faith you have in yourself is more than enough.
- Everyone isn't set out to cause your downfall like anxiety made you believe.

Anxiety Management Affirmations For The Overwhelmed Black Woman

Sometimes, everything becomes overwhelming. Most people think anxiety comes in only when things are going wrong. No, this is not true at all. You can also become anxious when things are going just fine for you.

Sometimes, I get overwhelmed with all the good days and wonder why I was having a lot of good days. Sounds crazy, right? But this is actually a thing. Good days can be as overwhelming as bad days. Also, anxiety can also set in when you have a standard to maintain. For example, you are the best student in your school. Getting the best result is your standard, your lifestyle. Even without trying so hard, you'd subconsciously desire to maintain that standard or supersede it even. Performing below your standard could lead to a lot of anxiety for you.

When anxiety begins to steal the shine in your life, don't make the mistake of waiting for it to go away. Deal with it the very moment it steps in. Deal with the disturbing thought and deal with the panic before it grows into something you cannot handle easily. Also, remind yourself that you are the boss. Bosses take charge, you take charge. Speak to that anxiety and have it bow to your command. Affirmations can help you manage your anxiety as much as you want. So, come with me let us walk with all elegance through these anxiety management affirmations.

1. I manage my anxiety with ease.

2. I take charge of my responsibilities well.

3. I am deserving of all the good things that happen to me.

4. I do not run away from taking big steps.

5. I make good decisions.

6. I am not overwhelmed by worries.

7. I do not attract stress and hard labour.

8. I am excellent at managing my anxiety.

9. I don't give up when it gets tough.

10. I have enough time to chase my priorities.

11. I give all my attention to the things that matter.

12. I am in control of all my emotions.

13. I starve myself of my distractions.

14. I dissociate myself from everything that stops me from doing my duties well.

15. I manage my time effectively to accommodate all that I need to do.

16. I step into my powers with ease.

17. I do not know how to give up.

18. My anxiety can never steal my shine.

19. I stand tall despite my anxiety.

20. I bounce back bigger and better.

21. I am deserving of every good thing I get.

22. I can fix this one too.

23. I am great at handling things.

24. I do not bow to pressure.

25. I go through this difficult phase and come out unscathed.

Key Points

- You have all it takes to control your anxiety.
- Anxiety doesn't last forever, neither does pressure. You'll get through them.
- You are deserving of good things, do not let them overwhelm you.
- You are great at dealing with your responsibilities.

Affirmations For Black Women Battling Anxiety

Every day, thousands of black women battle with anxiety in various forms. In their homes, workplaces, personal lives and a myriad of other places. Dealing with any form of mental trouble could be so overwhelming sometimes. Also, people do not really seem to understand mental illnesses and how they affect people. This is why you'll always find people who ridicule people with mental illnesses. But, this shouldn't discourage you from getting help when you should.

A lot of studies have shown that getting help early enough for mental illnesses increases your chances of recovering faster and better. The moment you realize that something is wrong, do not shield it. Get help. It is actually a thing of great courage to get help for mental illnesses. I am not unaware of that at all.

Also, don't feel bad for anything at all. It happens to the best of us too. Do not let anyone shame you into keeping mum about your situation. It is very detrimental. Not to you alone, but also to your family and loved ones. Believe me when I say you can pull through your anxiety.
Do not be afraid. You won't deal with it all alone. I am here for you like I have always been. I'll hold you tightly as you walk on the beautiful and rough road that leads to healing. Let us begin.

1. I have all it takes to pull through my anxiety.
2. Getting the help I need is not synonymous to weakness.
3. I am worth it. I have always been.
4. Anxiety won't end me. I will end it.
5. I have all the courage I need to receive help.

6. Anxiety is not the end of my life.

7. I am a fighter, I'll fight this and win.

8. I am not ashamed to get help.

9. I fill my life with peace.

10. I refuse to be bothered by little things.

11. I dissociate myself from negativity.

12. I identify the root causes of my anxiety with ease.

13. I give no one the power and permission to shame
    me with my condition.

14. I do not surrender to my weaknesses.

15. I'll let no one trigger me.

16. I move away from my triggers with ease.

17. I have the ability to concentrate only on the things
    that matter.

18. I am amazing and loved.

19. My eyes are fixated on the beauty of my existence.

20. I do not struggle to get help.

21. I have the strength and courage to get therapy.

22. I walk boldly towards healing.

We have come to the end of this chapter. Did you have fun going through these anxiety affirmations? I bet you did. In the next chapter, we'll explore the beauty of sleep and wonderful sleep affirmations curated just for you. Turn the page and read on. I've got so much in store for you!

Chapter Four

The Value of Sleep To The Black Woman.

Sleep is like the golden chain that binds our health and body together.
—Thomas Dekker

I've had people ask for my skincare routine a lot of times. I have this gorgeous and silky skin that makes people stare at me more than once. When I hear people say there is no such thing as perfect skin, I resist the urge to walk up to them, pull them close and show them my skin. Yes, my skin is a thing of beauty. And in the words of John Keats, a thing of beauty is a joy forever. I know you too are interested in finding out the magic to the perfection in my skin. It is not on the high side, so you too can try it out. My ultimate skin care routine is good sleep. Sleeping as I should. Sleeping fully. No, I'm not making this up. There is something that adequate sleep does to your skin that not even the most expensive products can. Good sleep gives you a natural glow. That irresistible glow that comes with being a black woman.

But then, is a glowing skin all there is to good sleep? Of course not. There is a lot more to it. Various studies have shown that people are more productive when they get adequate sleep. I've tried this on myself, and I've gotten a lot of proof. I am the most productive when I get as much sleep as my body needs. This may sound quite unbelievable to you, but it is one of those truths that you should remember very often. You know, we deceive ourselves sometimes and overwork ourselves because we feel taking needed sleep would slow us down. We neglect the fact that getting sleep would help us a lot with our productivity and general output. Our bodies are made to require sleep. It is a necessity. Some people would try to make us feel bad for sleeping as though sleeping is a sin and not a healthy thing to do. Don't let anyone make you feel bad for sleeping. If anyone tries to, you might as well educate the person on the importance of sleep. Not only does it make you glow, it is also better for your health. As you make plans for your parties and meetings and dates, also make plans for sleep. Your body and health would be forever grateful to you. Do you see all the good work adequate sleep does for your body?

Some people wonder if sleep affirmations actually work considering that we are 'inactive' while asleep. You know, we're not doing any form of work while sleeping. This is a very wrong notion to follow. The main purpose of sleep is rest and rejuvenation. So, yes. The affirmations would work just fine even if you sleep. Affirmations are not as complex as we make them out to be sometimes. So, make your affirmations at any time you want. But somehow, people tend to make sleep affirmations just before they go to bed. I do it too. Saying my sleep affirmations just before bed always fills me with this surge of energy that makes me feel much more power than I am.

One other thing that makes me say my sleep affirmations is this: it helps me relax and empty my mind of the thoughts of the things that happened during the day. I'd climb into my bed and say my affirmations with power before I finally sleep. If you're a person that thinks so much before sleeping, saying your affirmations just before bedtime would do you a lot of good. Don't you think so, too?

I write this section for the sole purpose of opening your eyes and mind to see and understand the importance of sleep. I understand that you might have contrary views buried deeply in your subconscious. But, you and I will eliminate all of them armed with the power that affirmations carry. So, hold my hand one more time as we go on another affirmation journey. Let us explore sleep and all its beauty.

Sleep Affirmations For The Black Woman

1. I'll not let anything rob me of my sleep.
2. I'll sleep as much as I need to.
3. I do not battle with insomnia.
4. I fall asleep with ease.
5. The evidence of my good sleep shows beautifully on my skin.
6. Sleep comes easy to me.
7. I am not awakened by nightmares.
8. I dream beautiful dreams when I sleep.
9. I enjoy sleeping.
10. I make great plans for my sleep.
11. I am not too overwhelmed to lose sleep.
12. I sleep peacefully.
13. I am refreshed when I sleep.
14. I glow differently when I sleep.
15. I suffer no sleep disorder.
16. I give my body the pleasure of sleep.
17. I do not neglect my health by not sleeping when I should.
18. My dreams are filled with hope and positivity.
19. I am deserving of rest.

20. I. choose to sleep and rest. I will try again tomorrow.

21. I am thankful for a healthy body that sleeps with ease.

22. I am safe in my sleep.

23. My sleep strengthens me and fills me with new energy.

24. I wake up to a good body.

25. I wake up joyfully as my most authentic self.

26. I am grateful for all the things I achieved today. My sleep will fill me with more energy that will help me do better tomorrow.

27. My eyes close in joy.

28. My wellness is top priority to me; I do not neglect my sleep for any reason.

29. Nightmares have no place in my sleep.

30. I begin a new day well rested and refreshed.

31. I am more productive when I get good sleep.

32. I am worthy of great rest.

33. I am in control of how I sleep.

34. I develop healthy and beautiful sleep habits.

35. I do not let the internet make me lose sleep.

36. I enjoy the unique relaxation that sleep alone can give.

37. I am not consumed by anxiety that I'd lose my sleep.

38. I wake up rejuvenated and strong.

39. I empty my mind of thoughts that would keep me up all night.

40. I distance myself from bad sleeping habits.

41. I wake up with a glow, not eye bags.

42. I refuse to see the time I spend sleeping as wasted time.

43. I step into great strength when I sleep.

44. I dream beautiful dreams in my sleep and they come to pass.

45. I do not give anyone the permission to make me feel bad for resting.

46. I fall asleep with a lot of ease.

47. I am healthy and strong.

48. I embrace the beauty and serenity of sleep with my arms wide open.

Key Points

I have singled out the core points that you should remember always in this chapter. Find them below!

- The time you spend sleeping is not wasted time.
- You are worthy of pleasant night rests and the most beautiful of dreams.
- You glow up when you embrace the peace and strength that sleep gives.

- Good sleep enhances your productivity much more than you can ever imagine.
- Good sleep is one of the best skincare products ever. You don't find it in stores.
- Sleep makes you healthy. Embrace it with love.

Good Sleep Is Adequate Self-Care

For many black women, self-care is all about expensive lotions and skincare routines, long hours in the spa and food. Inasmuch as these are essential parts of caring for one's self, they are not all there is to self care. It is much more beyond that.

To care for yourself is to take care of yourself from the inside out. I used to have a very limited view of self-care in the past. The usual skin care, good hair and good food are the kind that a lot of people know. I'd finish going through my routines and still feel drained. I knew that wasn't close to normalcy at all. In fact, it was miles and miles away from it.

I knew I had to do something about it. I needed to experience the relaxation and warmth of true self-care. I wanted to feel something different. Something that was beyond good skin and a beautiful face. It was at that point that I began to take care of myself the most. It wasn't easy one bit because I was used to a certain lifestyle. I had to unlearn, relearn and adapt to new situations. That, my dear, was the beginning of my journey to true and adequate self-care.

In the course of my self-care journey, I discovered a lot of things. One of the best things I discovered was the power of sleep and the role sleep plays in self-care. This is what I want to share with you in this section. You should know that your self-care processes are incomplete without sleep. Why is this so? I'll explain to you in a very lucid way.

Sleep plays a great role in self-care because it is the core of true relaxation. Most of us indulge in self-care processes like massage, manicure and pedicure, exfoliation and others because we see them as avenues through which we can peel stress off our skins. The main purpose of self-care is relaxation and stress relief. When self-care fails to do these well, it would suffice to say that it didn't achieve its purpose. This is why you should embrace sleep. It is one of the most important self-care processes that a lot of us ignore.

It would interest you to know that getting good sleep would make the other self-care processes work better. The body thrives with relaxation and not tension. This is why sleeping well can help you fight eye bags and wrinkles more efficiently than lotions. Doesn't this amaze you? It would take a while for you to adapt to sleeping well if you're used to getting very short sleeps. But, this is one adaptation that you'll be grateful for for a very long time because the goodness it brings lasts for a very long time. This goodness expresses itself through your skin. It glows up your skin. You want to rock gorgeous skin when you're old, don't you? I know you want to. And that is why I urge you to embrace adequate sleep today and make it an essential part of your self-care.

I have curated relaxing self-care affirmations for you in this section. They'll help you rise into the knowledge of true self-care and the great beauty of sleep. Hold my hand tightly, let's go through these affirmations together. It will be worth all the while.

Adequate Sleep And Self-Care Affirmations

1. I take care of myself from the inside out.
2. I embrace good sleep with all that there is in me.
3. Sleep is the core of my self-care processes.
4. I glow up with ease because I have embraced true self-care.

5. True relaxation finds me with grace and ease because I have embraced the power of sleep.

6. Sleep finds me ready every day.

7. I have made sleep the core of my self-care.

8. I do not neglect my self-care for any reason.

9. I invest in my beauty through sleep.

10. Good sleep is one of the most beautiful things that has happened to me.

11. I sleep when I need to.

12. I am grateful for the rejuvenation that sleep gives me.

13. I throw away all the unhealthy self-care processes that I used to embrace.

14. I care for myself with so much love.

15. I do not take my self-care lightly. I am aware of its importance.

16. I do not find it difficult to relax when I want to.

17. I choose to care for myself wholly today.

18. I adapt to healthy changes with ease.

19. My self-care is worth it.

20. I catwalk into the elegance that self-care heralds.

I have compiled the most salient points in this section for your ease and reading pleasure. Find them below.

- Good sleep is the core of self-care.
- Good sleep is one of the loveliest skincare products ever.
- Sleeping well makes you glow.
- Sleep rejuvenates a person.

I Deserve All The Sleep that I Can Get

I have met lots of women who feel undeserving of sleep. Yes, this is actually a thing. The question now is, why would anyone feel undeserving of sleep? This could stem from various reasons. The first that I'd tell you about is trauma.

Say a woman's house got burnt while she was asleep, or her child got into great trouble while she slept. Mind you, these are just instances that I am using to drive my point home. Any woman that has experienced any of these would spend a long time healing from the trauma. She'd always find a reason to blame herself for 'letting' it happen. You'll hear her say things like; it happened because I slept. It's all my fault. I can't forgive myself for this.

The woman might even need some therapy to be able to deal with the trauma. The crazier thing is the fact that trauma never really goes away sometimes. It hides somewhere in you and wait patiently for the perfect time to make you aware of its presence in your life. It has a way of making you feel evil in situations where you meant well and tried your best. Now, how long would you let trauma rule your life? How long will you let that guilt thrive? How long will you ditch sleep? Don't tell me it's forever, please.

To combat this guilt that comes with sleeping, you have to first understand that it is not your fault. Yes, it is not your fault. No one makes grievous mistakes deliberately. No normal human loves to self-destruct. You have to accept that what happened happened. Then, you move on the path that leads to healing. Healing is no easy journey, but I trust that you will do well at it. You are a black woman who is powerful enough to do impossible things. As you walk the healing path, you will gradually begin to understand that you deserve your sleep. In fact, you deserve as much sleep as you can possibly get. And you can get it.

Another category of women who feel less deserving of sleep are people who value their productivity so much. You know, those ones that are more than willing to work their asses off to get what they want. Those ones who desire to leave bold marks in this world. Women who thrive on big ambitions and dreams. It is a wonderful thing to do all you can to fulfil your dreams. But it is not a wonderful thing to throw sleep away while at it. Remember the relationship between sleep and productivity that I talked about in a previous section? Sleep enhances productivity. I know it might sound counter-productive to you now. But, it isn't at all. When you sleep well, your body will function optimally. So, my dear woman, remember to sleep well and take necessary rests as you work on smashing those goals. Also, your tribe can manage affairs when you sleep. I understand how well you want to manage everything by being up most of the time. I know you are greatly needed. But, don't let this overwhelm you or make you quit sleeping. Sleep first, then attend to your affairs later. You need a healthy body to do everything well. Don't you think so, too?

This section is all about powerful affirmations for you who feels undeserving of sleep. Walk this affirmation walk with me as I lead you back into good sleep and rest. It is time to welcome rest into yourself again. Shall we begin?

Affirmations for The Black Woman Who Feels Undeserving Of Sleep

1. I welcome absolute rest and good sleep into my body again.
2. I am deserving of all the sleep I get.
3. I thrive the most when I sleep well.
4. I forgive myself for all the times that sleeping caused me to make mistakes.
5. I forgive myself for my mistakes.
6. Sleep fills me with peace.
7. I refuse to see sleep as a synonym for laziness. I am good and strong.
8. I welcome myself into adequate sleep again.
9. I deserve great rest.
10. My body is refueled by the peace and tranquillity of sleep.
11. I am not consumed by the busyness of my day that I would lose my sleep.
12. I am not a superhuman. I sleep to regain energy.
13. I empty my mind of everything that causes me not to sleep well.
14. I am not overwhelmed. I am in control.
15. I do not sleep to wake up lazy.
16. Sleep increases my productivity.
17. I strip my sleep of nightmares and restlessness.

18. I sleep with ease and elegance.

19. I attract the most gorgeous of dreams when I sleep.

20. I deserve the peace I feel when I sleep.

21. I give no one the permission to make me sleepless.

22. I am no insomniac.

23. Sleep looks very beautiful on me.

24. I bloom in my sleep.

Key Points

I believe these affirmations will welcome you back into true rest and graceful sleep. I have curated key points that you should always remember. Try to recall them as often as you can. You'll be glad that you did. Find the key points below.

- You deserve all the sleep that you get.
- Sleeping is not a counter-productive venture, it increases your productivity much more than you know.
- Forgive yourself wholeheartedly for all the times that sleeping made you make mistakes.
- Care for yourself by sleeping well.
- You are no super human, sleep when you have to.
- Your brain thrives greatly with the tranquillity that sleep gives.

We have come to the end of the sleep affirmations. I hope you had a wonderful ride. Now, we'll begin another journey of affirmations. This time, we'll explore beauty affirmations and what beauty really means. Let's go!

Chapter Five

Beauty Affirmations For The Black Woman.

Beauty begins the moment you decide to be yourself.
—Coco Chanel.

Read the above quote carefully. Now, read it again and let your brain absorb it wholly. When people are asked what the definition of beauty is, they'd most likely mention a certain eye color, skin tone, hair texture and even lip type! Have you noticed that some modeling agencies are big perpetrators of these stereotypes? They make it look as though beauty is limited to a certain tribe. But, I am glad about the black women revolution going on in our world today. Now, no one dares to teach us what beauty is or what it should be. It makes me wonder, why do people think beauty is limited to a certain standard? Why do people try to make others feel small because they do not fit into their definition of beauty? No one, dear black woman, has the right to fix you into a box.

I love gardens. Beautiful gardens. In all my years of exploring various garden types and styles, I have come to know this one thing. The most beautiful gardens are those that contain many flowers. There is so much beauty in variety, you know. I see this world as a garden of some sort too. The world is a garden, you and I are the various flowers that make up the garden. The beauty of the garden is largely dependent on the variety between you and I. The distinction between us is what makes the garden a thing of endless beauty. Whenever anyone tries to make you feel less of yourself for being uniquely beautiful, let the person know this.

Being treated with disdain is one thing a lot of black women have had to deal with at some stages of their lives. This is especially peculiar to the black women who choose to be themselves audaciously. You know, when you refuse to follow the crowd, the crowd would try to make you follow it by intimidating you into submission. But, we are black women whose ancestors do not know how to surrender. I've seen black women being sent out of corporate places and parties for wearing their hair with pride because afros are not presentable. As funny and sad this may sound, it is the truth. In fact, it is but one of the few things that black women go through.

My dear black woman, I want you to know that you are more than enough. Do not give any soul the permission to make you feel like you are not. You are whole and you are more than enough. Let this stick to every part of your heart.

I write this section for all black women who have been made to undergo the torture of beauty stereotypes. Women who hid their truest beauties to fit into societal stereotypes. For you, I write with vigor and joy and revolution. We'll begin a journey of affirmations again. The time has come again for us to speak power into ourselves and flaunt our daring beauties with all the pride there is in the world. Hold my hand, let us begin our affirmation walk!

I Am Enough.

1. My beauty is too large to fit into small boxes.
2. I am as beautiful as I am. I am the best I can be.
3. I love every part of myself.
4. I am more than enough.
5. I teach the sun what it means to shine.
6. I am beautiful forever.
7. I am effortlessly beautiful.
8. I bear so much positivity inside me that it glows on my skin.

9. My skin gives gorgeous a new and brighter meaning.

10. I do not compare myself to anyone.

11. I exude great beauty and charm.

12. I glow with effortless grace.

13. My soul is beautiful.

14. I am a breathing perfection.

15. I love how I look.

16. I am beautiful on the inside and the outside.

17. No one can make me feel small.

18. I do not embrace the world's stereotypes on beauty.

19. Everything about me is art.

20. I care for my skin with ease.

21. Being beautiful is no struggle for me.

22. I fall in love with the magic that I am everyday.

23. I love the shape of my body.

24. I wear my skin with pride and confidence.

25. My beauty attracts wonderful people.

26. I light up the world with my beauty.

27. I am my most original self.

28. I am audaciously elegant.

29. I create my own style.

30. I do not live on public approval. My approval is all
    that I need.

31. I have an irresistible charm.

32. My smile has a lot of beauty.

33. I am a perfect combination of rare intelligence and elegance.

34. I am the Queen of my territory.

35. I am grateful for all my features.

36. People are attracted to me.

37. I have the most gorgeous pair of eyes.

38. The texture of my hair is standard.

39. I am hot and I know it.

40. I have a graceful carriage.

41. No one can shrink my amazing self.

42. I make every dress beautiful and perfect.

43. I am the sexiest woman there is.

44. I make everything around me exceedingly beautiful.

Key Points

In the words of John Keats, 'a thing of beauty is a joy forever. I want you to remember this everyday because you are a thing of beauty. You are enough. Beautiful and enough. Below are the key points I curated specially for you in this section.

- You are the best kind of beautiful.

- You are unique in your own way, don't let anyone make you feel otherwise.

- You are too spectacular to fit into any stereotypical boxes.

- You teach the sun the art of shining.
- You are enough, and that is all that matters.

I Accept Myself

Dr. Steve Maraboli said; *When I accept myself, I am freed from the burden of needing you to accept me.*

This is one of the most beautiful quotes I have ever seen on self-acceptance. A lot of people go on and on about self-acceptance without even knowing what it is. Self-acceptance is more than just telling people to take you as you are or saying you can't change for anyone. To accept yourself is to embrace the whole of you. The perfections, the flaws and everything in between.

It is human nature to seek validation from other humans. It is one of the most burdensome things I have ever known. You know, I used to think that it was possible to be truly loved by everyone. How wrong I was. I realized the impossibility of being a sweetheart to everyone quite early in life, and I am very grateful for it.

If you are among the people who are yet to realize it or people who realized it quite late, don't feel bad at all. Growth is beautiful irrespective of when it happens. Each and everyone of us is made of different pleasing and displeasing characteristics. Some of the features we consider very pleasant could be quite disgusting to other people. This is why it is impossible for you to please everyone. Trying to please everyone is like trying to keep water in a basket. It never works.

It is for this reason that you must accept yourself. Embrace yourself with all of your good and bad. When you accept yourself, you loosen yourself from the sorrow that is embedded in seeking acceptance from other people. Also, you must accept yourself first before other people can accept you. Self-acceptance is not an easy thing at all, but it is a very wonderful thing to do. It'll help you love yourself and appreciate your uniqueness more.

Begin your self-acceptance by making peace with the fact that you are a human who makes mistakes and not some robot that is designed to do everything a certain way. When you make peace with this fact, every other thing becomes easier. Then, you begin to embrace yourself with open arms. Don't be selective in your embrace, please. Do well to embrace the perfection in your waistline, the music in your voice, the small breasts, the shy face, the dreamy eyes. Every single thing. You know, it takes a fine blend of flaw and perfection to flesh out elegance.

When you've accepted all of you, you'll see all the charm and magic that you are. You don't have to worry at all about going on your self-acceptance journey all alone. I'm with you to hold your hands and help you navigate through the rough paths. Through every affirmation that this section will be home to, I hold your hand to show my solidarity and to guide you. Now, let us begin.

Beauty Affirmations For Self-Acceptance

1. I love all of my features.
2. I am the best version of myself.
3. I am uniquely beautiful
4. I love the kind of woman that I am.
5. I am beautiful in every part.
6. I am a flawed perfection.
7. No one's opinion of me matters to me.
8. I love and accept all that there is to me.
9. I forgive myself for all the times I let people's definition of me steal my joy.
10. I send peace, acceptance and courage to my doubts.
11. I do not stay in toxicity to get accepted.
12. Every part of me plays a great role in who I am. So I embrace every part with love and kindness.
13. I quit apologizing for being myself.

14. I am full of confidence.

15. I do not seek for validations in places I cannot find it.

16. The only approval of myself I value and cherish is my own.

17. I nurture my body with care and attention.

18. I absolutely adore my body.

19. I celebrate the wonders of myself everyday.

20. I sing my best songs without apologizing to anyone on how my voice sounds.

21. I am myself unapologetically.

22. I am all the magic that I need.

23. All the validation I seek to thrive resides in me.

24. I let go of all the negative energies that pull me backwards.

25. I let go of all the insecurity I feel about myself.

26. I believe in my own power and ideas.

27. I am in a loving relationship with myself.

28. I'll not let what people think of me steal my joy.

29. I discard every hatred I have ever felt for myself.

30. I live my life graciously.

31. I become more beautiful with the break of every dawn.

32. I'll not destroy myself with hate and negativity. I am exceedingly kind to myself.

33. I forgive myself for all the times I looked down on myself.

34. I open my eyes to see all the awesomeness that lives in me.

35. I trust in my ability to take great care of myself.

36. I love myself deeply everyday.

37. I adore my body with everything in me.

38. My physical appearance isn't all the beauty there is to me. I am even more beautiful on the inside.

39. I am not overwhelmed by people's perception of me.

40. I radiate so much black excellence.

Key Points

My dear black woman, I hope these self-acceptance affirmations filled you with so much love and goodness. Remember everyday that you are the standard, and that you are the finest shade of black. I have curated amazing key points for this section just for you.

- You are the perfect definition of black excellence.
- No one's definition of you matters but yours.
- You are flawed and perfect all at once.
- Accept yourself in every way, and you'd see all the greatness that you bear.
- You are full of beauty.

I Am The Truest Fashionista Ever; Black Women Fashion Affirmations

I remember meeting this black woman at a party. She had this shiny skin that could pass for a new mirror. She's one of the most beautiful black women I've seen all my life. But thinking about her now, I wonder if she ever realized how beautiful she was. How much power the stare in her eyes possessed.

I remember that black woman and the discomfort on her face when she danced. She wore this flowing English dress that seemed to stifle her smile. I could tell that she wasn't comfortable in that dress at first glance. I wondered if anyone influenced her into wearing the dress. But I can't tell because I had no conversation with her. I was just an admirer admiring her gorgeousness from a distance.

A lot of black women have been ridiculed for dressing the way they do. If there's something a black woman pays a lot of attention to, it is her dress. Black women do not wear clothes simply because they want to cover up. They wear clothes to express themselves, tell their stories and live their truths. None of the black women I know loves to dress vicariously through anyone. They rather dress for themselves. But this is sadly difficult sometimes because some people have embarked on a mission to make black women feel bad for dressing the way they love. You'd find this behavior almost everywhere. In the office space, the churches, even at parties. It is that bad.

If black women continue to give in to the demands of people who want them to quit showcasing black excellence through their fashion sense, we might be heading towards a fashion era that is devoid of black women fashion in every way. That would be very terrible. Once a race begins to lose the major things that differentiates it from others, it would begin to head towards extinction. But I trust in the power of black women and black excellence not to allow this to become reality. Black is the color of power, black is culture, and culture must thrive. We don't thrive by mere words of mouth, we thrive much more by taking action.

I write these black women fashion affirmations for this reason. To strengthen all black women, make them appreciate the wonders of black fashion, and encourage them to embrace their own fashion styles. Don't look at me with confusion and anger yet, dear black women. I understand that it is not an easy thing to do. I also know that you possess all the power you need to do these. But I'm not letting you do all of it alone. I'll help you through the whole process by holding your hands and filling you up with positivity through it all like I have always done. Shall we begin?

Fashion Affirmations For The Black Woman

1. I make every dress perfect.
2. I wear my culture on my clothes.
3. I uphold black excellence through every piece of clothing that I wear.
4. My fashion sense makes me stand out from every crowd.
5. I have perfect skin that compliments my outfit.
6. I am blessed to be a black woman.
7. I have the truest fashion sense ever.
8. Beauty knows me by my name.
9. My foremothers dance in glee when I dress like the black woman that I am.
10. I'll have no one intimidate me into wearing clothes that I do not fancy.
11. I am very elegant.
12. My skin is an embodiment of the brightest stars.
13. My thick hair is the standard.
14. My fashion styles determine the trends.
15. I make the atmosphere joyful with the brightness of my clothes.

16. I am beyond beautiful. In fact, beautiful is a weak word to describe me.

17. I rock my styles with so much panache.

18. All heads turn to have a second at me when I walk past.

19. Fashion homes model designs after my styles.

20. I give fashion a newer and prettier meaning.

21. I portray black excellence with everything that I do.

22. My fashion style opens doors for me.

23. My fashion sense tells the stories of a generation of great women.

24. I am not consumed by society's idea of fashion.

25. I create my styles with ease.

26. If elegance were human, it would be me.

27. My body makes clothes into perfection.

28. Everything I wear turns out perfect on me.

29. My fashion style takes me to my roots.

30. I am as fashionable as I can be and that is the most important thing.

31. I am not afraid to dress the way I desire.

Key Points

My gorgeous black woman, I hope these fashion affirmations help you in finding the road that leads home.

Home, where the trueness of black women's fashion resides. Below are the key points for this session.

- Your fashion sense tells the stories of generations of black women who knew and embraced black fashion in all its forms.
- It is okay to stand out all by yourself.
- Your fashion styles set new paces for fashion homes.
- Do not give anyone the permission to intimidate you into wearing clothes that you do not love.
- You are elegance in all its forms.
- You have a perfect body that makes every dress you wear perfect.

A lot of black women are ridiculed for the hair texture and skin type that they possess. Some of these black women have been made to believe the fallacy that their skin is not pretty enough and that their hair is bad. Since when did thick, full and bouncy afros become bad? When people do not understand a thing, they try to destroy it. This is the thing that people try to do to black women. They do not understand all that melanin and kinky hair. They are such a beautiful pair that people wonder the mystery behind that kind of beauty. But instead of admiring it, they'd rather ridicule it openly and envy it in secret. When you understand this simple logic, you'd begin to understand all the hate that is shown to black women because of their hair and skins.

Isn't it ironic how afro themed hair care and skincare products sell out quickly in the stores? Have you not wondered about this before? Who are the people purchasing these products if afro is as ugly and classless as some people try to make it seem? This should send a message home. Melanin is the truth and kinky hair defines class. Trust me, I do not say these to you to make you feel good about yourself or boost your self-confidence in any form. I am simply telling you the truth that has always been hidden from you. I understand that you might have gone through so much trouble and bad treatment for rocking your skin and your hair. That might make you believe that your afro isn't all that worth it. To love your hair and skin wholly, you would need to embrace everything about the black excellence. Doing this isn't very easy because of everything that society has portrayed about black women's beauty. But it is an achievable thing. My friend, I'm not asking that you do everything at once. Not at all, it is a gradual process. Begin by first dissociating yourself from the lies and malicious talks. Then you go further by falling in love all over again with your skin and your hair. Appreciate the beauty of that glossy skin and its softness. Then you admire that gorgeous forest that grows on your head. You don't have to worry so much about doing it all alone because I am always with you to help and guide you as you navigate your beauty with ease and joy. I write every affirmation in this session just for you. Hold my hand and let us call gorgeousness into you. Shall we begin?

1. I love my melanin and how it differentiates me from the crowd.
2. My hair is a crown of beauty.
3. I love my skin and how it glows.
4. My hair is soft and free from breakages.
5. My hair grows from beauty to beauty with each passing day.

6. I do not allow anyone to intimidate me for being uniquely beautiful.

7. My skin tone and hair texture are dreams.

8. I afford the right diets my hair and skin needs with ease.

9. I create enough time to care for my hair and skin.

10. I choose the best products for myself with elegance.

11. My complexion is so amazing.

12. My hair resists breakages and dandruffs.

13. I embrace my birth marks with joy.

14. I accept my skin with all of its perfections and imperfections.

15. I absolutely adore my hair.

16. I style my hair in the most classy ways.

17. I manage my hair with ease.

18. I am proud of my hair type and texture.

19. I get good value from all the money I spend on grooming my hair and nourishing my skin.

20. My skin is strong and powerful.

21. I derive pleasure in caring for my skin and hair.

22. My skin glows like the sun.

23. I am grateful for the gorgeousness of my skin.

24. I am confident in my skin and hair.

25. I am as classy as I can be.

26. I celebrate my perfect hair and skin.

You know a black woman from the uniquely gorgeous texture of her hair and the silky nature of her skin. A black woman's hair and skin contain so much beauty that some people try to make themselves feel good by ridiculing her. It is high time this behavior stopped! I have curated the key points for this section that celebrates black women's excellent hair and skins.

- You are flawlessly beautiful.
- Your hair and skin add so much to your beauty.
- Discard all the lies that you were once made to believe about black excellence.
- Glow with pride. Suns like you do not thrive in hiding.
- Remember that you are as classy as you can be.

Again, we come to the end of a chapter. Tell me, did you have fun exploring these beauty and fashion affirmations? Do you feel more powerful now? Have you decided to step into your powers? Black women are so powerful. I do not want you to neglect your own powers. Make everything you do count. Do things the way you want them done. This is your one life. Be audacious!

We'll begin a new affirmation journey in the next chapter. We'll explore joy and its goodness! Come with me, let's speak joy into our wonderful lives.

Chapter Six

Joy Affirmations For The Black Woman

We cannot cure the world of sorrows, but we can choose to live in Joy.
—Joseph Campbell.

Life is filled with a lot of stress and trouble that one needs to work hard at one's happiness. Joy is one of the greatest emotions I know. Many people have defined joy in various contexts. Some say it is the state of being happy and content with all that there is around you. Others say it is happiness. For me, joy is more than just feeling. It is that light that floods your life and illuminates every darkness. It is that warmth that shields you from life's coldness. It is that fresh spring flower that blooms with ease and a lot of beauty.

Sometimes, we tend to think that joy is a special package that comes with a perfect life. But I put it to you that it is a fallacy. If joy was present only to people with perfect lives, no one on this green earth would know joy. Every life has its own lows and highs. Moments of despair and moments of exceeding hope. Memorable and regrettable moments.

Do you see that joy is not reserved for a special class of people? It is one of life's beauties that goes into anywhere it is welcomed. Yes, you invite joy into your life. You create your own joy. Joy begins to trickle into your being the moment that you realize that you have the power to create it as you want. Yes, it is trickling into your being right now because you have come into the realization.

No one can possibly cleanse the world of all the sadness that clings to it. But it is possible to live in joy despite all that happens in the world. No, I am not asking you to be oblivious of reality. Rather, I am asking you to focus on making your life out to be one that welcomes joy. You might think you are undeserving of joy when you let the world's idea of 'a perfect life' overshadow your reason. You don't need perfection to welcome joy. Joy and perfection are two different entities. Remember this always. That things are not going as planned for you is no reason to deny yourself of joy. In fact, joy has a way of making you stronger. Joy opens your heart up to hope. And when hope comes, you get the strength that you need to try again. Tell me, don't you want to taste joy? I bet you do. When you find joy, you'd never want to let it go. I tell you this from my own experience.

Now, you might wonder how to welcome this joy that I speak so keenly of into your life. Joy is no tax collector, so you don't have to worry about paying a price for it. All you have to do is welcome it into your life and it will be all yours. You can begin by stripping yourself of all the negativities that steal your joy. Be kind to yourself. You know, you are the biggest cheerleader you could ever have. Then you unlearn all the bad definitions of joy that the world made you believe at some point in your life.

Tell yourself that you are deserving of joy. Embrace your present life and work on an improvement with glee and not hate. Slowly, steadily, joy will build an amazing residence in you. I know you really want this joy. You'll get it.

My dear, I won't leave you alone to create your joy all by yourself. I'll hold you up like I have always done through the other chapters. I'll guide you through affirmations that will lead you into creating an endless flow of joy. Shall we begin?

I Begin My Day With Joy

This section is all about joy affirmations curated specially to bless your morning. You know, morning is a very powerful part of the day. It is in the morning that you make plans and decide how you want your whole day to turn out. This is why you should never take your morning lightly. Now, dig into these joy affirmations for your morning!

1. I invite joy in all its wholeness into my life this morning.
2. Joy rises into my life brightly like the morning sun.
3. Joy dwells in me from this morning until the end.
4. My joy is not a one time thing. It lasts for a long time.
5. I find joy in everything.
6. I give no one or anything the permission to take my joy away from me.
7. I spread joy and positivity to everyone I come across.
8. I am more than ready to carry joy.
9. I strip myself of everything that would make it impossible for me to have joy.
10. I choose joy today.
11. I am strengthened by joy.
12. I am exceedingly joyful despite the negativities around me.
13. I have made peace with the fact that I can't end the sadness in the world. I also come into the realization that I have all the power I need to create my own joy.
14. I step into my joy with ease.
15. The joy in me is so great that all the world sees it.
16. I do not allow the world to steal my joy.

17. My smile bears joy.

18. My morning is blessed with so much joy.

19. I give no room to sorrow.

20. I am joyful from the inside.

21. I wake into joy!

Key Points

Your day would turn out much greater and happier when you speak joy into it. That's why I encourage you to take morning affirmations for joy seriously. Below are the key points for this session.

- You have all the power you need to create a joyful day for yourself.
- Choose joy in the morning, and joy will cling to you.
- Joy strengthens.

I Choose Joy Above All Things

Many things in this life are subject to our choices. You have the power to make choices and decisions for yourself. But, some options seem to have more power over others. Don't get confused, black woman. I'll explain what I mean here to you in very clear terms with a very short story.

I remember this Tuesday in Spring a couple of years ago. I don't know why I find it difficult to recall the exact year it was. Well, not remembering the year won't affect the story in any way. So, I'll go on with my narration. That Tuesday remains one of the most remembered days in my life to this day. I had woken up early to get to work in time that morning. I had so much work on my desk that I wondered how I was going to fix it all. Not like worrying about it made any difference, I just couldn't help it. I used to worry a lot.

I got to work early enough and started my work for the day. Not without exchanging greetings with my colleagues of course. Everything was going fine until my boss arrived at the office two hours later. I knew something was wrong the moment he arrived because of his unusual sternness. My boss was usually an easy going and kind man. He was always cheerful too. He also had this permanent smile on his face. But on this Tuesday morning, the smile lost its permanence. He wasn't smiling at all. The atmosphere in our large office was so tense. It was so silent that we could almost hear ourselves breathe. It was scary. No one had any clue what the problem with our boss was, so we all decided to let sleeping dogs lie by just doing our work more carefully and being faster at it. That worked for a very short while. We were too troubled to even work as efficiently as we used to. That's the thing with tension. It has the power to make the fastest person into a snail.

I was quite close to my boss. Not the boss-staff relationship. It was more like a cordial friendship. I respected his boundaries even with the closeness. It was this closeness that made me decide to ask him what the problem was with all boldness. But before the words could form in my mouth, he dismissed me with a languid wave of his right hand. It was at that point I knew that whatever it was that stole his smile and made him behave in such a manner was a very serious thing. How right I was. Nothing on earth could have prepared me for what followed.

The suspense in the office was finally lifted when my boss called me to a private space and offered me a sack letter for no reason. He said my services were no longer needed at the firm. For a moment, I thought it was a big fat joke. I couldn't believe it. I was one of the best workers in the firm, so I couldn't even figure out the rationale behind the sack. That hurt me the most. My boss paid no attention to my tears. He wouldn't tell me why I got sacked either. That was the part that hurt me the most. I really wanted that closure. But he wouldn't give it. And there was nothing I could do about it.

When I finally accepted that my job was over, I hung around the environment hoping that he would call me back and say it was all a mix up. Oh, how I wished and cried for that. Sadly, it never happened. The whole incident threw me into serious depression. I felt like my life was over. It was just too much for me to bear. Also, being sacked without a reason made it harder for me. I spent two weeks gloating and contemplating suicide. My mental health was a big mess. Exactly three weeks after I lost the job, I sat my ass down and talked to myself for a long time. I made myself realize that gloating and wallowing in my depression could do nothing. It was on that day that I chose joy. Yes, joy is a choice that you alone have to make for yourself. Know this.

Now, let's go back to what I said about some options being more powerful than others now. Getting depressed was the more powerful option. It was the easiest thing to do in that situation. It would have taken so much strength for me to choose joy on that first day. This is why I say choosing joy can be difficult sometimes. But it is always worth it, believe me. The strength that came with choosing joy helped me apply for better jobs. In the end, I got a better one. I did not share this story to inspire you or something, I shared it to make you realize the power of choosing joy above all things.

This section is all about choosing joy no matter what. I wrote these affirmations just for you. You too should learn to choose joy, always. So, let's begin to affirm!

1. I choose joy no matter the situation.
2. Unfavourable circumstances won't steal my joy.
3. All the pains I have gone through do not define my story.
4. I am the most joyful soul I know.
5. I forgive myself for all the times I made myself suffer.
6. I choose joy even in difficult situations.
7. Everything turns into joy for me
8. I am not weighed down by obstacles.
9. My obstacles are stairs that lead me to higher heights.
10. I'll know joy all the days of my life.
11. I choose joy even when it seems crazy.
12. I am not consumed by sorrow.
13. I stand firmly on the strength that joy gives to me.
14. I am exceedingly joyful about my existence.
15. I distance myself from melancholy and its troubles.
16. I am aware that life isn't all rosy, so I won't crush my joy by expecting greatness in everything.
17. I am the chief creator of my joy.
18. There is so much joy within me.
19. I distance myself from killjoys.

20. I find help with ease when I get depressed.

21. Joy surrounds me on every side.

Key Points

Sometimes, life will present you with very tough situations that'll dissuade you from choosing joy. If you keep on waiting for things to eventually get better before you choose joy, you might have to wait for a very long time. It is for this reason that I urge you to choose joy at all times. Below are the key points for this session.

- You are the chief creator of your joy.
- Forgive yourself for all the times you chose sorrow and let joy flow into you.
- Do not let bad situations steal your joy.
- Do not wait for joy, choose it everyday, and it will come to you.

I Invite Joy Into My Being

If you wait for joy to come to you spontaneously, you might have to wait for a very long time. This is because joy hardly comes like that. You have to do the choosing. Joy comes to you the moment you choose it. The moment you open up your arms to it.

Sometimes, people would wait for a lifetime in search of joy and end up not finding it. What mystery that would be! So, I am letting you know today that joy clings to whoever invites it. Don't spend so much time waiting for joy to find you of its own accord. Invite it into your being and it'll flourish there. Inviting joy into your being is one of the easiest things ever. It doesn't require your money and it doesn't make you sweat. You only have to make the decision. Then you open up your heart to it. That, my dear, is how to invite joy. Invite joy into your life day. Also, open up your heart to the small and big things alike. It is an open heart that can find joy in places where other people can't. It is an open heart that can explore the essence of joy in all its forms. Again, you won't be inviting joy into your being all alone. I'll be holding your hand to lead you, guide you, and strengthen you as usual. Now, let us begin to invite joy into the whole of your being.

1. I open my heart up to joy.

2. I find joy even in the hidden places.

3. I do not struggle to find joy.

4. I burst forth with joy everyday.

5. I invite joy into my being with the break of every dawn.

6. I'll not wait all my life for joy to come to me. I choose it and I create it.

7. Joy clings to me everyday.

8. Joy flourishes in my heart everyday.

9. I am exceedingly joyful.

10. My joy lives until the end of time.

11. Joy knows my name.

12. I attract joy.

13. I spread joy wherever I go.

14. I am surrounded by joy.

15. Joy comes to me easily.

16. Joy blooms in my heart and soul.

17. I choose joy.

18. I am empowered by joy.

19. I do not regret choosing joy.

20. I open every part of me to joy.

Key Points

- You'll find joy when you open your heart to it and invite it into your being.

- Life is much more beautiful with joy in it.
- Choose joy everyday. It comes at no cost.

Now, we have come to the end of this chapter with joy. Tell me, gorgeous soul, does your heart leap in joy? Does your soul burst forth with joy? I believe it does. Life bears so much grief that living without joy is one of the saddest things ever. For every part of your life, choose joy, create joy, spread joy and live joyfully. Embrace these affirmations wholly and you'd find your own joy clinging to you.

A new chapter begins again. This time, we explore affirmations for independence. Independence is one of the greatest attires that one can wear. And that is why I will adorn you with it in the next chapter. Come along with me!

Chapter Seven

Affirmations for Independence for The Black Woman

I always did something I was a little ready not to do. I think that's how you grow. When there's that moment of 'Wow, I'm not really sure I can do this', and you push through those moments, that's when you have a breakthrough.
—Marissa Mayer

Independence is one of the greatest things ever. We need independence to thrive in a competitive world like ours. You'd wonder, what is this independence all about? What is all this fuss about independence?

My friend, I understand that you might be so full of love and kindness that you'd expect the same measure from the world and everyone around you. I am sorry to disappoint you, but I must tell you this. There will come a time in your life when you would have to stand all by yourself, be your own cheerleader, pat yourself on the back and encourage yourself. There will be demanding times, but they won't stress you too much if you're rooted in independence already because you'd surely know how to take care of your affairs properly without any external influence. Do you see why I urge you to learn how to be independent now?

It's okay to be afraid and unsure. It's okay to detest failing, it's okay to cry. It's okay to fear what would become of you should you fail at this independence thing. You know what's not okay? Not trying. Yes, not striving for that independence is not okay. It is an essential thing. Before I could boldly stand on my own and say I was independent, it took me quite a long time. You know, I used to have this loving perspective of the world. I used to see the world as one big family where each and everyone of us was required to cheer the other on. I had good people around me, so I didn't see the flaw in my thinking. I only realized it when I stepped into unfamiliar grounds. Places that required me to stand all alone. It was then I realized that nobody owed me shit. Excuse my French, please. This is the one truth that you should know. I'm not asking you to hate people or not seek help when you can, I am only telling you that we are not entitled to people's kindness, warmth, love, money, compassion and other things that we tend to think we are entitled to. Of course, it is human behaviour to crave these things and give them back in return. But, this world is not all that black and white. Do you get it?

It Is for this reason that you must try your hardest to attain self-independence. Somehow, life is much easier when we are solely dependent on ourselves. We won't have to deal with the emotional baggage and trauma from depending on other people. A question is rising in your heart, isn't it? I can tell.

How does depending on other people cause us trouble? I'll answer this question with a very short story.
Two students are writing an exam together. These students are very close friends, so they share a lot of things together. One of the students studies hard, while the other doesn't. The hard-working student promises to help the lazy student pass the exam by helping him out in the examination hall.
Exam day comes, and for some weird reason, both students are made to make use of a different sitting arrangement as opposed to the one they were used to. Due to this, the hardworking student passes the exam with flying colors while the lazy student fails woefully.

Now, let's look at it this way. If both students had studied, the lazy one wouldn't have failed. He failed because he depended on someone else to pass the exams. This is just an example. Worse things have happened to people and are still happening because of the absence of Independence.

Walking the independence path is not an easy thing to do. But trust me, it is totally worth it. I won't leave you alone to walk the path of Independence all by yourself. I'll be holding your hand as always through these powerful independence affirmations written just for you. Let's begin, shall we?

1. I trust fully in my own abilities and strength.
2. I am not afraid to do all that it takes to stand firmly on my feet.
3. I am the greatest cheerleader I could ever wish for.
4. I am aware of my weak points, I have all it takes to turn them into strengths.
5. I take advantage of every opportunity to be more independent.
6. I do not allow privileges and kindness to get into my head so much that I forget my independence.
7. I love and treasure my independence with the whole of my heart.
8. I am blessed to be this independent.
9. I do not waiver when I have to do things by myself.
10. I flourish in my independence.
11. Being independent is the most beautiful thing that has ever happened to me.

12. I cut away everything that steals my independence.

13. I have all the courage I need to walk away from situations that threaten my independence.

14. I do not give anyone the power to crush my independence and my power.

15. I am totally in control of all that concerns me.

16. My opinion of myself is the best and greatest there would ever be.

17. I thrive more when I'm independent.

Key Points

Did you enjoy these independence affirmations, I trust you did. I have more in stock for you! Before I go on, take your time and savor the key points for this session.

- You have all it takes to be independent.
- You have all the courage you need to walk away from the people and the things that threaten your independence.
- You are the greatest cheerleader you could ever have.
- You have the power to turn your weaknesses to strengths.

I Am Financially Independent

Black women glow the most when they are financially independent. Depending on anyone for finances is very frustrating and limiting. You'd have to explain what every money you get goes into. You'd be afraid of spending money on the things that make your heart dance because your benefactor doesn't fancy them. You'd have to tame your desires and give up a lot of things. Also, you'd work your ass off to be able to enjoy a small amount of luxury.

Financial independence is every black woman's dream. A lot of black women have attained it, and more of them will. Financial independence is more than just being able to wear cool clothes and live in a decent home. Financial independence makes you live the kind of life that you desire. Not only that, it also helps you not to stick to limitations that you would have surpassed but for your finances.

A lot of people hold the belief that financial independence simply translates into very fat bank accounts. This is a little part of it, but there's still a lot more to it that you do not know yet. Having a fat bank account simply translates to you having money in just one place. I don't really fancy that.

I love to spread my money across different profitable ventures. By this, I mean investments.

Investing money would generate more passive income. You know why I call it passive? It's because I do not have to work for it. I'd enjoy the dividends of my investment while my capital is still intact. What more wonderful thing could there be? Dear black woman, learn to invest money in stocks and good businesses. It is one of the best ways to emancipate yourself from poverty and the troubles that come with not having enough money. I need you to know one thing before you dabble into investments. You have to prepare yourself for losses just as you anticipate the huge dividends. You know, the market fluctuates sometimes. Also, investment is a risky venture like business is. But, it is a risk worth taking.

You might have to take a couple of classes to be able to understand how the financial market works. There are also available training sessions by professionals that you can consider. That is the price that you must pay one way or the other. Don't let this price discourage you at all. It is worth it. Every day, I understand that nothing is truly free in this life. Save for the kindness that we get from people and other gifts, humans have to pay certain prices for things. If you understand this, it'll help you so much. Also, you wouldn't depend on people or blame them when you don't take action.

I understand the struggles that come with financial independence. But, don't worry too much about it. You won't go through it all alone. I'm with you as always to lead you through life changing affirmations for financial independence. Hold my hand, and let us begin.

Financial Independence Affirmations For The Black Woman

1. I attract wealth.
2. I am well equipped and fully ready to receive the wealth that I seek.
3. I manage my finances very well.
4. Money is a tool that'll help me reach my goals.
5. I invite money into my life.
6. I refrain from spending poorly with ease.
7. I am not consumed by my desire for money that I begin to seek it the wrong way.
8. I attract wealth.
9. I have rich and powerful ideas that lead me into wealth.
10. I invest my money in the most profitable ventures.

11. I am grateful for financial literacy.

12. I am blessed with an innovative mind that births millions.

13. I do not invest with greed.

14. I am confident of living my biggest financial dreams.

15. I connect with people that are interested in my financial growth.

16. I forgive myself for all the poor financial decisions I once made.

17. I am not ashamed to seek the financial expertise of experts when I get confused.

18. I have all it takes to improve my financial strength.

19. I distance myself from impulse buying and other negative habits that stop me from saving.

20. I value money and I handle it greatly.

21. I do not spend frivolously to impress anyone.

22. I get good dividends from my investment.

23. I make the most incredible financial decisions.

24. I'll become as rich as I have always dreamt no matter what

25. Wealthy looks really great on me.

26. I depend wholly on myself to rise into wealth.

27. I am happy because I know I am certainly going to reach the level of financial independence that I desire.

Key Points

My dear black woman, financial independence is not an empty dream. Do not let anyone discourage you at all. We believe that these affirmations would be of immense help to you. Before we proceed to the next session, do well to note the key points below.

- You have everything it takes to attain financial independence.
- You become richer when you eliminate bad spending habits like impulse buying.
- You can become as wealthy as you aspire to be.
- Your financial goals will become more attainable when you connect with people who share similar money dreams with you.
- Investing rightly can make you rich.

I Am Emotionally Independent

Emotional independence is one of the greatest types of Independence that any black woman could possibly know. Emotional independence is all about being able to exercise absolute control over your emotions and emotional life. To be honest with you, emotional independence is quite difficult for almost everyone because of how powerful our emotions could be. Emotional independence is difficult, but it is not impossible. Remember this always. It took me some time to learn how not to be easily influenced by my powerful emotions.

In the past, I used to ignore people who wronged me and treated me like I didn't matter because I didn't want to hurt their feelings. I used to be all sweet and kind to everyone. Even people who were mean to me were not left out. I was taken for granted because I was that perfect description of a good person. An angel. One major incident happened with a person I used to call friend before I realized what I was doing.

I used to have this person who I loved with all my heart. No, not romantic love. It was platonic affection. I would do everything I could to make this person happy and comfortable, but this person would never do the same for me. At first, I would make up silly excuses for this person's terrible behaviour towards me because I was really scared of accepting the glaring truth that reality had presented. It continued this way until I could no longer bear it. I connected all the pieces of the jigsaw puzzle together and I realized that this person was just a parasite who stayed around me to take advantage of my kindness. It was a very painful realization for me. I do not regret anything about it at all. Does it surprise you? I expected it to. That singular incident taught me a lot of emotional intelligence. The learning process was very painful, but it was worth it in the end. Mind you, it didn't rob me of my kind heart nor goodness. Rather, it opened my eyes to see that not everyone deserves it. I also learnt to keep my emotions in check. Being emotionally weak costs one too much. If you're not very careful, you could end up suffering a very serious breakdown.

My dear black woman, there is nothing cute about giving an arm for a person who wouldn't give a finger for you. Sometimes, our emotions overshadow our reason and make us turn blind to these things. One of the greatest forms of slavery ever is emotional slavery. It makes you sit in a room that shrinks you because you are too weak or afraid to leave. It keeps you in a toxic relationship because you feel you might never find a lover as passionate as your abuser. It makes you pile up excuses for people who treat you like a piece of dirt.

The list goes on and on. It never ends. But I know that you have all it takes to bring emotional dependence to an end in your own life. Like I said earlier, it is not an easy thing to do. But it is always worth it. You must understand that emotional independence is not a magical thing that happens just once. It is not the burst of a balloon. It takes time. Quality time. Emotional dependence is a psychological thing that sticks to a person like a tattoo. It doesn't go away at once. Little by little.
You can begin the journey to emotional independence by cutting away every single thing that makes you dependent. You would need a good amount of will power to do this well. It is totally okay if you are unable to do it all at once. You can as well do it little by little. Take small and steady steps. When the small steps accumulate over time they become big steps. You know that, don't you?

When you begin your emotional independence journey, do not make the mistake of going back to the things you left behind because you 'miss' them. This is one terrible mistake that many people make. Doing it could ruin the whole detachment and independence process for you. You might have to begin all over again. To avoid this, do everything you can not to ever go back.

The journey to emotional independence is a very stressful one. But you won't go through the stress and rigors all alone. I'll hold your hands carefully and tightly while I lead you through some strengthening emotional independence affirmations written just for you. Shall we begin?

1. I am in control of my emotions.
2. I do not give my emotions the power to dictate my life.
3. I am not easily influenced by my emotions.
4. I reciprocate the energy I get from people with so much ease.
5. I forgive myself for all the times I allowed my emotions lord over me.
6. I am not consumed by my emotions.
7. I refuse to give my emotions the power to overshadow my reasoning.
8. I have made peace with my emotions, I do not live in denial of them.
9. I will not let toxicity into my space because of my emotions.

10. I cut myself off from everyone and everything that manipulate my emotions.

11. I open myself up to gain emotional independence with elegance and ease.

12. I will never put myself up for abuse because of my emotions.

13. I step away from emotional manipulators.

14. I thrive the most when I am in control of my emotions.

15. I have mastered the act of calmness even when I am in a bad place.

16. I do not suffer any emotional trouble.

17. I accept my emotional flaws and I am willing to work on them.

18. I am powerful enough to do all it takes to gain emotional independence.

19. I accept that emotional independence is a process. I am willing to go through it all.

Key Points

My gorgeous black woman, remind yourself everyday of the power you possess. You have every single thing it takes to gain independence in every area of your life. Your emotions are inclusive. Below are the key points for this section.

- You have all it takes to become emotionally independent.
- Emotional independence is a process, it is not a one time thing.
- Everything could become a mess if you let your emotions overshadow your reason.
- Accept your emotional flaws and work on them.

I Make The Best Decisions All By Myself

Decision making is one very important aspect of our lives. It takes quite a lot to make good decisions. A lot of people find it hard to make their own decisions. Does this surprise you? People can still make decisions without necessarily knowing what decision making is all about. Some people also make their own decisions by consulting other people and finding out what they think about the decisions they are considering. This is actually a nice thing to do. One would make better decisions if one consults with the right people. This behavior only becomes a problem when the individual is unable to make independent decisions.

Independent decision making is all about being able to make good and wise decisions without the interference of other people. You know, at some point in your life, you would have to make decisions. Some of these decisions would require urgency. A bad decision is capable of ruining a lot of things for you and the ones you love. In a case of urgency where your yes or no could fix or mar things, who would you first consult before taking action? Yourself. The earlier you learn this, the better for you. You have to master the act of independent decision making. You'll never regret it.

Just like emotional independence, independent decision making might take you a while to fully master and practice. This is simply because habits die hard. Especially habits like this one that become a part of us. But, it is not impossible. No matter how dependent you are on other people when you need to make your decisions, you can still become independent. It only takes time.

The first step that you should employ as you begin to master independent decision making is acknowledgement. You have to acknowledge your dependence and inability to make your own decisions at that point in time. Living in denial of it would do you no good, really. Acknowledgement is that big step that you must first take. Afterwards, speak to yourself from the depth of your heart. Remind yourself that you possess a great brain that can help you make great decisions. Of course, being intelligent isn't all there is to making good decisions. But, reminding yourself of that intelligence, versatility, open mind, rationality and other important factors would surely increase your self-confidence. Do you know why self-confidence is important in decision making? It helps you trust your own decisions. Sometimes, people don't trust their own decisions. This is not because those people are bad at making decisions, it is because they lack self-confidence when it comes to decision making. Such people would still be afraid even after making the best decisions in the world. It is for this reason that I urge you to be confident of your own intelligence and ability to independently make good decisions for yourself. You have to be in charge of every area of your own life.

At first, when you begin to make your own decisions, you would want to go back to the old style of consulting other people. It is a normal feeling. Don't let it bother you too much. Do not give in to it either. My friend, that is the thing with habits. But you have all the power that you need to fight it off. Whenever the feeling comes knocking at the doors of your heart, remind yourself yet again of the price you paid to get to that level. You did not go through a lot of thought and growth processes to fall back to dependent decision making just like that.

I understand that the journey to independent decision making is no easy one. But I am certain that you can win. I'll be with you to strengthen and guide you through the process by taking you through powerful affirmations for independent decision making. Hold my hand and let us begin. Shall we?

1. I trust in my ability to make great decisions independently.
2. I am not afraid to decide major things in my own life.
3. I embrace independent decision making with all of my heart.
4. I refuse to be irrational and overly emotional in my decision making.
5. I make good decisions with a lot of ease.
6. I am aware of the importance of independent decision making.

7. My decision making process is not influenced by unimportant things.

8. I do not feel guilt for the times I could not make my own decisions.

9. I make the best decisions concerning my own affairs.

10. I am not pressured into making decisions that are bad for me.

11. I have a very brilliant thought process.

12. My decisions matter the most in my own life.

13. I give no one the power to bully me into making decisions that I do not like.

14. I am full of wisdom, I apply my wisdom in my decision making.

15. I do not let anyone make me feel terrible for making the best decisions for myself.

16. My decisions are valid, I'll not change them to fit in people's expectations of me.

17. I do not depend on other people to make decisions for myself.

18. I make good decisions even within a short time frame.

19. I am at peace with the fact that not all my decisions would turn out the way I expect them to.

20. I respect the decisions of others.

Key Points

Independent decision making has become a necessary skill that every one should possess. I believe these affirmations would lead you gallantly into the beautiful world of independent decision making. Below are the key points for this session.

- You have all it takes to make good decisions independently.
- Do not feel guilt nor beat yourself up for all the times you depended on people to make good decisions.
- Independent decision making is a process. It is not a one time thing. Be patient with yourself.

Again, we have come to the end of a chapter. Did you enjoy these independence affirmations? I trust that you did. Before we go on to the next, I want to advise you to always employ these affirmations in your daily life. You'd be amazed at how much independence that you would gain.

The next chapter is all about healing. You know, no one thrives by carrying so much hurt around. Come along with me, we'll explore affirmations for healing in interesting ways in the next chapter. Shall we begin?

Chapter Eight

Healing Affirmations For The Black Woman

Instead of saying, I'm damaged, broken, and I have trust issues, say, I'm healing, rediscovering myself, and starting over.
—Horacio Jones

At some point in our lives, we go through pain. Some of these pain could be light. Light enough for us to heal from them very quickly. But some could be very deep. So deep that we begin to think healing is an impossible thing. But I'll remind you that healing is never impossible no matter what. The only truth is that healing requires a lot of courage. It takes courage to even accept that you are breaking apart, that you have embraced so much sorrow, that your heart bleeds.

Several years ago, I experienced one hell of a heartbreak. I felt like dying. My whole world became dark. I wished to die or at least become oblivious of all that pain. The pain bore deeply into my bones. I thought I would be miserable for the rest of my life. But, look at me now. Full of joy and so much love. Healing of any kind only begins when you are ready for it. When you open up your heart to it. Healing first begins with acceptance. You know, a lot of people feel disappointed in themselves when they go through certain situations. They'd feel weak and powerless. Some would feel like the most terrible people on earth, some would curse at the world's injustice and weep deeply about it. In all of this, do not cause yourself more pain by living in denial of your hurt. You have to understand that it could have happened to anyone. You also have to understand that these things don't happen because you are a bad person. They happen because they can. It is okay if you want to be a little hysterical before the acceptance. It is okay to cry and cuss at fate. But it is not okay to be at a low place forever. You know that, don't you?

My darling woman, I am urging you to drop that baggage of pain that continually steals your joy. No matter what happens, you are deserving of joy. And most importantly, healing. When you heal, joy will flow effortlessly. Healing is not wearing fake smiles in the midst of people and pretending it no longer hurts. Healing is all about embracing the hurt, letting go of it and not letting it decide your life anymore. You are a queen who is in charge of her own life. Pain is too small to influence your life till the end. No, I'm not trying to belittle your pain. Rather, I am letting you know that pain is unworthy of ruling your magnificent life. You deserve something great and beautiful and kind. Today, step into the path of healing and embrace it. Also, remember to walk away from all the things that break you. Don't worry, I won't let you walk the path alone. I'll hold your hand as always and walk you through powerful affirmations for healing. Believe me, you are going to heal. You are going to smile again. Now, shall we begin?

1. I welcome total healing into my existence.
2. I'll no longer allow the pain I experienced to rule my life.
3. I acknowledge the hurt and all that it brought, but I'll not wallow in them. I choose healing.
4. My past experiences do not define me.
5. I give nothing the power and the permission to steal my joy.
6. I am worthy of healing.
7. I believe in my ability to heal and be joyful again no matter the depth of the pain.
8. Healing comes easy to me.
9. I'll not pretend to have healed when I have not.
10. I understand that healing is but a gradual process. I am willing to go through all of it.
11. I believe in my unique ability to heal from every fall.

12. I am happy to heal.

13. I understand the essence of healing, I desire it with my heart. And I know that I'll get it no matter what.

14. I have all the courage I need to walk away from everything that breaks me.

Key Points

When pain is acknowledged, healing becomes much easier. This section is all about healing and rising above the pain. Find the key points for this session below.

- Healing begins to happen when you acknowledge the pain and decide to not let it govern you anymore.
- You have all it takes to heal.
- Be bold enough to walk away from all the things that cause your pain.
- Remind yourself always that healing is not an impossible thing to achieve.
- Nothing possesses the power to stop your own healing.
- You are in charge of your own life. Live it as such, my dear black woman.

Healing of The Body

Do you feel so much pain in your physical body that you wonder if it'll ever go away? Do you suffer from an illness? Does it hurt a lot? Does it break you from the inside? I want you to know one thing. You'll find this healing that you seek, it will come to you, never to disappear ever again. Your body is not a home to illnesses. It is a home to good health, peace of mind and absolute love. You deserve a healthy body and all the goodness that heralds it. And you will get it. No, these are not just words. They will come to pass. Say them to yourself everyday with power.

While you make affirmations for good health in your body, please do not make the mistake of ignoring your medications because you are expecting some sort of miracle to happen. I have seen a lot of people do this. You know, they'd abandon their medications and begin to disobey their doctor's instructions. Healing doesn't work like that at all. It is one thing to acknowledge the illness and weakness in your body, it is also another thing to heal. Healing requires you to diligently take your medications. Your medications are like catalysts that trigger your healing. If you don't take them, how will healing come?

Also, a lot of people shy away from medications because of fear. This unexplainable fear of things going wrong or getting worse because of the medications. When people are like this, they'd subconsciously look out for stories of medicine killing people, infections making people paralyzed and other similar stories like these ones. I think this behavior is a human thing. Whenever we humans find a thing scary, we begin to look out for scarier things about that thing to reaffirm our stance.

My friend, that's a very toxic way to live life. Doing that will make you blind to healing. That's not the only thing it does. It also fills your mind up with a lot of negativity. Negativity has a great power. It weakens you beyond your imagination. And, I am sure that's not what you want for yourself. To know healing, you have to master how to eliminate negativity. It slows down healing. Going to good hospitals can help reduce your fear. Do you know why? The chances of facing complications and being treated the wrong way is lesser in good hospitals with qualified health care personnel compared to substandard hospitals. The only downside to it is that you would have to spend more money on health care. The truth is, quality health care is not cheap.

But, this won't be so much of a problem to you if you have health insurance. Health insurance companies work hard to help you get quality health care at the cheapest prices. You should consider getting one. You mustn't be ill before getting health insurance. In fact, it is a necessity. Don't let anyone tell you otherwise.

Choose healing and decide to see the best things. Think healing and embrace healing. You'd be surprised at the amount of healing that you'll know. Choosing healing is not very easy. No thanks to sad stories people hear and the pessimism that comes with being ill sometimes. None of these should discourage you. You have the power to not allow them. Remember this always. In this section, I'll hold your hands tightly like I have always done. Then I'll walk you through some wonderful affirmations for healing in your body. I write each and every one of them for you. I pour all my love in them. Now, let's begin your healing journey. Shall we?

1. I have good health in my life.
2. I acknowledge my pains, and I know they'll go away.
3. I do not give my illness the power to dictate my life.
4. I'll walk through this and leave unscathed.
5. This pain will not steal my joy.
6. Good health comes easy to me.

7. My medications work beautiful wonders in my body.

8. This pain will not be the end of me.

9. I eat healthy foods. I take off all unhealthy foods from my diet.

10. I am healthier and stronger than ever before.

11. My cells work towards healing. Every organ in my body is receptive of good health and strength.

12. I welcome happiness and peace and good health into my life.

13. I release all toxins and disease causing organisms from my body.

14. I do not take my medications in vain, they will work efficiently and help me heal fully.

15. I entertain thoughts of healing alone. Negative thinking has no place in my mind.

16. I have a very strong immune system that works to ensure that I am healthy.

17. I am encompassed by healing energies.

18. I have an amazing body.

19. I am grateful for good health.

20. I take care of my body.

21. I indulge in only healthy habits.

22. I release every negative emotion that is making me unhealthy.

23. My body gets every nutrient it requires from what I eat.

24. I am full of unstoppable energy.

25. I am very delighted to be alive.

26. I radiate positivity, strength and good health.

27. I develop a healthy lifestyle.

28. I am deserving of good health.

29. I am open to discarding everything that works against my health.

30. I love and adore my body. I forgive myself for the times I didn't care for my body well.

31. I am not overwhelmed by the pain and discomfort I feel.

Key Points

Good health is one of the greatest things anyone could ever have. That is why I am exceedingly glad that I led you through these powerful healing affirmations. Below are the key points for this section. Remember them daily, would you?

- You are deserving of good health.
- Your thoughts affect your health. Think and embrace positivity always.

- Love your body, nurture it like a tender child. Do not forget to forgive yourself for the times you didn't treat your body right.
- Healthy foods would help you heal faster. Ditch all the junk.
- You'll walk through your illness and leave unscathed.

My Heart Is Healed; Affirmations For Heartbreak

A heartbreak is one of the saddest things that could ever happen to anyone. It's sadder when you tried all you could to make it work and it never did . You'd cry and wonder where it all went wrong. You'd see pictures of your lover and cry your heart out. Your favorite memories might even begin to haunt you. For someone like me who has experienced a couple of heartbreaks, I understand how it steals one's happiness and makes one second guess every act of kindness. It is that terrible.

When the relationship is over, don't blame yourself for anything. It only worsens everything. I can attest to this. The first time my partner broke up with me, I contemplated suicide. It was my first relationship and I had wished it would end with a happily ever after. You know, I wanted a perfect love story where it's all rosy and sweet. When my partner sent me the breakup text, I felt like a part of me died. That is the thing with loving people. When you love anyone, especially in a romantic relationship, you give a part of yourself to that person. When the relationship ends, you'll try to get that part of yourself back. That's almost impossible. The hurt and detachment would literally ruin you. You'll find yourself breaking up at the slightest thing.

When that break up happened, I spent days gloating and wondering what went wrong. I kept on trying to find out what I did wrong. I still faulted myself even in situations where I did nothing wrong. I was desperately in love. I didn't even realize when I started apologizing for the things I didn't do. I did every single thing I could to make my partner take me back. But it was all futile. I desperately needed some closure, but my partner didn't give it. It made me think so much and wonder what I did wrong. I was blind to all the toxicity in the relationship. The verbal abuse and everything. I always felt like I wasn't enough. At some point, I began to do things I usually wouldn't do because I wanted to keep my partner. I didn't realize I tried too hard until it ended. A good number of black women stay put in toxic relationships because of the fear of losing their partners. It's one of the most toxic things ever. You are too full of beauty and intelligence to be treated like dirt. When the relationship begins to shrink you and shape you into what you do not like, do yourself some honor and catwalk away like the Queen that you are. It is not an easy thing to do, but it is worth it. It'll save you from future heartbreak.

Now, remember that the first step to take in order to heal is to accept the reality of the break up. Not like there's anything that you can do about it. Then, don't blame yourself for anything. Don't blame your partner either. It ended because you both wouldn't work out. Don't gloat about it. Also, don't hurt yourself by trying to live in denial. Pretending it never happened only makes the pain go deeper.

The mending of a broken heart is a very gradual process. On some days, you'd party and celebrate your healing. On other days, you fall into deep sadness because your favourite memory of your partner made you cry. You'd heal sometimes and relapse sometimes. But the ultimate truth is that you'd definitely heal no matter what. You have to take little and steady steps as you navigate your way around healing. You'll need a good amount of courage too. Then self-control. It is self-control that'll keep you from calling your ex at the slightest opportunity. It is courage that'll make you slowly discard the things that trigger your tears no matter how much those things used to mean to you. Do you understand this?

One more thing. Take as much time as you need to heal.
Don't make the mistake of getting into a new relationship
immediately because you want to prove a point to your
former partner. It is a very dangerous game to play, and
you'd be the only one that ends up hurt in it. You don't need
to prove anything to your partner. Your healing and
happiness is all that matters. Let this stick.

Don't fret, you won't walk through this healing alone. I am
with you as always to lead you through sincere and
beautiful healing affirmations. Your heart won't stay broken
forever. Hold my hand and let us begin.

1. I am grateful for all the good times I had in my past
   relationship. I regret nothing at all.
2. This break-up is the beginning of a beautiful phase in
   my life.
3. I am happy to begin my life afresh.
4. I choose to be happy despite the hurt.
5. I am my own happiness.
6. I choose healthy relationships.
7. I love myself at all times.
8. I accept my hurt, and I'll do everything I can to heal
   from it.
9. I do not wish my former partner any pain.

10. There is so much love in me.

11. I am grateful to have loved and be loved.

12. I let go of the hurt.

13. I am not afraid to open my heart to love.

14. I know that I'll find the love I deserve someday.

15. I heal with elegance and ease.

16. I forgive myself.

17. My life is beautiful the way it is.

18. This heartbreak won't ruin my love life. I'll have a wonderful relationship with my new partner.

19. I'll never give up on who I am for the sake of a relationship.

20. I have all the courage I need to walk away from a toxic relationship.

21. I am grateful for the lessons my previous relationship taught me.

22. I attract my dream partner.

23. I believe in my ability to heal.

24. There is a better person waiting for me.

25. I do not give up on love.

26. My heart is whole.

27. I understand that healing takes time, I am ready to go through the process.

28. I'll love and laugh again.

29. I am worthy of love.

30. I am too beautiful to be stuck in a bad relationship. I
   walk away with all elegance.

Key Points

You'll heal from the heartbreak, you'll find your dream
partner and you'll love again. Below are the key points for
this session.

- You'll heal from the hurt.
- A failed relationship doesn't define your love life.
- Don't be afraid of walking out of a toxic relationship.
- You are worthy of love.
- You heal faster when you don't live in denial of your
  pain.
- You are whole.

Affirmations For Mental Healing

When we talk about good health, most of us just think about
our physical body. But, that's not all there is to good health.
Our mental health is one aspect of our health that we do
not pay a lot of attention to. Mental health includes our

psychological, emotional and social well-being. Anything that affects our mental health has the power to affect our physical body too. This is one great reason why we should never ignore our mental health.

There's this popular misconception that a lot of people hold about mental health. They think it doesn't just come, that it is always caused by something. No, this is not always the truth. Sometimes, one can begin to face mental health problems out of the blue. I'll use depression as an example. I used to think that I could never get depressed because of the great life I had. I mean, I live my life on my terms and I am able to do the things that I desire with a lot of ease. Why would I get depressed? I thought like this until a strong wave of depression hit me from nowhere. I began to lose interest even in those things that made my whole existence nearly perfect. At first, I lived in denial of it. I felt greatly disappointed in myself. What reason did I have to fall into depression?

I lived in my denial for a while. I had to get a therapist. It was that kind therapist that sat me down and educated me about mental illnesses and how they could happen to just anyone. I did a lot of unlearning, and I'm absolutely grateful for all of them. Now that I have talked about this misconception, I will talk about the triggers. Your triggers are simply the things that cause a fall in your mental health. Those things that cause mental illness. Triggers could be anything. They could be your own thoughts, people, memories, situations and a lot of others. Some people suffer a lot of mental health issues because they find it difficult to identify their triggers.

To have good mental health and to be able to recover from any mental illness quickly, you need to learn how to identify the things that cause your mental illness. Doing it all by yourself could be very stressful sometimes, so you can always do it with a therapist. Don't be ashamed to talk about what you go through with a therapist, it's one of the first and greatest steps that you can ever take towards true healing.

My dear black woman, you have to learn how to guard your mental health with jealousy. Guard it and treasure it with everything that you are. There's something I want you to know. You do not have to indulge anyone or anything that robs you of good mental health no matter how 'tempting' it appears to be. Nothing, my dear, is worth your mental health. If your mental health is unstable, it would affect a lot of things in your life. Not just your physical health, but other important things like your productivity, relationships, finances and a lot of others. Do you realize how important your mental health is now? Never trade it for anything. Whenever you notice that your mental health is unstable, do not ignore it. It could grow into something terrible. Get the help you need.

I know that walking this path of adequate mental health care is not an easy thing to do at all. But I know that you can do it. I trust in your abilities. All of them! I won't leave you alone to walk the path all alone. I'll be with you as always and hold your hands and walk you through some powerful mental health affirmations written just for you.

1. I take absolute charge of my mental health.
2. I am not ashamed to seek health for my mental issues.
3. I guard my mental health with jealousy.
4. Nothing is worth my mental health.
5. I have all the courage I need to walk away from anything that threatens my mental health.
6. I love and cherish my mental health.
7. I have all it takes to heal completely from mental illness.
8. I do not give my trauma the power to rule my life.
9. My mental illness doesn't define me. I am so much more.
10. I do not live in denial of my mental illness.

11. My mental health flourishes greatly.

12. I walk away from everything that triggers me with ease.

13. I do not keep my triggers close for any reason.

14. I am not ashamed nor afraid to open up to my therapist.

15. I have all I need to heal.

16. My mental healing is not an impossible thing, it'll come to me no matter what.

17. I break free from every single thing that torments my mental health.

18. I do not entertain anything that affects my mental health.

19. I have access to the kind of therapy that I need.

20. I have the finances I need to take care o of my mental health.

21. I do not ignore my mental health.

22. I am not afraid to dissociate myself from anyone that makes me fall into depression.

23. I do not blame myself for my mental illness.

24. I am aware that a mental illness is not a death sentence, I'll heal and be joyful again.

25. I do the things that make me joyful.

Key Points

Embrace mental healing as much as you embrace physical healing and you'd see how well you would function. Below are the key points for this section.

- Your mental health is worth it. Do not keep your triggers close.
- Do not be ashamed of getting help, getting help doesn't make you weak.
- Be strong enough to walk away from everything that makes a mess of your mental health.
- A mental illness is not a death sentence, you'll heal, and you'll be joyful again.

We have come to the end of this chapter! It was such a beautiful and heartwarming thing to go through these affirmations with you. I hope these healing affirmations strengthen you and help you heal in the most beautiful ways. The next chapter is all about affirmations for black women in leadership. It promises to be a very rewarding chapter. Read on, let's explore it all together!

Chapter Nine

Affirmations For Black Women In Leadership

Leadership is not about titles, positions and flowcharts. It is about one life influencing another.
—John Maxwell

Whenever leadership is mentioned, most people tend to only think of being in the position of power. You know, all that authority and power. The titles and the privileges that come with position. But, leadership is beyond that. John Maxwell reaffirms in the quote I wrote at the beginning of this chapter. To be a leader is to oversee the affairs of a certain group. To be a leader is to ensure that everything about that group tilts towards the right direction. Leadership involves a lot of management and care more than it involves the use of power. This is why passion and dedication are one of the major attributes of good leaders. If a leader has no passion for the office, the leader may not be able to do a very good job.

Black women make great leaders. Black women are strong, resilient, powerful and full of intelligence. Believe me when I tell you that black women are one of the most intelligent people on earth. This might cause a question to brew in your heart. Why then do black women shy away from contesting for offices? There are a lot of reasons for this. Some black women shy away from power because they believe the false narrative other people sold to them about black women not being good enough to occupy positions of power. This is one big lie that some black women have been made to believe. If you believe in this lie, I put it to you that it is a fallacy. Take it out of your heart today and thrash it. It holds no atom of truth.

There are also black women who do not contest for offices because of fear. The fear of not being able to do it right. Leadership is very overwhelming, but you can do it awesomely if you put your heart to it. You have the unique ability to do anything you desire if you put your heart to it. Yes, you are powerful like that. Letting fear govern your desire for leadership would make you unable to reach your potential. I understand your fears. Your fears are valid. But your fears become very strong when you give it power. You give your fear power when you let it take deep roots in your life. When you let it determine the outcome of your life. My dear black woman, don't you want an adventurous, beautiful and fulfilling life? I know you do for sure. It is very achievable. But how can you achieve it with fear? How can you step out of conformity if you are afraid? No way at all. You have to kill that fear.

Look around you today. There are lots of black women doing great things in leadership. For them, I'll write the affirmations in this session. A lot of black women agitate for revolution. But only few black women are willing to do what it takes to bring the revolution. These women are found in leadership. Are you a black woman in leadership? Does it get overwhelming sometimes? I know it does. But you can win no matter what. You can leave your mark in this world of ours.

I understand how overwhelming being in the leadership sector is, but I urge you not to throw in the towel. I am right there with you to encourage you, cheer you on and strengthen you. Hold my hand and let us walk through some powerful affirmations for black women in leadership together.

1. I do absolutely well in leadership.
2. I have all it takes to be a leader.
3. I embrace quality leadership only, mediocrity does not thrive in my space.
4. I am willing to lead other black women like me into the revolution that they seek.
5. I thrive in leadership.

6. I am no despotic leader, I lead with kindness, love and fairness.

7. I care about the opinions of my followers.

8. I incorporate true democracy into my leadership.

9. I am the best leader there is.

10. I am not overwhelmed by the difficulties that come with leadership.

11. I am deeply loved and valued by my followers.

12. I am not afraid to stand for what is right.

13. I am not afraid to stand up to oppressors.

14. I give leadership a more beautiful and brighter meaning by being a very good leader.

15. I make decisions that favor my followers and every single person under my leadership.

16. I am not afraid to lead.

17. I am blessed with enlightened and understanding followers.

18. Leadership is not a struggle for me.

19. I lead with passion, I am not blinded by the power that comes with my position.

20. I do not intimidate my followers into obedience. I make them see reasons with me instead.

21. I am grateful for being able to lead.

22. I value my followers greatly.

23. I am the best version of myself even in leadership.

Key Points

Dear black woman, I hope these affirmations help you in your quest to become a great leader. Below are the key points for this section.

- You have all it takes to lead.
- The opinions of your followers matter. Do not impose anything on them.
- Do not be blinded by the power that comes with leadership. It could ruin you.
- Be fair and honest in your leadership.
- Believe in your dreams and vision, do not let anyone intimidate you into silence.

Affirmations For Black Women Looking To Venture Into Leadership

A lot of black women do not venture into leadership because they do not get the push they need. Some people love to be motivated into action. While others just do their thing all by themselves. The first group of people are larger in population than the second group. There is no difficult science behind this. When people motivate you, you'll feel this sense of support and love. You'll know that you're not alone. The truth is, when we are pursuing anything, we tend to give more energy to it when we know that people are solidly behind us. For a thing like politics where winning or losing is a major thing, we'd desire more motivation and support than ever.

But what happens if there is no one to support us the way we want to be supported? What becomes of our ambitions if the only support we have is ourselves? Do we abandon them or do we forge ahead? Abandoning them looks like the easiest thing to do, right? It is, but it isn't. Abandoning your ambitions because you did not find the support you need is not a great thing to do. You'll end up hurt and sad in the long run. You may hate yourself for not trying at all. Believe me, regret is one of the worst feelings ever. It'll make you beat yourself up and hate yourself. The powerlessness of it all is even more terrible because you won't be able to do anything to erase the past. Traveling back in time is the perfect thing to do, but it exists only in the world of fiction. This is real life, dear woman. You have to know that you are all the motivation that you need. Your support and love for yourself will take you far. When people see you excelling and moving mountains all by yourself, they'll be interested in joining your cause. Success has many friends is no cliché at all. It indeed has many friends. That's why people would fight against a cause at first and later support it because they want to identify with success.

I believe you have your answer now. Don't you? If you're in search of motivation or a push, look deeply within yourself and you'll find all that you seek. The passion that you have for what you do will motivate you. Your big dreams will motivate you. The goals of your leadership will motivate you. Leadership mostly comes with a lot of opposition. You have to get ready for them. Don't expect everyone to welcome you with open arms or smile with you. All you really have is you. Your supporters come second. You're curious about why this is so right? See, you may treat people with all the kindness and love that you know and still have them treat you like shit. Naturally, you would expect people to treat you the way you treat them, right? I used to think like that too. But I have long learnt that the world doesn't work like that. People won't always treat you the way you would treat them and things won't always go the way you plan. Know this and know peace.

Also, don't try to get into leadership by buying your way through people's hearts and bringing out your true self later. It doesn't end well. Not only do you break people's trust, you also teach them not to support you later. Don't make the mistake of wearing a mask to be loved, be your most authentic self. The people that will love you will love you and the ones that will support you will. Pretence is a dangerous game to play.

Don't be afraid to go into leadership, you can win big if you work towards it. I understand that leadership is no stroll in the park too. That is why I'll be giving you all my love and support. I'll hold your hand through every line in this section and walk you through powerful affirmations I specially wrote for every black woman who is looking to go into leadership.

1. I have all it takes to lead.
2. I am my biggest supporter.
3. I am willing to learn all that there is to becoming a good leader.
4. I'll do exceedingly great in leadership.
5. I'll not become who I am not to be loved by people. I'll be my most authentic self.
6. I am proud to be in leadership.
7. I am not afraid to go into leadership.
8. I'll achieve all of my leadership dreams.
9. I don't gloat over poor leadership, I'll go into it and change the narrative.
10. I am the dream of black women leadership.

11. I'll win on every side.

12. Leadership comes easy to me.

13. I am governed by my passion and love for leadership.

14. I am deeply loved and supported.

15. I lead with wisdom and confidence.

16. I am not afraid to lead.

17. I trust in my leadership skills.

18. I open myself to learning things that would make me a good leader.

19. I am not consumed by leadership.

20. I am a wonderful leader.

21. I have all it takes to be the kind of leader I have always dreamed of.

22. I'll perform more than my expectations.

23. I am ready to give my best to leadership. I'll not be blinded by power or money.

24. I understand that leadership is more than just office work. I'll be the leader that works above it.

Key Points

My dear black woman, do not be afraid to go into leadership. You have everything it takes to do it excellently. Below are the key points for this section.

- You have everything you need to become a leader.

- Do not let the wealth or power that comes with your office stop you from executing your dreams.
- Open yourself to learning all the time. It'll make you a good leader.
- Don't complain so much about the state of leadership, go into it and change the narrative to a better one.

Affirmations For Black Women Being Intimidated In Leadership.

A lot of black women have conquered many obstacles surrounding black women leadership. A lot of black women have risen into leadership. One would think this is all there is not knowing there is more in store. I used to think that every other obstacle would cease to exist the moment black women debuted into leadership. I was so wrong. It is saddening that a lot of black women still face problems while in leadership. The most common problem that they face is intimidation. Does this amaze you? It doesn't amaze me so much, really. People are greatly threatened and frightened by the enormous power and audacity that black women show in leadership. So they try to silence black women by intimidating them into silence. I'm not making this up. Engage black women in leadership in deep conversations and you'll be amazed at how much this intimidation has eaten deep into black women leadership. But I beg of you, do not let it deter you. Black women come from a history of Amazons and great women who trampled anything that tried to kill them to death. No one can end the power of a black woman unless she gives that person permission. Are you awed by this? Don't be. It is the truth about you. This is the truth that they do not want you to know. They do not want you to know it because the more self-aware you become, the more difficult it would be to intimidate you.

How can black women deal with the issue of intimidation in leadership? Do they back out or not? Giving up is never the option in cases like this one. Running away from a bully empowers the bully to trouble you more. You fight a bully by standing up for yourself. In high school, I had a bully in my class. He'd torment us, forcefully take our snacks and force us to do his school work for him. We'd do everything he commanded because we were afraid of being intimidated and beaten. None of us ever dared to speak up. Our silence empowered the bully. The bullying continued until I could no longer bear it. I had to become the Devil's Advocate. I reported to our teacher. Our teacher dealt seriously with the bully and the bullying stopped for a while. It started again. This time, I was the only target of the bully. My crime was reporting to the teacher. The bully made life so much hell. At that point, I realized that reporting to the teacher wasn't the best solution. I had to fight for myself. There comes a point in your life where you would have to stand up for yourself. It was that point in my own life. It met me afraid and without preparation.

One day, I got into a fist fight with the bully. I don't know what gave me that courage till this day. Before anyone could stop us, I had beaten the bully to a pulp. I cried in amazement. I never knew I could win such a bulky frame in a fight. It was too good to be true. That fight caused a turning point in my life. I humbled the bully.

Most people that intimidate black women in leadership are like this bully. Their weapons are always fear, intimidation and the manipulation of power to suit selfish interests. My dear black woman, I urge you to stand up for yourself and fight them off like my younger self. You don't know how powerful you can be until you try. If you're too afraid to fight all alone, tell your sisters, other black women like you. When black women unite, they become invincible.

I won't leave you to fight the intimidation all alone. I'll hold your hands and bear you up like I have always done by taking you through powerful affirmations. These affirmations will help you fight with strength and courage. Shall we begin our walk through the affirmations?

1. I have all the courage I need to stand up to anyone that intimidates me.
2. I give no one the permission to intimidate me into silence.
3. I am worthy to be in leadership.
4. I cannot be trampled by anyone.
5. My leadership gives room to no mediocrity.
6. I attract people that believe in my leadership dreams.
7. I have the best support system.
8. I am not afraid to stand up to a system that is designed to oppress.
9. I give no one the power to silence me into submission.
10. I lead with wisdom.
11. I do not compromise my office for any reason.
12. I do not indulge in criminal acts to stay relevant in office.
13. I am not afraid to stand up for myself.
14. I attract black women in leadership whose dreams align with mine.
15. I join forces with other black women to fight oppression.
16. I am not silent in the face of oppression.

17. I'll cause a positive change in black women's leadership.

18. I dissociate myself from everything that would make leadership difficult for me.

19. I am not afraid to be my truest self even in leadership.

20. I am too powerful to be intimidated by anyone.

21. Black women leadership will grow from strength to strength in my time.

22. My leadership bears a lot of excellence.

23. I am willing to incorporate new and productive strategies into my leadership.

24. I support no form of intimidation.

25. I am aware that the bully is only as strong as I make it.

26. I lead wisely even in private establishments.

27. My good leadership skills are evident even in my personal life.

28. No intimidation can end me. I end it.

Key Points

Intimidation ends when you stand up to the bully. Remember this always and muster the courage you need to fight anyone that tries to shrink you into yourself. You have the power you need to fight. Below are the key points for this section.

- You have all it takes to fight anyone that intimidates you.
- Do not bow to intimidation. Stand your ground. The bully becomes afraid of you when you stand your ground.
- Be willing to incorporate new ideas and great strategies into your leadership.
- Do not make the mistake of indulging in crime to stay relevant in leadership. You most likely won't love the outcome.

We have come to the end of this chapter, I hope these affirmations for leadership strengthens you and empowers you for the next big thing that you wish to embark on. The next chapter will be all about self-confidence affirmations for gorgeous black women like you. Come with me, let's explore it all together!

Chapter Ten

Self-Confidence Affirmations For Black Women

Your success will be determined by your own confidence and fortitude.
—Michelle Obama

Sometimes, when I see people cry about how no one believes in them, the first question I ask is 'do you believe in yourself?' This is a truth that you must know. Your confidence in yourself is what propels other people to believe in you. A lot of people have very twisted views of self-confidence. Self-confidence is not being defensive or trying to shut people up when they try to point out things that you don't want them to point out to you.

Self-Confidence is your ability to trust in your own judgement, qualities and yourself. Self-confidence is that driving force that propels you to take up tasks that other people find challenging. Read the quote at the beginning of this chapter again. Let it sink deeply into you. Your success will be determined by the level of your self-confidence. I realized this truism a very long time ago, and that is why I am extremely daring. You never know how well you can excel in a thing until you try. Self-confidence pushes to try. Without self-confidence, you'll hold back even from doing things that you can do with effortless ease.

There comes a point in everyone's life where they would have to stand up for themselves and encourage themselves. The truth is, people may not believe in you all the time. Especially in situations that seem absurd or when you begin to dream some very big dreams. At that point in time, you may begin to think that people are not wicked or unkind because they do not believe in your biggest dreams. It would interest you to know that that's not often the case in most times. They do not believe in you simply because what you bring to the table is strange to them. They would need some evidence to hold on to before they can really believe you. So, you have to believe in yourself first. For instance, someone tells you there's a time traveler in town who can take you through time. In this case? What would be your first reaction? You'd most likely call it bluff because of the absurdity of it all. But the moment you see some solid evidence, your unbelief would be cleared. In this example, you are the time traveler who needs to perform the magic and the people are those who wouldn't believe in you until evidence is provided.

Do you understand how it works now? Your self-confidence is paramount. Being confident in one's self is not an easy thing to do. Sometimes, the doubt will creep in when you least expect it to. It is in moments like that that you would need to step up and remind yourself of what you stand for. While you do that, also remember to remind yourself of the power you possess to make that thing come true. Think of the good things that self-confidence helped you achieve and do not be afraid to take the big leap.

I know how demanding this self-confidence thing can become, and that is why I'd be supporting you along every step of the day. I'll hold your hand through this page and lead you through some energizing and motivating self-confidence affirmations written specially for you. Shall we begin?

1. I believe in my dreams. And I am aware that I have everything I need to realize them.
2. I am confident in myself even if no one else is.
3. I trust in my abilities and strengths.
4. I give no one the power to take away my self-confidence. I guide it with so much zeal and jealousy.

5. I give myself the freedom to step away from everything that makes me lose faith in myself.

6. I am highly confident in myself, and I believe in my dreams no matter how absurd other people might find them.

7. I am confident in my abilities to accomplish great things.

8. My self-confidence helps me rise to the top with so much ease.

9. I eliminate self-doubt in my life.

10. I am aware of the value of self-confidence, I work hard to gain mine and I sustain it with ease.

11. My self-confidence is a very powerful feature about me.

12. My self-confidence makes me know when to leave a place that continually shrinks me.

13. I am not afraid to undertake big projects.

14. I can do anything I put my heart to.

15. Self-doubt has no place in me.

16. I set the standard with my self-confidence.

17. I attain the greatest heights because I embrace self-confidence.

18. My self-confidence ushers me into a lot of goodness.

19. Self-confidence looks beautiful on me.

20. People believe in me greatly because of my self-confidence.

Key Points

My dearest black woman, your self-confidence is one of the greatest attires that you can wear. It stands you out from thousands. Below are the key points for this session.

- There is no single thing that you cannot do if you put your heart to it.
- Do not be afraid to take on big projects and opportunities.
- Your self-confidence is attractive, do not let anyone make you feel otherwise.
- Dare to try!

I Step Out Of My Comfort Zone

Some black women do not reach their apex because they do not step out of the confines of their comfort zones. Not stepping out of that place that offers you a lot of ease stops you from reaching great heights.

At some point in my life, I stayed put in an average job simply because I was afraid of what would happen if I began to venture out and explore big opportunities. I didn't understand the source of this fear at first. It wasn't because of qualifications. I had great ones. I was passionate about what I loved doing, but I still found it difficult to venture out. It took me sometime to realize that despite the great skills I possessed, I lacked something very important. Self-confidence. The absence of self-confidence in you can make you seem like the least bright person in the room even when you're the brightest. There is this thing that self-confidence does to a person that I am yet to find a perfect name for. It makes you stand out brilliantly. It makes your work become more glaring and beautiful. That's how beautiful it is. You know, people believe in you as much as you want them to. If you're not confident in yourself one bit, why would you expect anyone to be confident in you? It doesn't work that way at all. You have to do it first. You have to put in that work.

Sometimes, you'd relax in a mediocre place and endure poor treatments not because that is what you deserve, but because that is what you have chosen. Believe me, not daring yourself to go all out isn't beneficial at all. You might even begin to regret it later. You should know that you have all it takes to do the things that you want to do. Don't be afraid of venturing out into big things. You are deserving of it. Stepping out of your comfort zone is one of the best things that you could possibly do for yourself. It helps you grow and makes you open to more opportunities.

Don't feel overwhelmed by these at all. You don't have to do it all at once. No one does that even. You have to start with some basic steps. Then you progress into bigger ones. To step out of your comfort zone, the first step that you should take is reprogramming your mind. Do you find this strange? I'm not exactly surprised. You know, that fear or complacency that holds you back from stepping out of your comfort zone begins from your mind. That is why I put it to you that the first step is reprogramming your mind. You'd have to unlearn a lot of things. You'd have to unlearn how to accept mediocrity with open arms, how to stay in places that do not benefit you and how to follow the norms.

Stepping out of your comfort zone would make you realize that beauty is not always in conformity. Sometimes, it is in you giving yourself the power and confidence to be the odd one out. Today, I urge you to step out of your comfort zone. I understand that you need a good dose of self-confidence to step out of it. I'll help you by going through some powerful affirmations with you. Hold my hand tightly let us begin our affirmation journey. I'm ready, are you?

1. I have all it takes to excel beyond my comfort zone.

2. I am worthy of great things. I am a great person, and I won't let anyone make me feel less of it.
3. I do not embrace the complacency that comes with being in my comfort zone.
4. I dare myself to step out and reach for the greatest things.
5. I am confident in all of my abilities.
6. I do not find mediocrity attractive nor beneficial.
7. I have all I need to step out from a boring conformity.
8. I do not conform to anything that shrinks me.
9. I cease everyday to remind myself that my comfort zone is not where my apex lies.
10. I'll reach my apex and I'll flourish greatly.
11. I am not afraid to step out of my comfort zone.
12. I embrace self-confidence with the whole of my being.
13. I am grateful for the blessings that self-confidence brings.
14. I stun everyone with my gorgeous self-confidence.
15. I am beautiful the most when I'm confident in myself.
16. I wear my self-confidence with so much pride and elegance.
17. I gracefully step out of my comfort zone.
18. I am ready and willing to take up new challenges and tasks.

19. I am not overwhelmed by the stress and fear that leaving a comfort zone sometimes bring.

20. I believe in all of my dreams.

21. I give my comfort zone no power over me.

22. I am not enticed by my comfort zone. I step out into greatness.

Key Points

Dare to step out of your comfort zone. Dare to take up great opportunities. Dare to take charge of your self-confidence level. You have everything that it takes, remember this always. Below are the key points for this section.

- You have everything it takes to step out of your comfort zone.
- The apex that you seek to reach doesn't reside in your comfort zone, you have to step out and reach for it.
- You do not have to conform to be accepted, you can set the standard.
- Wear your self-confidence with a lot of pride. It looks very great on you.
- Do not embrace the mediocrity that the comfort zone offers. You are worth a lot more.

I Am Rooting For Myself Even If No One Does

Do you love the title of this section? I chose this title for the sole purpose of strengthening you, I hope you love it. Have you ever thought of this question, what becomes of me if no one roots for me even with my self-confidence? Do I throw self-confidence all away or beg people to root for me?

I am somewhat certain that questions like this one do arise in your heart from time to time. My friend, they are nothing to feel bad about. They simply show that you are a human with a very active mind. The truth is, I've been in quite similar situations to these ones. No one believed in me. They didn't see the things I saw in my own ideas. It was very frustrating, but I think it equipped me for the future. It made me make peace with the fact that people won't always support me, especially when there's nothing to show for it yet. In the earlier section, I talked about how people give their support more when they see evidence. I'm making you remember it again, it is one thing that you must know. We are not entitled to people's kindness. You know that right? Knowing this fact and making peace with it would make you not falter nor lose your self-confidence when people don't support you as you would desire them to. So, what do I do when no one roots for me no matter how confident I am? It is simple, I root for myself and not give up. I know you just rolled your eyes at me for making it sound like a stroll in the park. It isn't, I am aware.

You'd have to take some steady and gradual steps. The first step that I'd recommend you start with is strengthening your belief and confidence in yourself and your ideas. How can one do this? You can do it by first reminding yourself of that passion that drives you to try your hardest.
That passion that keeps you up at night. That self-confidence that has seen you through your most difficult rejections. Then you go ahead to ask yourself one question. 'Do I really want to do this? Can I get this?'. In these, you'll find your answer and you'll be strengthened. There's this thing that passion does to you. It makes you serious, and it fuels your creativity and strength more. It'll even help you belief more in yourself.

One more step that you should take is this. Try your best to distance yourself from the people and things that cause you not to root for yourself. You do not need any negativity to thrive. In fact, negativity will shrink you much more than you can imagine. Yes, you have to stay away from that person that ceases every moment to tell you how absurd your dreams are and how achieving them is nothing but an imagination. This might come off as selfish, but it isn't at all.

Again, I remind you not to accommodate people that shrink you and make you doubt yourself when you need support the most. One thing you should know is this, people like that could diminish your self confidence level. Yes, people can do this to your self-confidence. No matter how self-confident an individual is, the moment that individual begins to absorb too much negativity, the individual would most likely end up affected.I do not want this for you, and I know that you do not want it for yourself too.

Rooting for yourself all alone with no one's support is truly not an easy thing to do, but it becomes easier when you have a great level of self-confidence. In this section, I'll help you walk through the beautiful and demanding act of rooting for one's self all alone by taking you through some powerful self-confidence affirmations written just to root for your gorgeous soul. Now, shall we begin?

1. I will forever root for myself even if no one else does.
2. I am aware that the greatest support I will ever need comes from me, I'll support myself until the end.
3. I do not open my space to anyone that shrinks me.
4. I know how to walk away from the people and the things that shrink me.
5. I am blessed to be able to root for myself.

6. I am grateful for every support I get.

7. I am confident in myself until the end.

8. I'll never throw my self-confidence away no matter what.

9. I am confident in the manifestations of my biggest dreams.

10. I root for myself with the whole of my heart.

11. I derive joy in rooting for myself.

12. I am confident that all the work I put into myself will not become wasted effort.

13. I love myself a lot, I'll root for myself every day.

14. I give no one the power to discourage me.

15. I give no one the power to make me feel terrible for supporting myself end believing in myself the way I do.

16. I bear no grudge against anyone for not supporting me, I am happy that I get to support myself.

17. I am at my highest point when I support myself.

18. I reach my apex with ease when I support myself.

19. I am aware that I bear all the support that I could ever need.

20. I root for myself with a lot of joy.

21. I derive pleasure in taking responsibility for myself.

22. I possess all the strength I need to do all that I am supposed to do. I leave nothing to chance.

23. I love myself for all the goodness that I bear.

Key Points

My dear black woman, I hope this section makes it much easier and beautiful for you to support yourself as much as you need. I hope it takes you deeper into the realization that you have all it takes to root for yourself as much as you desire.

Below are the key points for this session.

- You are the support that you need.
- No one can truly root for you as much as you root for yourself.
- Do not give anyone the permission to make you feel terrible for rooting for yourself. You are worth it, you have always been, and you will always be.
- Do yourself some good by walking away from people who diminish your self-confidence level while you root for yourself.

Chapter Eleven

Courage Affirmations For The Black Woman

I learned that courage was not the absence of fear, but the triumph over it.
—Nelson Mandela

Whenever courage is mentioned, the first thing that comes to most people's minds is the absence of fear. Many people believe that a courageous person is a person without fear, but this is not true in any way. To be courageous is to do things that make you afraid. You are afraid, but you do it anyway. You don't think you can land the job, but you apply anyway. You don't think your boss would approve a raise, but you ask anyway. This my dear, is what courage is about. Courage makes you do the things that make you afraid, it doesn't kill your fear.

Courage is one essential attribute that we need to live life. Without courage, you would keep on holding back and never go for the things you love because you are wholly dominated by fear. Fear paralyzes the biggest vision, it makes a big person feel small. Never give in to it. I understand that fear is a normal feeling. I get afraid sometimes. But I am not dominated by fear. Courage demands that I try at least. It demands that from you, too. You have to understand one thing, courage doesn't in an any way make light of your fear or ridicule it. Rather, it asks you to overlook that fear and go for the next big thing. There's this thing about not trying. It fills one with so much regret. It's better to try a thing and fail at it than not try at all and regret your actions later. You'll also save yourself the big trouble of imagining what could have been. There are two ways to this thing, it's either it works or it doesn't. Focus on trying your best. It's either you win or not. When you begin to see it this way, you'll realize that fear is what you make it to be. It is only as powerful as you make it. Now, you choose, would you give fear so much power over you or not?

Life involves a lot of risks. It takes so much courage to take risks too. If you spend your life avoiding risks at all costs, you might end up not leading a very interesting life. Most of those things that you wish to own live in the risks that life would present before you from time to time. It's either you go for it, or you ignore it. The ball is in your court. Remember this every day. But, I'll advise you to take risks. Please note that not all risks are worth taking, some are out rightly stupid. Yes, there are good risks, and there are bad risks. Engaging in a game that can claim your life because you want to belong with your friends is a bad risk to take. Come to think of it, what would you gain from a bad risk like this one? Nothing at all. You'd end up losing so much. Investing in stock is a good risk. You know, it takes a great deal of courage to invest money. You'd battle with so many what if's before you eventually do it. Now, what do you stand to gain when you invest? Financial freedom. Do you see the difference between the good and the bad risk? I hope you see it very clearly. Before you take any risk, always try to think carefully about it. Think about what it could cost you, think about what you stand to gain. Doing this will help you make good decisions and courage would help you execute them.

I know all the fear and doubt that comes with walking this courage path. Sometimes, you'll feel crazy about certain things. Other times, fear would overwhelm you. In all of this, do not let courage go. Do the things that make you afraid. Leap for the heights that awe you. Apply for the positions that you dream of. You'll be amazed at the outcomes. I won't leave you alone to take this courage walk alone, I'll hold your hand like I have always done and guide you through some wonderful affirmations for courage. Hold my hand, let's begin.

1. I am courageous enough to take big steps.

2. I acknowledge my fear, but I will not let it dominate my life.

3. Courage looks so gorgeous on me.

4. I'll do all that I set my heart to.

5. I am not overwhelmed by fear.

6. I am as courageous as I can be.

7. I embrace courage with the whole of my being.

8. I excel the most when I am courageous.

9. I come from a history of black women who dominate fear. I too shall dominate my fear and win.

10. I excel through the power of courage.

11. I do not know how to give up on the things I love.

12. People love me for my courage.

13. Courage opens up great doors for me.

14. I am happy that I am courageous.

15. I take risks, and I excel in them.

16. I am not afraid of taking risks.

17. I am exceedingly great.

18. I loves and value courage greatly.

19. I am a very courageous woman.

20. I'll achieve every single thing that once scared me.

21. I am grateful for all the times I let courage triumph over fear.

22. I forgive myself for all the times I let fear dominate my life.

Key Points

My dear black woman, embrace courage with the whole of your heart. It will make you excel more than you have always dreamed. It is the courageous ones that make history. Remember this every time you are tempted not to choose courage. Below are the key points for this section.

- Life contains a lot of risks, take the good ones.
- Do the things you want to do no matter how scared you are.
- Courage is not the absence of fear, it is doing great things even in the presence of fear.
- Forgive yourself for all the times you let fear win, celebrate yourself for all the times that you were courageous enough to go after the things you wanted.

Courage Affirmations To Overcome Fear

Fear is one of the most terrible emotions I have ever known. Fear is an innate thing, but that doesn't mean that you should let it gain so much dominance in your life. If you do, you would regret it for quite a very long time. Most times, great fear doesn't just come to you all by itself.

Something triggers it. It could be a thought, a past experience, an individual. The trigger is like an open door through which the fear can come in. I like to think of it as an open wound and fear as an infection. When the wound is open, it would be very easy for the infection to get in. Do you get the drift?

Whenever I notice fear coming into me, I try to block it off by not paying mind to the thing that triggers the fear. It is a method that has worked a lot of times for me. I think you should try it too. I know you wonder about the possibility of shutting fear away forever. I've wondered about it too, and in my wondering I found answers. It's not possible to completely shut fear away from one's mind. Do you know why this is so? It is so because fear is an innate thing. It's just inside us like every other emotion. We all knew fear even as little children. But the good thing here is that we can manage fear and live a great life with it. If we can live with other emotions that we feel, why can't we live with fear, too? No reason at all.

The first step that you should take towards managing fear is the identification of your triggers. You have to find out those things that make you afraid. Fear management is easier, faster and more efficient when you know the things that trigger your fear. You know, it is always easier to treat a known disease than an unknown one. But, fear doesn't always come with triggers. Sometimes, it just saunters through your mind and starts looking for something to feed on in order to make you afraid. Fear would spin up a thing that would never happen and watch you quiver in terror. After identifying what triggers your fear, the next step you should take is control the triggers. You can do this by thinking less about those triggers and distancing yourself from them. This is a very effective method. Walk away from the trigger and watch every other thing cower.

Courage is yet another great thing that you should wholly embrace if you must control your fear. You know, fear works to ensure that you do not take the big steps that you need to take while courage works to ensure that you take those steps. Out of these two contrasting things, fear is the easiest to go to. And that's why a lot of people tilt towards it. Courage is the harder and best option. Not only does it help you in the pursuit of your goals, it also helps you control your fear effectively. That is why I advise you, my dear black woman, to follow courage with all your heart.

There is one more thing that I would love you to know. Fear has a very faux power. Yes, it is not all that powerful. Fear is only as powerful as you make it. Fear swallows you up when you give it power. I'll share my story with you. Have you ever witnessed a high jump? It is a sport where people are made to jump over set heights. I used to be sorely afraid of jumping even the lowest heights because of how fearful I was. Whenever I deigned to try, I'd think about the high chances of me jumping wrongly and ending up with a permanent scar that would make me hate high jumps until the end of my life. This fear continued for a long time until the day I decided to try. I still do not know what inspired me to jump on that day. The crazy thing is, I tried jumping very very high. I did it! I couldn't believe my eyes at all. It felt like a sweet dream. After that day, I began to jump more and partake in more sports. Especially the ones that scared me. That experience taught me a beautiful lesson that I am sharing now with you. Fear is only as big as you make it. Do the things that scare you and make you gasp in surprise. Life would be a lot of boredom but for things like this. Do not allow fear to dominate your life. Be courageous in this life! You have all it takes! I know it.

Taking the courage path is not an easy thing to do at all. I say this from my own experiences. But you don't have to worry about how to walk this courage path all alone because I'd be holding you up as I have always done through the pages of this book. Together, we'll be courageous.

1. I cease to give fear power over my life.

2. I am aware that fear is only as powerful as I make it. So, I'll take away every power from fear and be in charge of my life.

3. I embrace courage with the whole of my being.

4. I quit giving up on the things I love without even trying.

5. I make peace with either winning or losing. I'll no longer be afraid to try.

6. I stun the most when I am my most courageous self.

7. I am so courageous that fear trembles at the sight of me.

8. I eliminate fear from every area of my life.

9. Courage comes easy to me.

10. I conquer fear with a lot of ease.

11. Fear doesn't control me, I control fear.

12. I am too big to be controlled by fear.

13. I'll go for the things I want even in the midst of fear.

14. I am grateful for all the times I dared to try even in fear.

15. I am not consumed by fear.

16. I am exceedingly courageous.

17. I am blessed to know courage.

18. I love courage, I'll be courageous until the end.

19. Trying doesn't scare me anymore.

20. I bloom greatly even in my fear.

21. My fears do not define me, they are just a small part of the wonderful woman that I am.

Key Points

My dear black woman, I hope fear doesn't dominate your life anymore. I trust in your unique abilities to kill fear. Below are the key points for this section.

- Fear is only as great as you make it.
- Your fear doesn't define you.
- Afraid? Try anyway.
- You are in control of your fear. Remember this always.
- Don't hold back anymore because of fear, dare to try. You'll be happy you did.

Courage Affirmations For Love

Has it ever occurred to you that you need a very generous amount of courage to love? But, that's not the way the movies show it. I know, I know. In the movies, you meet someone you love, emotions rage and you both fall in love. Life would have been less complicated if loving was this easy. There wouldn't be a lot of pain and heartaches. A lot of black women are emotionally damaged today because they loved the wrong people. Yes, it is possible to love the wrong person. Who exactly is the wrong person? A wrong person is that person that makes love into a bizarre thing for you. The wrong person leaves you with bruises and makes you regret ever knowing what love is. You'd wonder, are these wrong people the bad people of this world? No, they're not. The truth is, the wrong person for me might be the ideal person for you. The perfect person even. This is where compatibility comes in. Being with a person you're not compatible with makes love sour. If you and your partner are not compatible with each other, you'd end up being the wrong people for each other. This is how it works. Do you get the concept of the wrong person, now?

A lot of times in the past, I shut away people I loved and people who loved me because I lacked the courage to love them. I'd second guess every single act of kindness toward me and think everyone was set out to hurt me. Sometimes, this fear of getting hurt or broken stems from past experiences with love. We don't know how deep a failed love relationship hits us until it is time to open our hearts to love again. But it doesn't always arise from bad experiences. Some people are just naturally afraid of becoming vulnerable and free in love. I am that kind of person. I know how it feels. I'd make lots of excuses to avoid meeting with people I even admired because I was afraid of loving them deeply. I didn't do these things because I hated love. I did them because I lacked courage. I lacked that courage that one needs to love wholeheartedly. I'd read love stories and smile when people fall in love. I loved the idea of love and I loved to see people fall in love. I only loved love when I wasn't the one in it.

As I grew older, I knew I had to do something about it. I had to work on my love life. I started by coming to terms with the fact that not all relationships would lead into a big thing or end beautifully. Then, I made one big decision. I decided to let myself love as much as I wanted to. I decided to stop holding back. My dear woman, it was so difficult for me. I didn't just know how to go about it. All I knew was that I wanted love without wanting it. This is confusing, right? I faced a lot of confusion. It took me quite a long time to understand that not everyone that wants a thing with me comes with the intention of hurting me or breaking my heart into a thousand shards. It was at that point in my life that I first became aware of how lovable a person I was. I am grateful for all the steps I took towards loving. But I am most grateful for the courage I mustered to love. If you keep on stopping yourself from loving because of fear, you might regret it for a very long time. Give yourself the freedom and the courage to cherish the little moments and dwell in them. Fall in love and appreciate that love. If it lasts forever, beautiful. But if it doesn't, also beautiful. Pick the lessons and move on with your life. Appreciate yourself for daring to love in a world like ours that's too weak and cowardly to love. Would you?

Being courageous in love is not an easy thing at all. But I can make it easy for you by taking you through powerful affirmations that would help you build all the courage that you need to love. Hold my hand and let us begin, shall we?

1. I'll dare to love as deeply and passionately as I desire.
2. I embrace all the beauty and goodness that is found in love, I will quit shutting myself away from love.

3. I am aware of how much of a lovable person that I am. I will accept love with the whole of my being.

4. Fear no longer dominates my love life.

5. I have all the courage I need to love as much as I desire.

6. I am patient with myself as I build courage in love.

7. My love life is filled with courage and not fear.

8. I love love, I won't let fear take it away from me.

9. I refuse to believe that everyone is set out to hurt me and make me regret loving.

10. I am positive that I will get the kind of love that I have always dreamed about.

11. I am courageous enough to stop walking away from love.

12. Love is the best thing that has ever happened to me.

13. Never again will I be a coward in love.

14. I forgive myself for all the love I have ruined and the hearts I have broken by not being courageous enough to love.

15. Love doesn't frighten me anymore, it empowers me.

16. I am blessed to love and be loved back in return.

17. All the energy I put into loving is not wasted energy.

18. I am courageous enough to open my heart to love.

19. I am not afraid of vulnerability.

20. I am courageous enough to live and cherish every moment that love brings to me.

Key Points

My dear black woman, you are deserving and worthy of love. It is high time you summoned courage and opened your heart to love. It is one of the most beautiful things ever. Below are the key points for this section.

- Love is a very beautiful thing, do not be afraid to open your heart to it.
- Love comes with a certain level of vulnerability, embrace it.
- Not all love stories will end with a happy ending.
- Forgive yourself for the mistakes that you have made in love.
- Do not let fear rob you of the love that you desire.

We have come to the end of the courage chapter! I hope you enjoyed reading it as much as I enjoyed writing it. Now, go ahead and apply what you've learnt in this chapter. Be as courageous as you can be, you'll thrive more in this world with loads of courage. The next chapter will be all about stress management. Come with me, let's explore!

Chapter Twelve

Stress Management Affirmations For The Black Woman

Our greatest weapon against stress is our ability to choose one thought over another.
—William James

A lot of black women learn how to work very hard, but they do not learn stress management. Stress management is a necessary skill that everyone should possess.

Studies show that people deal with more stress when they do a job that they do not really love. Does this mean that people that do the jobs they love do not face any form of stress? They definitely do. Stress is almost inevitable in every kind of work. Mind you, when I talk about stress, I do not talk about physical stress alone. Mental stress and other forms of stress are included. In fact, it is easier to deal with physical stress than mental stress. A good massage session, food and enough sleep could be all you need to effectively deal with physical stress sometimes. But it isn't so with mental stress. In some cases, you would have to see a therapist.

Inasmuch as hard work is important, stress management should also be encouraged. Stress decreases productivity a great deal. This is one thing that many people fail to realize. They think that the time taken to rest is wasted time. No, it isn't at all. I see my resting time as an investment in my well being for increased productivity. Resting when I become stressed is one of the best things I've ever learnt. Not only does it calm me down, it also keeps me away from breakdowns. You have to make conscious efforts to manage your stress levels because when you look at things from surface level, you'd think you really do not have time to rest. You never know how much unnecessary work you put so much effort into until you take your time to do a personal stress evaluation.

One great method that can help you manage your stress is making a list of important things that you should do. It's a simple and interesting way to manage stress. Make a list of the most important things that you need to attend to. Doing this will make it easy for you to cross out the things that are not really important. Everyday, we wake up and think of things that we need to do without giving proper thought to those things. Before you indulge in some things, ask yourself questions. Is this important? How would this help me reach today's target? You'll realize that questioning yourself like this would help you develop the habit of focusing majorly on the most important things in the long run.

You should also try to make peace with the fact that you can't do everything at once, you're no superhuman. No, I am not asking you not to aim as high as you want. I'm simply asking you to take deep breaths and rest when it gets overwhelming. Stress shortens your lifespan, take those rests and continue later. Believe me, your body will thank you for it. Allow yourself to do the things within your power first. You do not have anything to prove to anyone about your strength. Black women do not show off their strength, it shows by itself. You don't have to juggle so many things at once to appear strong. Doing that doesn't show your strength, rather, it shows how desperate you are to show off your strength. That, my friend, is a great sign of weakness. The only opinion about your strength that should count is yours. Know this and know peace. I beg you, my dear black woman, take rests and manage your stress well. You'd love the glow that it will bring to you.

I know how difficult it is to manage stress effectively all alone. That's why I'll support you by going through some powerful and effective stress management affirmations with you. Let's dig in!

1. I take rests when it becomes overwhelming. I'll not let stress ruin me.
2. I embrace the goodness and importance of effective stress management.
3. I do not glow in stress, so I'll take rests instead.
4. I love to manage my stress levels just as I love to work hard.
5. Everyday, I remind myself that stressing so much doesn't translate to great work. I do great work and stress less.
6. I cannot surrender to stress.
7. I love to manage my stress.
8. Taking rests doesn't make me weak.
9. I refuse to see rest time as wasted time, it is an investment into my well-being.
10. I care so much about my health, I'll not let stress make a mess of my mental health.
11. I do not find stress attractive in any form.
12. I walk away elegantly from the things that stress me for no just cause.
13. I distance myself from all forms of stress.
14. I can do my work greatly without a lot of stress.

15. I have wonderful stress management skills.

16. I am at peace with the fact that I can't possibly do everything all at once. So, I refuse to bother myself with the things I have no control over.

17. I dissociate myself from the people and things that increase my stress levels.

18. I do not find it difficult to say no to stress.

19. I am happier when I am not stressed.

20. I am happy that I can take a rest when I want to.

21. I am not overwhelmed by stress.

Key Points

Stress doesn't make your life beautiful in any way, master the act of doing away with it. Below are the key points for this section.

- Prioritize everything that you do, do not leave out space for stress.

- You are no super human, take rests when you need to.

- Learn how to walk away from the things that stress you out.

- Say no to stress when you can.

I Am Not Controlled By Stress

A lot of black women live their lives under the total control of stress. They give stress a lot of power that it becomes a master in their lives. Do you find it surprising? I don't at all. I've seen women who say that stress keeps them going. These women embrace the toxicity in stress so much that it begins to appear beautiful to them. It is quite similar to the Stockholm syndrome. But I don't think this is all there is to it. I mean, who thrives on just stress? The truth is, some of us use stress as an escape route from our realities. I'll use myself as an example. I'll share a life experience with you in the next paragraph.

I work very hard when I'm stressed or dealing with a problem that I do not want to face. Do you know why I do that? I simply use work as a daily distraction instead of facing the major thing eating me up from the inside. Working hard in such conditions is one coping mechanism. But coping mechanisms can become toxic too, can't they? Some of our coping mechanisms are not all that safe. In our bid to escape one problem, we end up creating another one for ourselves. This is one of the saddest things ever. And in the end, we end up with more stress. What a bad way to deal with a problem. If you're like me who uses stress as an escape route from reality, you've got to stop. The dangers that it brings outweighs the good that it does. Facing the problem is not an easy thing to do, but it is the best thing to do. Whenever the desire to escape the problem with stress comes up, tell yourself that you have to woman up and face it! Escaping from the problem doesn't make it go away. Rather, it makes it lurk in the corners. And one day, it'll pounce on you with greater ferocity. This is the thing with escaping from our problems and hiding from them. We only empower the problem. Don't be afraid to stand up to your problems.

A lot of people have glamorized stress so much that people would engage themselves in avoidable stress in order to hold the busy narrative. Everyone wants to be busy. You need to understand that being busy every time doesn't translate to being a great worker. You can work smartly without having to stress yourself so much. Don't give stress any control over your life. This is your one precious life, why would you give stress so much control over it? Take charge of your life. You have to unlearn these fallacies that people have made about stress. Begin by telling yourself about the importance of rest in your life. Restructure your life to accommodate rest. Plenty of it. You'll be more productive when you rest. My dear black woman, you do not have to be busy all the time. Yes, you do not have to work around the clock every time. It is okay not to be busy on some days. It is okay not to be overly engrossed in activities every minute of your life. A lazy day with good food and sweet sleep is no curse. You deserve some of that peaceful and great self-care. No one can get it for you but you.

At some point in your life, you would have to make certain decisions concerning stress. You'll have to stand up for yourself and say no to stress. You know one thing? It is what you allow that thrives. It is the stress that you allow that chokes you. Believe me, you are capable of ending stress in your life if you want to. Remember I once mentioned that you are much more powerful than you know? It is a truth that you should embrace. It is high time you stopped giving power to stress in all its forms.

So, my dear black woman, cease to let stress control your life. I know it is not an easy thing to do. But, I can make it easier for you. I'll give you all of my support by going through powerful affirmations that can help you stop letting stress take control of your life . You'll love them! Now, let's dig in.

1. I am in control of my life, I'll no longer give stress any power over me.
2. I do not give stress the power to rob me of my happy rest.

3. I take breaks when I'm overwhelmed.

4. I do not give stress the permission to dominate me.

5. I am not busy every day. I set time aside for rest.

6. I refuse to go with the misconception that stressful work is hard work. I don't do stressful work, I do smart work.

7. I trust in my ability to eliminate stress from my life.

8. I do not give my energy and time to the things that do not matter.

9. I am not consumed by stress.

10. I have total dominance over stress.

11. I unlearn all the lies that I believe about stress.

12. I possess great power, I am stronger than stress.

13. I do not work round the clock everyday.

14. I love resting.

15. I do not use stress as an escape route from realities, I stand up to my problems, and I face them with great solutions.

16. I do not fancy stress no matter how attractive it might seem to be.

17. I take rest seriously.

18. I am productive the most when I'm well rested.

19. I create time to rest and have fun.

20. Stress has no power to stifle out my inner joy. I am in control.

Key Points

Your life will become more beautiful and interesting the moment you decide to take control of it. Stress is only as powerful as you make it. Remember this all the time. Below are the key points for this section.

- You have all it takes to control your stress.
- You do not have to be busy every day. It is okay to have nothing to do on some days.

Create Something Beautiful Out Of My Stress.

I've been going on and on about the negative impact of stress in the past sections of this chapter. But, has it ever occurred to you that there could be positivity in stress? No, don't get me wrong. I'm not asking you to embrace stress. I'll explain what I mean to you.

Our perception of a thing and how we react to it plays a great role on how that thing affects our life. Simply, the way you react to a thing is a major determinant of how that thing affects you. I'll use stress as the major case study here. When we think of stress, we think of a thing that is set out to frustrate us and make us joyless. We try our best to run away from all forms of avoidable stress. But you'd agree with me that not all forms of stress can be really avoided, right? This brings us to an interesting question, what then can be done to free oneself from the grip of stress that can not be avoided?

It is a quite simple yet difficult answer. Detach yourself from the negativity of the stress. You know, instead of lamenting and suffering about your stress, let it motivate you to work harder. Some stress will only exist at certain points of our lives. The moment we cross over to new levels, they will end. Instead of letting a stress like that squeeze out all the joy in our lives, why shouldn't we let it motivate us instead? Of course, finding motivation in stress is not easy at all. But I have learnt that suffering sometimes propels us to work faster and harder so we can get a better life in a shorter time.

I understand how difficult it is to find motivation in stress, so I'll make it easier for you by leading you through some powerful affirmations curated just for you. Let's dig in, shall we?

1. I refuse to allow stress to make me suffer.
2. My stress propels me to work harder and faster.

3. This stress is a phase, it will pass away very quickly.

4. I have a very beautiful and interesting life.

5. Stress has no power to steal my happy life.

6. I am motivated by my stress to work harder.

7. I will not allow stress to make me into a toxic and sad person.

8. I do not wallow in stress.

9. This stress is preparing me for something great and beautiful.

10. I am not overwhelmed by this stress, I am in control of it all.

11. I excel greatly despite the stress.

Key Points

When you begin to see your stress as a tool that propels you for something greater, you'll work harder and smarter and reach your goals faster. Below are the key points that you should note.

- You have great power and control over your stress.
- You'll excel greatly despite all the stress that you face.
- Your life becomes more joyful when you allow stress to motivate you into working harder.

Again, we have come to the end of a chapter! I am excited. I enjoyed going through these stress management affirmations with you so much. Did you enjoy it like I did? I bet that the next chapter will be even more thrilling. But before we move to it, I'd admonish you to embrace stress management in its best forms. Not only does it make you exude a brighter and more beautiful black excellence, it also makes you healthier and happier. Now, let's go tothe next chapter. It'll be all about affirmations for positive thinking. Let's dig in already!

Chapter Thirteen

Affirmations For Positive Thinking For The Black Woman

You can't win in life if you're losing in your mind. Change your thoughts and it'll change your life.
—Tony Gaskins

We do not talk enough about the power of positive thinking. Thinking positively is one of the greatest things you can embrace if you are keen on changing your life for the better. Somehow, our thoughts reflect in our outward life. If there's anything that you must know, it is the fact that your thoughts play a very crucial role in how your life turns out . Go back to the quote at the beginning of this chapter and read it all over again. Do you feel the impact in those words? They aren't just words, they bear the truth that you need to know.

Many times, life will give you reasons to think as negatively as possible. Some things that happen will make you feel like the most miserable person in the world. But tell me, my dear black woman, will you let circumstances steal the power and goodness of positive thinking from you? Of course not. Dwell in positive thoughts and watch your life turn around for the best. Sometimes, you will feel so overwhelmed that you will want to 'feel' your grief and spend more time picking at the wounds. It is perfectly okay to feel this way. You're a human with complex emotions and thought processes. I don't judge you for letting yourself feel. Sometimes, letting yourself feel those strong emotions will help you heal from them faster. So, let yourself feel.

There are times I felt very stupid for thinking as positively as I did. I'd laugh at myself and wondered where I get all the energy from. Believe me, it is not easy to choose to think positively at all times. It is not easy to choose optimism over pessimism at every single point of your life. In fact, it is one of the most difficult things ever. Positive thinking doesn't mean that you will lose touch with reality, rather, you choose to see the good things and think the best thoughts. It'll make you have a better life. That's why I'd advise you to choose to think positively every day of your life.

I know how difficult it is to choose to think positively at all times. It is very demanding and exhausting. But it becomes easier with time and consistency. You should understand that it's okay to slip back once in a while. But, the best thing is forging ahead and not gloating nor beating yourself up for the times you fell and had to try again. I have curated a fine list of affirmations for positive thinking just for you. Let's dig in!

1. I live the best days of my life.
2. My life is an overflowing river of joy, love and all the goodness that I desire.
3. Nothing can steal my joy and peace.
4. All the hard work I do will pay off, I do not labor in vain.
5. I eliminate negative thoughts from my heart.
6. I am stronger than all the negativity in the world.
7. I am aware of the power of my mind, I utilize it to the best of my ability.
8. I am a very intelligent and amazing woman.
9. I'll sing my best songs with the most sonorous of voices.
10. I am blessed and happy to be me.
11. I excel greatly in all areas of my life.
12. I'll get my dream jobs with ease.
13. I do not struggle to stand out anywhere. I stand out by being my true self.
14. I am made for excellence.
15. Nothing can shrink me or make me feel small.

16. I am proud of myself and I am thankful for every progress I make.

17. I look gorgeous in every dress I wear. I am elegance in all its forms!

18. How joyful I am that I get to be me!

19. My smile warms the hardest hearts.

20. I do my jobs with a lot of excellence!

21. I'll realize all my dreams!

22. I am evidence that black is perfect and glorious.

23. I am not shaken up by circumstances, I am in total control!

24. I am a lovable and amazing person.

25. I thrive in all areas of my life.

26. I am greatly loved and cherished.

27. I am surrounded by amazing people who love to help me and see me flourish.

28. I make and keep friends easily.

29. I am perfect.

Key Points

Positive thinking will fill your life with all the beauty that you never knew existed. The time has come for you to ditch all the negative thoughts that lay in your heart. Embrace positive thinking today! Find the key points for this section below.

- Thinking positively will turn your life around for the best.
- You cannot do greatly if there's so much negativity in you.
- Embrace everyday with love, everyday is the best day of your life.

I Work In Line With My Positive Thinking

It is one thing to think positively, and it is another thing entirely to execute positive things. You know, thinking is another, and saying is another. Now that you have embraced the whole armor of positive thinking, you should ask yourself these questions. Are my actions in line with my positive thought process? Do I work towards this positivity that I desire and think about every moment? If your answer to these questions are no, you have a lot of work to do on yourself. I trust you to do it beautifully and excellently.

A student has a major examination to write. A very tough one. A lot of people have written the exams and failed. Only a few people pass that particular exam on their first sitting. This student is filled with a lot of positivity about the exam. This student believes that she will write the exam and come out with flying colors. Amidst all of the positivity and good thinking, this student doesn't study for this exam as she should. In summary, this student is a lazy but very positive student. Failure is almost inevitable for this student no matter how positive she is in her thinking. Yes, thinking positively isn't all there is to achieving success. You have to put in the work too. Do you understand this? Your positive thought process will be more prominent in your good grades when you work hard. Never make the mistake of abandoning the work you need to put in simply because you think great thoughts. You need to know that positive thinking is not a magic of some sort. It doesn't replace the work that you need to put in. Never forget this.

One thing that you must know is this. No matter how high the level of your positive thinking is, it won't singlehandedly take you to the heights that you desire to reach independently. A couple of great habits would be required to work hand in hand with your positive thinking. While you think positively about getting that dream job, do not forget to get the necessary skills for it. While you think positively about getting the best grades, do your part by studying as hard as you should. While you think positively about dominating your field, do the needed work. You don't stay relevant in a competitive world like ours by just thinking positively. If you try to do that, you'll get lost in the times. Keep this at the back of your mind and pull it out to have a look from time to time so you can know the major things that you should focus on.

I have heard a lot of black women complain about the persistence of their negative thinking despite how hard they work and how well they do things. My friend, I have been in situations like this too. I'd literally work my ass off and still wallow in self-rejection and very negative thoughts despite it all. It made me detest myself for a while. I mean, how could one be home to such a level of negativity? At first, I thought it was all a part of who I was. You know, just one of those people that always saw negativity in everything no matter how good those things were. This is one of the terrible things about negative thinking. It shuts you away from seeing all the good and beautiful things and appreciating them for that goodness. It only opens your eyes to see negativity and shortcomings. It took me some time to understand that all that negativity wasn't who I was. I think we are all born with clean, beautiful and neutral minds. But as we grow older, we begin to pick up habits and thought processes from the things we encounter. Some people are lucky enough to pick more good habits than bad ones, others are not that lucky. I know you're looking at me in disbelief now. You really want to ask if I'm aware that people can be born with different abilities and personalities. Right? My dear black woman, I know this fully well. I need you to understand that our habits and behaviors are greatly shaped by our environment and exposure. That's why people are able to build their own habits.

My dear black woman, I need you to understand that becoming a positive thinker is a process. A very gradual process if you were once deeply rooted in negativity and its cousins. You have to learn how to be patient with yourself. It is a process that you cannot skip. Rome wasn't built in a day is no cliché. It is a lot of truth. You can't become a positive thinker overnight. Take your time and go through the process. I love to take every process of my life seriously because I know they won't be there forever. They become memories quickly. So, go through them with all elegance when they come. You'll be happy you did in the coming times.

I know how difficult it is to embrace the power of positive thinking wholly. But, I'll make this great embrace much easier for you by holding your hand tightly like I have always done and take you through some wonderful affirmations that will help you work in line with all of your positive thinking.

1. My actions are in line with my positive thinking.

2. I am positive all round. I leave no room for negativity to leak through.

3. I do not do things that are contradictory to all the positivity that I confess in my heart.

4. I understand that becoming a positive thinker is a process, I'll treat myself with care as I go through the process.

5. I think positive thoughts everyday.

6. I get great results that reflect the beauty and power of my positive thinking.

7. I have a very beautiful and powerful thought process.

8. I am aware that whatever settles in my mind has the power to influence me greatly. I am very careful of what I let into my heart.

9. I have an active and brilliant brain that dwells in positive thinking.

10. I think positively without losing touch of reality.

11. I am happy that I can see positivity in most things.

12. I am blessed to be able to think the way I do.

13. My brain is the most gorgeous brain there is.

14. I do not dwell on the things that can go wrong, I dwell on the things that would work according to my plans.

15. I am glad that I think positive thoughts alone.

Key Points

My dear black woman, remember to always work in line with your positive thoughts. You can do it, and I know you will. Below are the key points that you should note for this section.

- Your brain is your powerhouse, fill it with a lot of good thoughts.
- Your thinking is capable of affecting your life, think positive thoughts.
- Becoming a positive thinker takes time, be patient with yourself.
- Think positively and put in the work! They go hand in hand.
- Your thought process is wonderful, remind yourself all the time.

My dear black woman, we have come to the end of this chapter! I had a lot of fun while going through these affirmations for positive thinking with you. They strengthened me in the most beautiful ways. I trust that you enjoyed it as much as I did. Tell me, did you? I urge you to take your time and grow into the positive thinker that you have always dreamt of becoming. I can't wait to see you excel at it. The time has come for us to step into a new chapter. The very last chapter in this book. Affirmations For The Black Woman On Authenticity. Do you know why I wrote this chapter last? I wrote it last in a bid to remind you to never forget to be your most authentic self in everything that you do. Now, let's begin to explore the last chapter! It will be a lot of fun, I promise you.

Chapter Fourteen

Affirmations For The Black Woman On Authenticity

Authenticity is the daily practice of letting go of who we think we are supposed to be and embracing who we are. —Brene Brown.

Authenticity is one of the best things you can wear. I love this quote by Brene Brown with my heart. Nothing sums up authenticity as concisely as this. Everyday, we rise to fight our places in the world. We meet people, experience cultures, unlearn and relearn. While doing all of these, we might begin to lose our true selves. Staying genuine and original is beyond posting beautiful and Afrocentric pictures of yourself and captioning them #natural. It is way deeper than that. Aren't you curious as to what makes people lose themselves? I'll share some of them with you in this chapter.

The greatest reason why people forfeit their authentic selves is acceptance. It is human nature to crave for love and acceptance in every place. In some places that we will go to, the people there will not accept us because we do not fit into their leagues. My friend, this is where a lot of people lose it. They'll begin to think that there's something wrong with them or their ideals. In order to get people to accept them, they will begin to drop those things that make them themselves. It works out most of the time. They'll be accepted. But come to think of it. Is an acceptance that takes away your authenticity a true one? Is it not a glamorized form of bondage?

A lot of black women lose their authenticity for conformity's sake. This is one thing I understand very well. With the great level of discrimination against black women in some parts of the world, black women are made to face a lot of pressure. Some of them never bow to this pressure. Others can't withstand it. So, they bow to it and give up the biggest parts of their identity. This is one sad thing. It is okay to lose other things in this world, but losing one's authenticity is not okay at all.

Lest I forget, there is also the class of black women who give up their authenticity because they feel it is not in vogue. You know, they give up their history and roots to take up a new one that they don't even understand well. This class of black women do not understand the gravity of giving up one's authenticity. They care about the rave of the moment and ignore their roots. Don't be this kind of black woman. Be the black woman that encourages her sisters to become themselves again.

The acceptance that comes with throwing your authenticity away doesn't last for a very long time, believe me. I don't think anyone really loves a person that gives up who she truly is because of acceptance from a certain group of people. The acceptance would last for a while, then it would fizzle out like a mirage. By then, the black woman will find it difficult to go back to her roots and she'll feel too awkward to even attempt blending into the new identity she got for herself. It is at this point that she'd begin to float on both sides. Neither authentic nor entirely fake. The confusion that comes with being in this condition can never be described properly. I do not want you to experience it at all. It's not a nice thing to know. But if you must know what it feels like, find women who have experienced it, ask your questions, and listen to all their stories.

My dear black woman, you have to learn how to stand up for yourself with all your might whenever anyone tries to make you lose your authenticity by imposing what you are not on you. Do you now know that you come from a generation of women who wrestled with vigor? You have every single thing it takes to retain your authenticity in a world that wants you to lose it. Do not give up your authenticity for any reason. Every day, the world will bring you things that it thinks you should be. Whenever it does that, bring out all that you are and embrace them with all the love your mother gave to you.

I won't leave you to walk on this authenticity path all by yourself. I'll support you as always by holding your hand and leading you through affirmations that strengthen. Now, hold my hand and walk this path with me. Would you?

1. I embrace my authenticity with so much pride and love.
2. I am proud to be who I am. I am happy to be who I am. I don't wish to be anybody else.
3. I flourish in the best ways when I am myself.
4. I wear my skin with a lot of pride.
5. I am a thing of beauty, and I am a joy forever.
6. I give no one the permission to stop me from being who I am.
7. I am grateful that I am myself.
8. I am in love with my roots and everything that came together to ensure that I exist in this time and season.
9. People marvel at the beauty and authenticity that I ooze.

10. I do not care about the acceptance that comes from anyone but myself.

11. I'll be my truest self in every day of my life.

12. I am the best version of myself.

13. I am in absolute love with myself and all that I am.

14. No matter how far I go from home, I'll never forget my roots.

15. I come from a descendant of gorgeous warriors, I'll win this fight that threatens to defeat my authenticity.

16. No matter the pressure I face, I will never give up on who I am.

17. I embrace myself with joy and pride.

18. I delight in how lucky I am that I got to be myself.

19. I know how to walk away from anything that tries to take my identity away from me.

20. I am not afraid to let go of anyone that doesn't value my originality.

21. My authenticity doesn't bloom in toxic places, I step out of all forms of toxicity no matter how glamorous they are made to look.

22. I am perfect just the way I am.

23. I am not ashamed to be myself.

24. I am not sorry for all the extras that I am. They make me who I am.

25. I'll always be myself no matter what happens.

26. I'll never allow anyone to make me into what I am not.

27. I love how I carry myself with so much pride and confidence.

Key Points

Everyday, lots of people will try to make you see reasons why you should give up on being your truest self. Do not give in to it. Nothing is worth your authenticity. Remind yourself of this as much as you can. Below are the key points for this session.

- Nothing in this world is worth your authenticity. Never give it up.
- You are gorgeous just the way you are.
- Do not conform to anything that steals your trueness.
- Wear your skin and carry yourself with a lot of pride.
- No matter how far you travel from home, do not forget the paths that lead home. That is where you'd find your authenticity the most.

Affirmations For The Black Woman Who Has Become A Stranger To Herself

A lot of black women have become strangers to themselves because they embraced the world's definition of authenticity. Remember what I said earlier, nothing is worth your authenticity. Never give it up. But all hope is not lost for every black woman who has become a person she no longer recognizes.

It's crazy how it all begins. It could be you compromising a few values because you want to conform to people's standards. You don't want to be left behind, so you do what you have to do. It begins little by little. You won't realize when you begin to become a person you had always wished not to become. In this life, there are a few things that you should never compromise no matter what. Authenticity tops the list. Whenever anyone tries to convince you why you should do that little thing, let the person know it isn't little. You just can't do it. Sometimes, that thing you consider little would be the catalyst that would cause you to do more things that you wouldn't do. Losing one's self is one of the easiest things ever. You'll always find things that will tempt you and make you want to give up on your authenticity. It takes a lot of courage and self-will not to give in to some of these things. Some of them know just how to make one weak. But I know that you are more than strong to overcome them all.

When you realize that you have become a stranger to yourself, what do you do? Do you gloat, or do you make efforts to become your best self again. The latter is the best thing to do, but it is not the easiest. Only a few women would not gloat on making such a discovery. It is okay for you to feel terrible and beat yourself for doing what you did. It is okay to allow yourself to feel those painful emotions as strongly as you want. But I beg you not to be unkind to yourself. Being unkind to yourself in such a situation is not in your best interest. You will only end up causing yourself more pain. I am certain that that isn't what you want. Give yourself some time and cry and feel your pain the way you want to. Then go on to acknowledge your mistakes. You'll find it easier to forgive yourself and rise again when you acknowledge your mistakes. It will take time, but you will become your authentic self again. You wil look into a mirror again, and you will find yourself and not a stranger.

I know how difficult it is to become friends with yourself all over again. But I won't leave you to do it all alone. As always, I'll hold your hand and lead you through affirmations that will strengthen you. I believe in you, you'll become your most authentic self again. Now, let us begin.

1. I fall in love with who I am all over again.
2. I am proud to be myself.
3. Never again will I give my authenticity for anything.
4. I am the most beautiful when I am original.
5. I will never quit being myself for any reason.
6. I forgive myself for becoming a stranger to myself.
7. I'll look into the mirror and find myself again.
8. I refuse to let my mistakes define me.
9. I'll never compromise my standards for any reason.
10. I will not become who I am not not in quest for acceptance.
11. I am kind to myself in everything.
12. I acknowledge my mistakes, and I am willing to correct them.
13. I'll be happy with who I am again.
14. I'll never forget the road that leads home again.
15. I am a descendant of strong and independent female warriors, never again will I cower at the sight of anything that would rob me of my originality.

Key Points

My dear black woman, be kind to yourself despite the mistakes you made. I hope you find it easy to keep on being your true self in all circumstances. Below are the key points for this section.

- Be kind to yourself.
- You'll become yourself again.
- Do not compromise your originality standards for anyone.

Conclusion

Action is the foundational key to all success.
—Pablo Picasso

Yay! We have finally come to the end of this affirmation book. It was one hell of a journey. I put so much love and strength and kindness into writing this book. For each word I wrote, I hoped that you would feel it deep in your bones. I reserved this quote by Pablo Picasso because no one could have said it better than this. I wrote this book for every black woman that she may be empowered, strengthened and feel safe in her own skin. I wrote this book to light you up, my dear black woman. But, lighting you up goes beyond you reading the pages of this book. You have to take action.

Before I talk more about taking action, I would love to know if you enjoyed reading this book. Did you love the ideas each chapter bore? I hope you did. I started the book with affirmations for your morning. Morning is a very important part of the day. It determines how a lot of things will turn out for you during the day. I hope that saying those morning affirmations with firm belief and energy will cause you to have better mornings and greater days. I wrote on the empowerment of the black woman because I am very conversant with the poor level of black women empowerment in our world today. My dear black woman, I hope that part of this book helps you rise and get started in your empowerment journey. It takes empowered women to change the world for the better.

I enjoyed writing about affirmations for beauty. A lot of black women have been told great lies that have made them blind to their beauty. My dear black woman, I urge you to embrace those beauty affirmations every day. I wrote it and dipped it in so much elegance just for you.

It takes courage for a black woman to walk towards empowerment and independence. I thought of this, and I poured my heart and soul into writing the chapters for courage, independence and empowerment. I bet you didn't notice this interconnection when you were reading this book. Does this make you smile? I hope it does. Black women are very pretty whenever they smile.

I wrote the chapter on leadership for every black woman in leadership. I am happy to see more black women go into leadership everyday. It is not easy being a black woman woman in leadership. It comes with a lot of troubles, stress and anxiety. But I believe in the beautiful power of the black woman to overcome them all. Also, I had this black women's leadership in mind when I wrote the stress management, anxiety and rest chapters. My dear black woman in leadership. You need these three to function optimally. Never turn them away no matter how busy you get. You need to be fit to be able to lead well. Don't you think so?

Black women love deeply and passionately. Some of them are very lucky in love. Others are not. For these ones, I wrote on healing and moving on. Then I wrote on self-love. My dear woman, you excel the most and love better when you love yourself first. That is why I am always of the opinion that you have no business trying to build a love relationship with someone if you do not love yourself first. Of course, there is no formula to loving. I wish you great love and happiness. But when it doesn't work out, I hope the healing affirmations help you move on. You'll definitely find the love that you desire.

Writing the last chapter of this book made me happy and sad at the same time. At first I was happy because I remembered black women I encountered in the past who wouldn't give up their originality for anything in the world. Originality is one of the greatest assets ever.
I became sad at the thought of black women who have become strangers to their own selves by virtue of giving up on their trueness for various reasons. If you belong to this

class of women, I hope you find yourself again. I hope you forgive yourself, and I hope that you always remember that nothing is worth your originality. You are perfect in all your flaws.

Now, I urge you to take action and create the kind of life that you have always wanted and dreamt of by employing what you have learnt in this book into your daily life. If you are unable to read this book as often as you desire, you could easily read the key points and get the needed value. My dear black woman, I truly enjoyed holding your hand through each affirmation. It was beautiful to reach you so closely like that. You are a gem.

I love you, dear black woman.

Thank You

You could have picked from dozens of other books, but you picked our book 999 Powerful Affirmations for Black Women

So, THANK YOU for getting this book and for making it all the way to the end.

Could you please consider posting a review on Amazon?

Posting a review is the best and easiest way to support the work of independent authors like me.

Your feedback will help me to keep writing the kind of books that will help you get the results you want.

It can be something short and simple ☺

Emotional Self-Care for Black Women:

Boost Your Confidence & Mental Health with a Powerful Program in 90 Days!

Learn to Love Yourself, Increase Motivation, Overcome Obstacles & Become a Strong Woman.

About The Book

Have you ever wondered why many black women do not live to
the fullest? In Emotional Self-Care for Black Women, you'll find
out why.
Many black women face different hurdles in their everyday lives,
from anxiety to depression, low self-confidence, poor self-love,
weakness, and many others. Many black women do not reach
their potential because of the significant obstacles.

I understand that obstacles are a part of human existence. Yes, at
some point in our lives, we would face struggles of some kind.
But it is dangerous when these struggles become a constant in
our lives. Not only will they begin to stunt our growth, but they
will also begin to steal our joy until it remains of it. But the good
news is this; we have tremendous power to control and dictate
what happens to us or not. A lot of us do not know how powerful
we are. We are much more powerful than we know. Until we rise
into the actual knowledge of our greatness and power, we will
have to keep dealing with some obstacles.

I'm pretty sure that you do not want that for yourself. I do not
want it for myself either. No one does. I know you're getting
curious about where I'm driving at. Don't be! I have come with
solutions for every black woman dealing with obstacles of various
kinds. Be it poor self-love to anxiety, lacking self-confidence, and
every other thing that you can imagine.

I recommend reading this book wholly and carefully to get the
best results. Don't be in a rush to finish it up that you read with
so much speed and end up not assimilating everything. Also, this
book will contain a ninety-day plan that will help you manage
your emotions better.

Even if you think you've reached the end of the rope and can no
longer go on, I assure you that this book will help you rise again.
The time has come for you to regain all that you lost. Are you
ready for this ninety-day journey to becoming the best version of
yourself? Add this book to your cart, and let's begin!

Disclaimer!

This book has no medical backings, and it provides no mental health guarantee. Also, this book claims no authority over medical knowledge. This book is written based on what flows in my heart and what I have experienced. Note this down!

Introduction

For us to feel good emotionally, we have to look after ourselves.
— Sam Owen.

Some of us are very caring and amazing until we care for ourselves. We do the most important things for people without ever remembering to do those same things for ourselves. Tell me, are you not deserving of love, kindness, care, and awesomeness? You very much are. You are more than worthy of all of these. Taking care of oneself is an art. You need to learn one great art to become the best version of yourself. I see caring for one's oneself as nurturing. In this case, you are the flower. It would be best to have all the care you can get to flourish abundantly.

Many black women have missed out on essential points because they did not know how to combine self-care into their lives and blend it perfectly. I understand this from the depth of my heart because I used to be like this too. I was a very kind person. The kind that people would regard as a saint. You know, I loved and cherished public acceptance so much that I didn't realize when I made myself into a foot mat that people could walk on. I was in search of validation outside myself. That search drove me crazy. It has a way of making you do things you usually wouldn't do and tolerate crazy things just because you want that validation so bad. It is one of the most terrible and traumatizing things anyone could ever experience. I do not want you to repeat my mistakes and cry the tears I have cried. Instead, please learn from them to know how to deal with the obstacles that I faced. This book is very personal; it contains so much about me. I had to pour so much of myself inside. This book won't read like some science book or something out of a university lecture room. I find that quite boring. Black women do not like boring because they come from adventurous places. I will make this book very fun and relatable by including many personal experiences.

I am incredibly interested in black women who lack motivation too. I am no magician, neither do I have the power to push them back into creativity. But, one thing is sure. I'll help them rise to their feet again and find themselves and what they lost by assisting them in navigating all the parts that lead to creative inspiration. Dear black woman, I need to let you know that not having the required motivation every day is not as disastrous as many people make it seem. So, don't feel pathetic a bit. I know that you'll rise and walk into your motivation again. I think people do better and greater when they create and keep their motivation by themselves. Letting your inspiration reside in other people is not good at all. People are like the weather. They are very fluid. What becomes of you and your cause if the person that bears it fails? You might crumble. You should be your source and maintain all the motivation that you need.

I put a lot of energy and love into drafting a ninety-day plan in this book for women who are yet to master emotional management. Most times, people tend to think managing one's emotions is about not showing weakness in the face of trouble or putting up a faux strength. Not at all, gorgeous black woman. Managing your emotions is much more than that. Proper emotional management will help you be at your best even in situations that threaten your peace of mind or ruffle you too much. To be at your best in this context doesn't translate to keeping calm when you need to open your mouth to speak. Instead, it is about filling yourself with the right emotions for various situations. Yes, there is a thing like' right emotions.' Your right emotions are the appropriate emotions you should display in multiple cases. The truth is, different situations call for different emotions. That is why I advise you to learn how to manage your emotions well to react to different conditions. I'll write other chapters and let this plan come towards the end of the book. I find it fascinating doing that. Remember that saying about keeping the best for the last. Aye, that one.

This book contains simple and fun English for your reading pleasure. The personal stories in every part of the book will make it even more fun for you to read. Don't you think so? I also took women who do not always have time to read as they would desire into consideration while writing this book. How did I do it? Every section of this book contains 'Key Points,' which summarizes the chapter. So, you can read these key points and get great value from them. Now, isn't that wonderful? I believe this introduction has warmed you up and prepared you for all the wonder that you and I will explore in this book. The time has come for us to begin.

So, open the next page and behold the wonder of the first
chapter. I'll be with you through every word and page. Read on,
gorgeous soul!

Chapter One

How To Deal With Negative Emotions

Many black women do not know how to deal with negative emotions. I have seen lots of them blame themselves for feeling negative emotions. I used to blame myself and feel ashamed for having negative emotions too. I always felt that everyone had their lives in order except me. Not that I had a bad life, no. I had a good life. The good life I had always envisaged as a bit of child. But I tried to feel better by lying to myself that my life wasn't perfect enough because the negative emotions came. Maybe I would stop feeling depressed if I got the newest model of my favorite car brand. Maybe my anxiety would go away if that one person that always made me feel the butterflies would at least notice me. I got these things, yet the negative emotions wouldn't just stop. They worsened. All the things I desired came to me quickly to prove that they were not responsible for my negative emotions. Knowing that the negativity was from the inside made me feel worse. I felt ungrateful and wicked for not being happy with all I had.

My ignorance of negative emotions and how they affected people stayed with me for a very long time, and I wallowed greatly in it. I walked into the light that knowledge alone can give when I finally had the heart to see a therapist about the issue. I restricted myself from getting therapy because I considered it abnormal and crazy. How could a person have a great life and still feel terrible inside? The first time I opened up to my therapist about the problem, he held my hand and smiled. He told me he knew what I was talking about, that he had experienced it too. I was shocked. It was so surprising to see that I wasn't the only one with the problem. It was even more pleasing that the therapist knew exactly how I felt. Even after a couple of sessions with the therapist, the negative emotions didn't disappear. Sometimes, I would listen to the therapist with great interest; other times, I could barely hear. But the therapist was a very patient man. Carefully and lovingly, he broke down all the walls I had built around myself. It took time. In all those therapy sessions, I learned so many things. My friend, emotions are not just emotions. They have a way of affecting our lives so much. Positive emotions have their way of lighting us up. Negative emotions also have their way of dimming our light. To reach your apex, you need to learn how to manage your emotions well and utilize them to your most significant advantage.

There is a truth that you must know about this emotion management thing. There is no perfect way to deal with emotions. One thing could work perfectly for you, and it might not work for someone else. I'll share methods and techniques that worked for me and how I employed them all. For someone like me who has encountered different kinds of people, I am well versed in emotions and how to manage them. So, you can trust me to be honest, practical, and kind with you as we journey through every page of this book.

Acceptance: a Vital Tool in Dealing with Negative Emotions

When people ask me the best way to deal with negative emotions, do you know the first thing I say? It is acceptance. You have to accept first that there is a problem before you can solve the problem. It might sound very simple and straight to the point, but it is not. Acceptance isn't all that easy and sweet.

Many of us deal with negative emotions today simply because we get to deal with the feelings without accepting them first. I am not asking you to revel in the negativity that negative emotions bring by acceptance. Instead, I am asking you to walk into the truth unafraid. What is the truth? That you are dealing with negative emotions and need help with them. I noticed that I healed faster from what I accepted than what I denied. I can tell you firmly that acceptance is the first and most crucial step you need to take if you succeed in dealing with all of your negative emotions.

It takes a lot of mental and emotional strength to accept negative emotions truly. Sometimes, you would try to make yourself feel good by choosing to live in denial of your reality. But no matter how much you do this, the emotions would still be there, lurking at your insides and waiting patiently to manifest. Untamed emotions have the power to ruin almost anyone. Do not ever make the mistake of giving your feelings a lot of energy. Most of our positive or negative feelings are not as powerful as we think they are. Yes, your emotions are not all that powerful. We are the ones that give power to our feelings. You know, the negative emotion eventually grows so much to become a monster capable of consuming you and making you sink into a lot of gloom.

I used to listen to sorrowful songs to elicit some catharsis in the past. Listening to sorrowful songs would make me cry, and crying always made me feel better after an episode of sadness. I thought it was an excellent coping mechanism. I only realized how bad it was when I became obsessed with sad music. I'd think up my sadness and weep. It became that terrible. Do not ever make the mistake of making negativity a part of your coping mechanism. It always doesn't end well.

***

You have to master the act of acceptance. It is a skill that you must possess if you genuinely desire to deal with your negative emotions. No matter how ugly, terrible, and heartbreaking those emotions you feel are, denying them won't do you any good. Denying them empowers them. It is perfectly normal to feel negative emotions. A lot of us do. But, we devise various methods to deal with them. The happiest people sometimes go through their bouts of negative emotions. Negative emotions do not come because you are a terrible person. Negative emotions happen because you are human, and humans are emotional beings who can feel a vast range of emotions. There's no need to beat yourself up about how you feel. You're not some work of AI which is programmed to feel a certain way all the time. You are a beautiful black woman with emotions.

Look deep into yourself, embrace and accept the truth of every negative emotion that you feel. Think of those emotions as minor problems that you can handle. You have all that you need to deal with them, trust me. You have to quit wallowing in your negative emotions. You have to wake up each morning and choose a positive emotion like joy. But this can't happen without acceptance. My gorgeous black woman, you are lovely even with the negativity you feel. Your emotions are only a sign that you are human. Accept them today. Acceptance will always make you do better and manage them better. Please do not be ashamed to accept them. It's one of the best things you could ever do to take charge of your negative emotions.

Key Points

I am writing this key points section to make everything easy and fun. This section contains the key points that I need you to remember always as you journey towards accepting your negative emotions.

1. Acceptance is a vital tool that you must embrace to successfully deal with your negative emotions.

2. Please don't beat yourself up for feeling the way you do, we are humans, and emotions make up a large chunk of our humanity.

3. Acceptance is the first step you need to take when dealing with negative emotions.

4. You have everything you need to fight your negative emotions and win. You are way stronger than you think you are.

5. Your emotions are strong, yes. But it is the emotion you give a lot of attention to that will thrive the most in your life.

Allow Yourself to Feel

Many of us feel trapped in our negative emotions because we do not allow ourselves to feel them the way we should. We are very quick at stopping our emotions just before anything happens. A lot of black women mistake this behavior for strength. You know, strong women do not shed tears when they should. Strong women do not spend a lot of time being emotional. Strong women do not allow help in their lives, and they rather sweat it out. Who made these rules? Again I ask, who made these rules? You have to unlearn these things. Being a strong woman doesn't translate to being a woman who hides her humanity and sensitivity. Being a strong woman doesn't stop you from exploring your emotions. But, do not allow your emotions to take absolute control of your life. I am afraid of identifying with the word 'strong' sometimes. I wouldn't say I like all the misconceptions that surround it. Many people think to be strong is to throw away all the softness that makes you human. No, that is not what it means to be strong. Do not call me strong if that's what it means to you.

I love to embrace my humanity and bask in the fullness of it. It is what makes me who I am. It is also what makes you who you are. You know, right? Never for any reason throw your humanity away. Doing that will make you into a woman that you will not love. I have often tried to harden my heart because of some bad encounters that I had in the past. Whenever I noticed the slightest shift in energy and behavior towards me, I'd quickly move away in a bid to protect myself from emotional troubles. Doing it saved me from many emotional problems and disappointments, but I regret it now. It stopped me from making meaningful relationships and being as human as I could be. I tried so hard to stop inhibiting myself from feeling, but I could not. I had gotten so deep into it that I had to invest so much energy in letting myself feel things the way I wanted to. Now, I don't do that anymore. I give no one the power to make me into a person I am not.

Now, you'd wonder. Do we allow ourselves to feel just the good things? Is it okay to let one's self feel negative emotions, too? The answer is yes. Let yourself feel both positive and negative emotions. Nothing expresses your humanity and human weakness more than the expression of emotions. Allow yourself to be as joyful as you want. Also, allow yourself to cry and feel the pain the way you want to. No, this is not bad advice. I promise. Feeling good emotions fills one with joy and strength.

Regarding the negative ones makes one heal faster. It is high time that people stop thinking negative emotions are synonymous with weakness. I have learned that shutting away negative feelings doesn't help at all. Shutting them away causes them to hide in the deepest parts of you. They'd lie in wait for triggers and descend on you on the days you least expect.

Shutting away negative emotions is like treating the symptoms of an illness without dealing with the root cause, which is the primary illness. At some point, the symptoms will disappear. You'll be under the illusion that the disease disappeared too. But it never goes away. It'll shelter itself in one part of your body and come out later. It always comes out worse. It is for this reason that you must deal with the root cause. Deal with the depression, fear, anxiety, and other negative emotions you feel. Allow yourself to handle them. Cry, wring your hands in despair if you want, scream out some sadness, feel it all you want. After feeling them all, what comes next? I know this is the question standing at the tip of your tongue now. I'll answer.

After feeling them, brace up and deal with them. It is one thing to let yourself feel emotions, and it is another thing to dwell for a very long time in them. Embracing your feeling has its unique way of making you heal very fast. After feeling it, pick yourself up and work towards putting an end to the negative emotions. My dear, you must understand that this whole thing is a gradual process. It doesn't happen all at once. But the more consistent you are at it, the faster it becomes. Some women can heal all by themselves, but some can not. That doesn't make them weak. If your healing or rising requires you to undergo therapy, do not be afraid or ashamed to experience it. It is your life, and you matter the most. Your opinion of yourself is the greatest there is, do not let other people's opinions of you take up so much space in your life. Remember, it is your own life.

Key Points

1. It is okay to feel negative emotions. But it is not okay to dwell in them.

2. Do not shut away from your negative emotions. Let yourself feel.

3. Basking in the softness of your humanity doesn't make you weak. It is proof that you are human.

4. You have everything that you need to deal with your negative emotions. You are a lot stronger than you think you are.

5. Do not let bad encounters stop you from showing affection and interacting with people. Do not give anyone the power to make you into who you are not.

Choose Positivity

Almost everything in life involves decision-making. Most things that go on in our lives result from our choices. Choosing isn't limited to any area of our lives. You can choose positive emotions in place of negative ones. Don't get ruffled yet, and I understand it is no stroll in the park. I have learned that most things that involve choosing are not very easy to choose from, no matter how simple they may seem to be. Sometimes, I like to choose something that goes on in my life. Other times, I'm not too fond of it. Decision-making is one thing that I cannot afford to do wrongly. A small decision could make or mar my life.

Your decision-making power can also help you fight negative emotions. How? Most emotions are either positive or negative. You can choose to go with the positive ones and expel the negative ones out of your mind. Of course, it isn't easy at all. The first thing I would advise you to do as you begin to choose positive emotions is the identification of your triggers. In simple terms, triggers are the things that propel your feelings. For example, you begin to feel very terrible after seeing a test result at school. You feel awful because you performed poorly on that particular test. We can say the poor performance is the trigger. Choosing positive emotions doesn't end at making the decision. That's where it begins. You have to take deliberate steps to make it easy for your choices to manifest.

Look deep inside of you and try to pinpoint all that spur your negative emotions. Are they things within or beyond your control? If they are within your control, do yourself and your emotional health the good of controlling them. What happens when they are beyond your control? That is the point where it all becomes somewhat tricky. Here, you'd have to devise a plan that can keep the trigger away from you as long as possible. My dear woman, I understand the fear that comes with detachment. Even if that one thing that you're detaching yourself from had shrunk you into a lot of smallness in the past, you'd still experience that fear. Humans seem to fear detachment more than they do a lot of things. With detachment, a lot of things change. But one thing is sure, detaching yourself from the things that trigger your negative side is a great thing to do no matter what.

After dealing with the triggers, you'll come to realize that choosing positivity is not as complex as you once thought. It is one thing to choose positive emotions. It is another thing to be consistent at picking them. Choosing positivity is not a one-time thing at all. It is something that you would need to do frequently. You don't select positive emotions today and dwell in negativity tomorrow. No, it doesn't work like that. With the dawn of every new day, you choose positivity all over again. You don't have to make it a routine. I find patterns as boring as hell. You could make it an enjoyable and easy process for you. I love to choose positive emotions through affirmations. I could decide to affirm ten wholesome things that involve positive feelings when I wake up. Something like this;

I embrace positive emotions today. I am not overwhelmed by any form of negativity today.
It looks fun, right? It is a lot of fun, and it is stress-free. It works great too. I think you'd love it so much. Just try it first and see the wonder it bears.

Key Points

Choosing positive emotions is no easy thing, but I trust in your ability and strength to do it and do it well. Below are the essential points for this section. Keep them close to your heart always.

1. Amidst all the negative emotions you feel, you can choose positive emotions if you desire.

2. Choosing positive emotions is not an easy thing, but I believe you can do it.

3. Do not be afraid to detach yourself from anything that triggers negativity in you.

4. Be bold in choosing positive emotions.

5. You have all it takes to fight your negative emotions. Yes, you are powerful like that.

My dear black woman, this is where this chapter ends. Apply all I have shared with you in this chapter to your own life, and you'll notice a significant improvement. Now, come along with me to a new chapter. The next chapter will be centre on self-love. Self-love is one thing that many of us do not fully understand. Trust me to unveil it to you in all its glory in the next chapter!

Chapter Two

Self-Love and The Black Woman

Love yourself enough to set boundaries. Your time and energy are precious. You get to choose how you use it. You teach people how to treat you by deciding what you will and won't accept.
—Anna Taylor.

I have come to learn that a lot of black women have very wrong definitions of self-love. Self-love is beyond posting gorgeous photographs of yourself on social media and using the caption #selflove. If it were this simple and plain, we would all love ourselves, and there would be no hate in the world, but self-love transcends this. True self-love is the most fantastic romance ever. Nobody can rob you of this kind of romance. It is deeper and more authentic than romantic relationships with other people who can let go at any time.

Now, what does self-love mean? Self-love is all about looking out for yourself in every area of your life. Self-love acquaints you with the truth that you are the first, most important, and most influential person in your life. No matter how much you love other people, do not forget that you come first. Sometimes, people forget this truth. They seem not to remember their importance in their own lives. Forgetting one's importance is one of the most dangerous things that can ever happen to anyone. In the past, I used to sacrifice a lot for people and do many uncomfortable things because I thought it was cool to express love to the people who mattered to me. Now, I am unlearning a lot of things. No, my heart did not evolve into stone. I am still full of love. But I am learning not to show love to people to my detriment.

Do you know that self-love is not selfish? Yes, you are not greedy for loving yourself the way you do. You are not a selfish person for choosing to love yourself with the whole of your heart. I'd love to recount a story my friend once shared with me. My friend had a classmate who everyone said was the kindest girl in school. Some said she was an angel. Do you know why this girl was called an angel? It was because she never said no to anyone. She was from a wealthy family who cared deeply about her and bent to her every whim. So, she always had the things she wanted. My friend admitted to envying her sometimes. Tell me, what fifteen-year-old wouldn't envy such a sweet life? Despite how gorgeous and rich that girl was, she had very low self-esteem and just a droplet of self-love in her. She greatly desired to be everyone's friend. She wanted to be loved by all. But that's an impossible thing. After trying to no avail, she resorted to giving gifts to her classmates. They would all jump at her and display faux affection towards her. They did that because they wanted the things they or from her to keep coming. Almost everyone in the class disliked how she threw herself in their faces. But who would dare confront the richest babe in class who gave everyone gifts like she was Father Christmas?

Her kindness continued for a while. Everything became sour when some greedy classmates coerce her to give away everything that she had nothing left for herself. She was able to do it for a while. When she got fed up with the whole thing, she stopped. No one knows what gave her the courage and wisdom to control. She faced a lot of hate, mockery, and subtle criticisms from the people she gifted the most important things. But, she never went back to her old self again until they all left school. Do you know what I told my friend when she shared this story with me? I told her that the girl began to love herself when she stopped being the sweet and cheerful giver. That was the point of realization for her. I still wonder what the propelling force was. I also wonder if she sat herself down and talked honestly to herself. Sometimes, you are the only one that can tell yourself the truth.

Just like the girl in this story, people may begin to despise you and call you selfish for deciding to stop sucking up to anyone and standing up for yourself, and loving yourself with all your heart. My dear black woman, pay them no mind. It is better to be labeled selfish for loving yourself instead of being called kind for giving your self-love up for anyone. I repeat this, do not let anyone rob you of the love you have for yourself.
If loving yourself requires you to be 'selfish' and 'distant,' do it. It might hurt at first, but you'd love the outcome eventually. Sometimes, people try to make us feel terrible for loving ourselves the way we do and carrying ourselves with so much elegance. Never give room for that. Do not let it thrive at all.

Many black women stay back in places that do not help them because they do not know the true essence of self-love. Self-love makes you walk out of a room that reeks of disrespect. Self-love makes you ignore the people who try to make you into who you are not. In our quest to be loved by people, we need to realize that we need to love ourselves first. Your love for yourself is what matters the most. You'd still feel horrible if a thousand people loved you and you did not love yourself. The journey to self-love is not an easy one. It is not impossible either. Are you willing to go on that journey?

Begin first by forgiving yourself for all the times you did not love yourself right. I ask this of you because people tend to beat themselves up about things they did wrongly in the past when they find out the right things. Count your past experiences as lessons that shaped you. No matter what happens, I do not find myself regretting some of the not-so-great things I did in the past. I don't regret them because they were all a part of my becoming. I think you should embrace this ideology too. Not only does it keep you from breaking up, but it also helps you learn from your mistakes and past experiences.

Today, decide to love yourself fully no matter what happens.

Key Points

Self-love is no easy thing. But it becomes much easier when you know your worth. Also, you must realize that you come first in your own life. Knowing this will help you love yourself as you should. Below are the critical points for this section.

1. You come first in your life.

2. Your opinion about yourself is the essential thing in your life. Every other one is secondary.

3. Your love for yourself is the most honest there is.

4. Do not compromise your self-love to please one. No one is worth your self-love.

5. Do not allow anyone to make you feel terrible for loving yourself the way you do. You are worth it, and you'll forever be.

People Love and Treat You the Way You Do To Yourself

The way you love yourself is the way people will love you. The way you treat yourself is the way people will treat you. Someone once said these words to me. That first time, it all sounded crazy to me. I wondered if people would genuinely treat me terribly if I treated myself terribly. I thought of human kindness and dwelled in it. People will be kind to me even if I don't treat myself well, and people are kind. It took me quite a while to realize that I am not entitled to people's kindness. Hold on. I'll explain this to you. Some of us are naturally kind and loving. We expect other people to be kind and caring like us most of the time. We do not prepare ourselves for the truth. The truth is, the world contains a variety of people, people who don't share the same beliefs as us. We have to prepare our minds for these kinds of people, so we don't feel hurt when we encounter them. I am excited about extraordinary times and good people, but that doesn't stop me from mentally preparing myself for people whose beliefs and attitudes differ from mine. These people are everywhere. You could bump into them in the stores, and you could meet them on the bus too. Anywhere. Meeting them unprepared is one crazy thing that could happen to anyone.

Like I told you earlier, it took me time to realize the integrity of those words. But now, I keep it close to my heart. You should, too. People will most likely do the same if you show yourself so much, love. If you treat yourself like a Queen, you'll get the same regal treatment from people. Come to think of this. You have this gorgeous dress that makes people drool when you wear it.

One day, you decide to make the magnificent dress into a rag by using it to clean. You expect the people around you to discourage you from using it as a rag, right? Or, they'd help you wash it and keep it safe. The chances of these happening are very slim. Most people would join you in using the dress to clean. If the owner can use this dress while cleaning, who am I not to? Then they'd go on and use it too. Do you understand the message I'm trying to convey with this brief illustration? People love and treat you just the way you do to yourself. Whenever you begin to notice that people treat you terribly, pause and think about how you've been treating yourself before those people; in that, you'll find your answer. I know you want to be loved and treated like royalty. But it won't just start happening. You have to put in the work by doing it to yourself first. Understanding this will help you a great deal.

Don't allow anyone to fool you into believing that you are not worthy of love and good treatment. You are more than worthy of it. From time to time, you might meet people who would try to scorn you into self-loathing. These people are adept at making people feel like they do not matter. I beg of you, do not give such people the opportunity to thrive where you are. No matter how great some of them pretend to be, never entertain them. It would help if you always looked out for negative signs like insensitive jokes, hatred, and other similar factors that very flashy personalities may mask. It would interest you to know that some of these people come dressed as your friends. They'd get into you by befriending you. As time progresses, you'll see that they do not mean well for you.

I used to have a friend that did these things to me. He'd call me arrogant for carrying myself the way I did and doing things the way I did them. He'd make me feel like I intimidated people with my presence by just being myself. Of course, I thought it was good advice at first. I thought I had a friend who cared about me so much. But my doubts began to grow when I found myself living a life I had once detested. I became highly reclusive because my friend said I was 'too much. I didn't realize how much I needed a brain reset until I slid into my solitude to have a heart-to-heart talk with myself. I'm the most honest person when it involves talking to myself. I thought about the strangeness I felt with myself and new behaviors. I realized I was a stranger to myself already, which had to change.

When I finished dwelling in my thoughts, I ended that friendship. It wasn't exactly easy because I had grown attached to that friend. But it was worth it in the end. Sticking with a friend who is against the great love you have for yourself is not worth it at all. Please don't make my mistakes. I shared my story with you because I was hoping you could learn from it. I hope you do. If you've been treating yourself poorly and not loving yourself as you should, the time has come for you to step up. Tell me, don't you want the royal treatment that comes with being good to yourself? Don't you want to inspire people to treat you great by first treating yourself great? I am confident that you do. It is no easy thing, primarily if you're used to not being good to yourself. But you can start now and still excel at it. Start with the little things. Respect yourself, carry yourself with pride, and love yourself. As time goes on, you'd grow into loving yourself in the most significant ways.

Key Points

Suppose you genuinely want people to treat you exceptionally and love you as you desire. In that case, you have to begin it with yourself first. The way you love and treat yourself is an inspiration to treat you. Find the critical points for this section below.

1. People love and treat you the way you love and treat yourself.

2. Prepare yourself to meet humans with varieties of characters the moment you step outside your home.

3. When you notice that people maltreat you, take a pause and evaluate the way you've been treating yourself.

4. Love yourself wholly.

5. Do not accept poor treatment from people.

On Self-Love and Forgiveness

Forgiveness is one crucial thing that a lot of people ignore. Whenever the topic of forgiveness comes up, what comes to your mind? To forgive is to let go of resentment, pain, anger, or vengeance you feel towards a person or a thing. Forgiveness makes you decide not to take revenge for the wrong done to you. It makes you not pay back evil with evil. Since I started this forgiveness part of this book, has it ever occurred to you that you need some forgiveness? Not from anyone but yourself. I'll make this easier for you and me by simply talking about self-hate and bitterness. You might wonder if there are people who do hate themselves.

Yes, some people do hate themselves. But self-hate doesn't just happen. Something always triggers it. There are a lot of things that could cause self-hate. For some, it is body shaming. For others, it is low self-esteem and depression. Then some people hate themselves for making mistakes and going through terrible experiences. Many people have done things that they are not proud to say. I have made a couple of errors that taught me lessons. I need to remind you that self-hate and self-love do not exist in the same place. You cannot love yourself if you hate yourself as they are two perfect opposites. They can't dwell in one person simultaneously.

And this is where forgiveness comes in. Have you truly forgiven yourself for that mistake that you made? Are you willing to move on and become a better version of yourself? Come on, let us explore forgiveness together. Growing up, I heard this phrase a lot. 'Forgive and Forget.' But in my adult life now, I know that it is an impossible thing to do. We don't forget. We can only forgive. Healing is one of the most gradual processes ever. You could try the best healing methods in one day, but you won't heal in just one day. You need to slow down and walk into your healing gallantly. Of all forms of forgiveness, I think self-forgiveness is the most difficult one. You'll wake up and blame yourself almost every day. You'll weep and wish to go back in time to undo a lot of things.

Self-forgiveness is no magic. On some days, you'll experience faux healing and think you've finally forgiven yourself, only to fall into sorrow later. Despite how difficult and demanding forgiving is very much possible. Pour yourself into it.

You can start by acceptance. Living in denial is terrible. It steals your peace. I know acceptance hurts, but it is a hurt that you need to embrace if you genuinely desire to forgive yourself fully. Tell yourself that what happened. Yes, you made a mistake, and you regret it. Forgiveness begins with acceptance. When you finish with it, give yourself some time to feel pain. It would trigger some cathartic tears. Crying makes me feel better every time. It doesn't only clear the fog in my head. It also reduces the pain in my chest. Don't you find it interesting how internal hurt begins to manifest as physical pain? It intrigues me.

Cry all you want. Then stop. Afterward, do away with the things that trigger your self-hate. They could be objects, people, and places. I understand that you cannot avoid all of these things altogether, but ensure to avoid the ones you can. Being exposed to too many triggers can mess with your healing process. Don't expect to heal at once. Go easy and take your time. Don't let anyone make you feel terrible for healing and forgiving yourself the way you do. Believe in your healing and forgiveness. You'll forgive yourself and stop hating yourself, trust me. It might seem impossible at first, but you'll see how you'll do it like magic.

How do I know I have forgiven myself? There are no perfect ways to know, my dear. But you'll see when you encounter a trigger and not falter. When the desire for revenge no longer burns inside you. When you successfully forgive yourself, you'll appreciate the beauty of self-love more and let it flow into you. Allow yourself to be full of self-love. Let it engulf you. It is one of the most beautiful things ever. Forgive yourself, then love yourself with all that is in you.

Key Points

I hope you forgive yourself with all the forgiveness that you need. Love yourself with joy and pride. You're a wonder! Below are the key points you could note for this section?

1. Self-hate and self-love do not thrive together. You have to make a pick from these two.

2. Healing and self-forgiveness are two very gradual processes. Be kind to yourself.
3. No one on earth can love you the way you love yourself.

4. Acceptance is the very first step towards true forgiveness. Please don't skip it.

5. Exposing yourself to your triggers can mess up your healing process. Try your best to stay away from them as much as you can.

6. Don't permit anyone to make you feel bad for healing and forgiving yourself the way you do.

Again, we have come to the end of a chapter. I hope you love this chapter, and I hope it does help you understand self-love better. I put a lot of love into this chapter just for you. Go on and forgive yourself. Fill the space that once housed your self-hate with nothing but love. Now, come with me. Let us explore anxiety together. Anxiety is another major thing that troubles black women

Chapter Three

The Black Woman Fights with Anxiety

Our anxiety does not empty tomorrow of its sorrows but only empties today of its strengths.
—C.H. Spurgeon.

Anxiety is one disorder that almost everyone experiences at some point in life. It usually comes with persistent worrying, and sometimes, fear about everyday situations. The worry that comes with anxiety isn't anything like the usual one that you and I know. This type comes with tremendous weaknesses and limitations. The kind of limitation that stops you from taking the one step you need to take to live your dream life. A lot of people do not understand anxiety. That's why they call it bluff when people with anxiety voice out the things that keep them from sleeping at night. My dear black woman, do not get sad over the actions of such people. Your feelings are valid. Do you know one thing that we should take seriously in today's world? Mental health education.

Anxiety is one disorder that can make a great mess of enormous efforts if ignored. It is a problem. But thankfully, it has a solution. Many black women are yet to find the help they need to deal with their anxiety because they do not accept anxiety. Many reasons cause this lack of acceptance—the most typical being that they consider it a terrible feeling. This great need for acceptance in the human race causes some people to lie to themselves and deny their glaring realities to be accepted by other people. I tell people, acceptance is a significant thing that you should embrace in the emotional self-care journey.

Remember the title of this book? It's all about emotional self-care. YOUR emotional self-care. I need you to know that acceptance is not something anyone can do for you but for yourself. You should also know that anxiety is no death sentence nor a contagious disease that you should hide. It is part of human life. Your anxiety level is way higher than other people's, which doesn't make you a terrible person. All you need is help to manage your anxiety. But, tell me, how can you get help for a disorder you claim not to have? It's impossible. Do you get my point now? In your acceptance of your anxiety, you will find the help you need.

Well, acceptance isn't the only thing there is to deal with anxiety. It is only the first. After acceptance, what happens next? Get help. Help means different things to different people. It is getting therapy and speaking to experts in anxiety disorder management. The truth is, no one can help you as much as a good therapist can in things like this. Sometimes, a good friend could give you the listening ears you need and a shoulder to lean your head. But your friend most likely won't be able to get you the help you truly need. Except your friend is a therapist, of course. I've met many people who overlook things they should pay attention to because they 'talked' to their friends. No, I'm not trying to make light of the help friends render. I'm simply trying to make you understand the importance of professional help in cases like this. Therapists undergo a lot of training to help you deal with anxiety, trust them to do all they can to help you. It isn't as easy as I make it seem, right? I know, Luv.

I used to be hesitant about therapy in the past too. I'd feel ashamed and wonder what the therapist would think of me later. I'd wonder if the therapist would see me as some pitiful human or someone who needed help. It took me a while to stop overthinking the whole thing. It was so overwhelming! There is no shame in getting help, and there is no shame in seeing a therapist. You do not only do yourself good, but you also help the people around you- your friends, family, colleagues, and other people you would have to meet in your life. When we suffer illnesses or face challenges, we are not always the only ones that suffer them. The people close to us and those who love us do, too. The bond we share with them always gets affected. You love your folks too much to watch them suffer for your sake, don't you? I know you do. Please don't make them suffer by giving your anxiety the power to eat deeply into you.

You could also fight anxiety by choosing to worry about a few things. Try to take your mind away from irrelevant things. Everything isn't worth your peace. It is perfectly okay to worry but don't let it get the better of you. You can minimize your worrying by creating a simple list of what you should pay mind.

This method is one of the most effective methods to deal with anxiety. Creating a simple list has a way of taking your concentration and worry from everything. It'll help you focus on the things on the list squarely. You would love it. I have always created to-do lists so long that I do not even remember the exact time I started building them.

Anxiety is not a one-day fight. You have to invest your time, energy, and resources into fighting it. Also, your victory in the battle depends majorly on you. Now, take a deep breath and ask yourself a question. Am I ready to win this fight? Yes! Your victory begins the very moment you decide to stand up and fight. You already have what it takes to win. At first, fighting anxiety may feel like a lost battle. But it is not. The emotional liberation and joy from winning are worth all the fight. Don't you think so, too?

Anxiety disorder affects the physical body as well. Ever been in a situation where you cannot breathe well because you're so anxious about what's going to happen next? I'll share a personal experience with you. I worked in a laundry store for almost a month. On a fateful day, something happened. We were about to lock up the store that day. I dealt with severe fatigue, and I couldn't wait to go home. I was about to leave when a man brought in some clothes for washing and handed them over to me. He said, "Alright, take these, just a top and a pair of jeans, get them all clean before uhm... Friday." That day was a Monday. I stood up from where I was and took the clothes from the man. I casually dropped them inside a small laundry basket and zoomed off. Coming in the next day, I couldn't find the clothes anymore. The shop was relatively small, so I checked every part of it properly in about five minutes. I came out with nothing. Immediately, I had a nervous breakdown. My head began spinning, and my heartbeat had become exceedingly fast. I had been employed there for less than a month, and a customer's clothes had gone missing? Bullshit. Throughout the week, it became a routine. Anytime I approached the shop in the morning, my heart would start beating twice as fast. I'd ransack the store again, and when I found nothing, the situation worsened. And it would be the same for about nine hours till I left for home. For seven days, I had that thing going on.

The owner of the clothes soon came looking to grab his clothes, and as I stood fidgeting before him, I decided to ask him what he had given me. Ridiculous right? "You're asking me what laundry I gave to you. How am I sure you haven't given my clothes to another person? I need the clothes for an occasion tomorrow!"

To make matters worse, he was a first-timer. What an impression! I said to myself, "you're gonna get sacked after this." I somehow managed to hold my ground, and of course, he had to remind me. It took a lot of courage to do that, by the way, something we're going to look at later on this lovely ride. To cut an already long story short, I hope I didn't bore you, though. After he explained how the clothes he brought looked like, I discovered it was sitting right in front of me all the while and I was looking at it for days but never knew it was the one. Due to the fatigue, I felt when he brought the clothes. My mind painted a red shirt and a blue pair of jeans and what he got was an orange-colored shirt and a couple of black pants! You know, as much as I was so happy, I was disappointed as well. What if I had developed a heart attack and collapsed? All because of what I thought I lost but was still there? Haha, the mind finds ways to play tricks on us sometimes. But as we grow, we should get acquainted with those tricks and know-how to handle them when they come. It's a simple story, but I hope you understand the illustration I tried to paint. Anxiety will come, but do your best not to let it get the best of you.

Key Points

The fight against anxiety can turn out to be victorious if you do it right. Doing it right simply means being patient with yourself and giving your very best. I believe in your abilities, and I am confident that you will win. Below are the key points that you should note for this section.

1. The fight against anxiety is a gradual process. Please, be kind to yourself.
2. You have fought many things with ease, and anxiety would be no exception.
3. Getting professional help is a great way to combat anxiety.
4. Pay mind to the important things alone.

5. Your victory against anxiety disorder begins with acceptance.
6. Anxiety has physical side effects.

Worrying Comes With No Gain

Worrying comes with no gain. It only knows how to drain you and leave you weak and frustrated. I think a lot of people do believe that worrying can change things. Sorry to disappoint you, darling. It has no gains at all.

I'm not judging you for worrying or getting worked up the way you do. I understand you perfectly. I have interacted with many people, black women especially, in living this life. I made a beautiful discovery. Worry is the fate of intelligent and active minds. Several studies have attested to this truth too. It takes a busy mind to think about things that most people ignore. But, you have to control your worrying lest it robs you of things that you cherish.

Instead of worrying, you could try finding a solution to the things that make you worry. That is one of the most effective ways to handle worry. I remember staying up late into the night sometimes in high school, worrying about how I'd fare in my exams. My friend discovered my excessive worrying and asked, 'why not study instead?' That one question changed me considerably. Whenever I begin to worry about things, I ask myself, 'why not fix it instead? Why not find a solution?' I listened to my friend that night and studied instead. I got a good grade on my exam, and I am forever thankful for that friend.

Whenever the worries begin to trouble you, seek out a solution.

Sometimes, this method won't work—when you have no control over the things that make you worry. Worrying about the things we can't change does us no good. I understand how difficult it is to stop thinking about things that make us worried but cannot change. It feels like hell. You'd feel this helplessness deep inside of you, but there's nothing you can do about it.

Worrying about things we can't change is of no benefit to us. It is not a behavior that we should embrace for any reason. My dear woman, please strive to stop beating yourself up about things you have no control over. For a long time in my own life, I did this thing. I don't think mine can pass as a worry, though. Maybe it is. When I was younger, I had these very chubby hands that made my classmates laugh at me. Kids find humor in absurd things sometimes. Some of my classmates said my hands looked like fat chicken laps. Sometimes, I'd cry and cuss out anyone who said mean stuff about my hands. I'd think about how to 'fix' my hands for hours at school. I think my performance at school would have been better if I didn't spend a lot of time worrying about my hands. My eight-year-old brain did a lot of work worrying about my hands. My folks at home always said I had the cutest hands ever, but I chose to believe the kids. I think humans have a knack for believing the bad things people say to them and throwing all the good ones into the bin.

Do you know what made me stop worrying about my hands? I sat my ass down on a chair and talked to myself. I am always the most honest person when it comes to me. I grew up that way. That day, I spoke to myself and acknowledged the truth that there was nothing I could do to make my hands like other people's hands. You know, I'm too full of uniqueness to contain a thing that is not me. Somehow, I saw beauty in my hands on that day. I didn't even realize when I stopped worrying about my hands altogether. It felt so beautiful. I had been getting myself worked up for no reason at all. Sometimes, I remember these things and laugh at myself. For those times, I put a lot of energy into worrying when I could occupy myself with exciting things. I was a child, and I am grateful for those incidents. They played very significant roles in my becoming.

Key Points

When you understand the truth that worrying bears no gain for you, you'll quit it for good. Anxiety makes it very difficult, but you are more than capable. You come from a history of women who fought the most significant wars and came out victorious; how could you not win? Winning is in your blood. Below are the key points that you should keep in your heart.

1. Worrying bears no gain for you—quit dwelling in it.

2. Take charge of your worries, don't get worked up for things you cannot change.

3. Anxiety is a common thing for active and intelligent minds. Go easy on yourself.

4. Instead of worrying, why not seek a solution?

5. You are more prominent than anxiety.

My dear black woman, we have come to the end of this chapter. I beg of you, employ what the anxiety chapter taught you into your life. You'd see how much positive change you'd record. Now, let's go on to the next chapter and explore courage!

Chapter Four

Understanding The Concept of Courage

"It is impossible to live without failing at something unless you live so cautiously that you might as well not have lived at all, in which case you have failed by default."
– J. K. Rowling

Courage is another concept I would like you to understand as I help you sail through this ninety-day journey of your life. Courage helps you to overcome fear.

I want to refer to the emotion, fear, as we go through this chapter. Some people believe fear is a virtue because they can benefit from it. Others believe it is not because of past experiences they've had with fear. I will not outrightly categorize fear as a virtue or a vice because it's simply an emotion. It is a natural human response to perceived danger and a critical feeling that can either make or mar a man or woman per se. It is how you deal with the fear that can be considered "virtuous" or not. For courage to exist, fear must be present. Else, courage would not even exist.

What causes fear? You probably are already trying to meander through some of the causes in your mind. Adorable! Well, I'll say fear comes when you perceive there is a threat of harm to you, either physically, emotionally, psychologically, natural, or even imagined. Yes, some people can get so afraid when they think something or someone is out to get them, but in the end, it's all in their imagination. I don't know if you've experienced that before? I'll explain.

As little children, we all had these, should I call them, crazy fears? It sounds a little bit off, though; let's move on. Personally, while growing up, I had a thing against horror movies. Whenever I came across a scary film with ghosts in a dark room or creatures who ate their victims alive all in the dark, my mind would tell me to turn it off, but I would do otherwise.

Yes, I was stubborn. At one point, I wanted to overcome that fear so bad that I stayed up late into the night watching a horror movie. The movie had to do with zombies and the sort. I was shivering under my duvet by the time I finished the movie. The worst part of it all was that I was alone in my room. I tried to get some sleep, but any slight movement or sound I heard or perhaps imagined, would make my eyes snap wide open. I'd cry terribly and blame myself for watching the movie. Yeah, I was that afraid. The fear didn't go away just immediately, but as time passed, I grew older and had this understanding that there was nothing to be scared of as it was just a movie.

I had a friend who never dared to sleep with the lights off. She'd go the extra mile by getting a lamp to light up the room if the lights ever went off. I told her there was nothing to be scared of, but she never believed it. I had to plead with her to try it, and after so many days of constant cajoling, she gave in. Now, she can sleep with lights on or off, and that's a big win for me, I guess. Yay!

Now, enough of the childhood fear stories. Let's get to some real-life adult situations of fear.

Have you ever been called up to stand before a crowd, and you're like, "No, I can't do this. You have to call someone else, please." You're begging whoever it is not to call you up, but they do so regardless, and the whole crowd is waiting and cheering you for you. When you eventually get on stage, you can't say a word at first, and you stand there, snapping your fingers and looking at the vast crowd. Cowering until you find the courage to speak or perform as the case may be. Standing and talking to the public in a situation like that sums up courage.

Cambridge Dictionary defines courage as the ability to control your fear in a dangerous or difficult situation. Even though you may be afraid, it is the choice and willingness to confront agony, pain, danger, uncertainty, or intimidation.

It is okay to feel fear in managing your emotions, but do not let it consume you. Fear can make you miss out on a lot of opportunities. It can hinder your progress in the sense that you were holding back for a long time, something you should have begun from the onset. You're a black woman, and by your color, you are strong. Absurd right? But it would be best if you realized that being black goes way beyond your skin color. It would help if you chose to be in charge of your fear. You will bend it to your desire and not the other way round. I'm not saying this because I want to say it or because it's that easy, far from it. I know how hard it is to overcome fear, but you have to try eventually. You have to start from somewhere, and you have to start now because time waits for no one.

You might be asking, "Where do I start from?" Or "how do I start?" Take a deep breath, begin with the small things. Doing the little things well would make you more courageous to take up the big stuff. Don't you think so, too?

Key Points

Courage is quite an intricate ability to master, but you have to exhibit it to make progress in life, even if it's just the little bits. You need to know your fear, understand it and embrace it. Only then can you overcome it and show courage. Below are the critical points for this section.

1.   Fear is simply an emotion. It is how to deal with the fear that can be considered "virtuous" or not.

2.   In managing your emotions, it is okay to feel fear but not let it consume you.

3.   Some fears are simply imaginary.

4.   It is hard to overcome fears, but you have to try eventually.

5.   Courage is the choice and willingness to confront agony, pain, danger, uncertainty, or intimidation, even though you may be afraid.

What Courage Entails

Courage entails intent and contemplation, personal fear, worthy or virtuous act, and self-endangerment. I want to shred it into bits for you, so let's have this scenario: You have a boyfriend or a husband, and you've been together for a year now. Let's call him

Zack. So, Zack used to be all-loving and caring when you started dating until a month ago when he began exhibiting some odd behaviors. He starts staying out late, coming home infrequently, and usually swaying like a palm tree and reeking alcohol. Zack is a shadow of himself, and you're worried. You try to talk to Zack, communicate with him, and ask him what was wrong and why he was the way he is now, but you know what he does? He hits you, and you can't believe what just happened. In the spur of the moment, you want to retaliate, tell him spiteful words and make him realize how much he's hurt you in the past days. You want to scream and cry and yell at him because he's being a jerk, but you're calm, and you don't even know what's happening anymore.
You decide to give Zack some time again, but he's grown worse, and the signs are now glaring that he's cheating. He knows you're aware, but he doesn't care, so you decide to call it a wrap, but Zack pleads for another chance. What the hell, right? I know. But you love Zack, and it's blinded you, so you forgive him.

Zack puts up good behavior for some months, and you're thankful that you stayed. It's a month to your second anniversary, and Zack repeats the same behavior. He hits you twice as hard this time, and you have a swollen face and a miscarriage. Now, you've had enough; you sit in your bathtub crying, remembering the good times you shared and how lonely and possibly miserable you would be without him. He's your everything and you don't know what you'd do without him. So you're afraid and at crossroads. You tell your friend, and she tells you to leave him. You say she doesn't understand you. You refuse to believe that Zack never loved you from the onset. You can call him a manipulator if you want. It's your anniversary date, and nothing's changed. You get no show of love even on your special day, but a pale "Happy anniversary," and that's the last straw that breaks the ice. So you take a deep breath and walk up to this monster you once loved and tell him it's over, never to look back.

Touchy story? That's up to you and really but not the point. It's only an illustration of what courage entails. The intent is what you wish to achieve. In this story, you intended to find peace and happiness elsewhere as the relationship was draining you. Contemplation, synonymous with deliberation and consideration, is a deep thought of the possible side effects of what you intend to do. Contemplation, synonymous with reflection and thinking, is a deep thought of the possible side effects of what you intend to do. What did you contemplate while reading the story? On leaving or staying? Giving him time to change? It's all the questions you ask yourself to make your decision. Then there's your fear. A lot of people would rather die than get out of a situation. They might be distressed in their marriages or relationships. Still, they would not leave because of what people say or what they gain from the individual. But it's wrong. What did we say about self-love? Your happiness first, black queen.

Your fear in the story is the fear of being alone because it's been a long time since you were that way. And you wonder how you're going to cope. This fear could be so overwhelming it would shake you till you bend to it, but be strong, and you'll overcome. It gets better in the long run, and you'd be thankful you made that decision. The virtuous act is that you were wise enough to realize that he was out of love with you if he ever was at all and that you'd ridicule yourself if you continue staying. How can a beautiful black queen be mocked in such a manner? You are PRICELESS, don't let anyone put a price on you. Show your worthiness by standing out. Where others choose to remain in toxic relationships or friendships, say NO, my black woman. Say No.

One more thing; self-endangerment. Did you consider the possibilities that could happen when you approached Zack for a breakup? What if he had hit you again and killed you out of anger this time? In meeting him for a discussion as crucial as that, you knew there were going to be risks, but you took them either way. That's what makes you courageous; intentionally committing any act or taking action after thinking despite the risks attached, primarily inspired by a worthy cause, perhaps in the presence of the emotion, fear. That's what courage entails, queen.

Also, more often than not, courage is confused with so many other concepts. These may include confidence, bravery, and fortitude. As they're not the focus of our chapter, I'll distinguish them from courage so you can further understand what courage is and relate to it on a personal level.

According to Wikipedia, Confidence originates from the Latin word, 'fidere,' meaning "to trust"; therefore, having self-confidence is having trust in oneself. So if you raise your hand when the teacher asks three students to volunteer themselves, without informing them of what they're to do, that's confidence. It's you stepping out in front of the class as a volunteer because you've done something like that or something similar before, so you can take a good guess of what it is. But how would you be so assured you can do whatever the teacher asks if you've not stepped out before? That's when courage comes in. As we now know, courage is the quality of mind or spirit that enables you to face difficulty, danger, and pain despite fear. You're the only one who knows the answer in the class, but you've never said a word since you've been in attendance. You're watching the teacher threaten to punish all the students for not knowing it, and with your heart throbbing and threatening to fall off, you raise your hand and speak up. That's courage. Courage is a prerequisite before confidence.

"When you're operating out of courage, you are saying that no matter how you feel about yourself or your opportunities or the outcome, you are going to take a risk and take a step towards what you want. You are not waiting for the confidence to arrive mysteriously." — Tribe of Mentors.

Courage and bravery are similar, but bravery is innate or like an instinct. Bravery is facing a dangerous situation without any fear. It's effortless. While courage is seeing a scary thing and acting, even though you're scared. Unlike bravery, courage is for a cause. A brave person can stand up to a bully without a thought. Still, a courageous person considers the reason and thinks it through, deciding to do so in the presence of fear. Being brave is excellent, as well as being courageous.

Last but not least is fortitude. In short and straightforward terms, it is advanced courage-the type of courage a black woman should have in the face of adversity. It is deciding to fight on and not give up despite the travails you may face.

Key Points

Knowing a thing helps a great deal in imbibing that thing. For that reason, I took my time to explain the whole concept of courage to you. Find the critical points for this section below.

1.   When you know what courage entails, you can begin your journey to becoming a better you, a beautiful black woman in total control of her fear. Work with intent and contemplation, personal fear, worthy or virtuous act, and self-endangerment. Master them, and you'll be loving your growth in no time.

2.   Always think your intentions through.

3.   Courage is mental strength.

Knowing The Types Of Courage

There are different types of courage. There's Physical, Emotional, Intellectual, Social, Spiritual, and Moral courage, but I want to talk about only three. I find that their knowledge has helped me a great deal and will also help you.

Physical Courage

When people think about courage, they get their minds on physical courage. It involves you risking discomfort, injury, pain, or even death at the expense of something more substantial. Now, this type of courage is so wild that I may not cover everything exhaustively, but I'll do well to touch on it as it needs to be.

I know how it feels as a woman to have a visible scar that makes people ask, "oh dear, how did you get this?" and stuff like that. That's because I have a very close friend who told me about the history of her scar. She was driving past a building when she noticed it was on fire and could hear screams and cries for help. They all sounded like kids, she told me. Know what she did? You can take a wild guess.

My friend stayed put in the car and called the fire department. Uh oh, not what you guessed? Keep reading. Did I mention my friend is so beautiful? She has this dark skin that glows, literally. No, she did not want to risk her beautiful skin, and truthfully, she was scared. I could see it in her eyes while she narrated her story. She was asthmatic, so she was scared of having an attack if she moved to save them. But minutes passed, 5, and then 10. Then she panicked. It's hard staying to watch people die and also leaving when you could do something. So she grabbed her inhaler and dashed into the building. The first thing she saw was the dead body, who happened to be the children's mother. She suffered electrocution in her kitchen due to some electrical faults. A fire started. Her children, who happened to be upstairs asleep, woke up a few minutes after the fire had spread to almost all parts of the house.

In summary, my friend could get to the children and get them calm after several burns. She said she saw death knocking at her door. She doesn't even know how she managed to take the children out before she collapsed. It's a real story, and things like that happen every day. Did you know even a little act of exercising takes courage? Even getting up after falling and trying again? Yes, Queen. Lance Armstrong said, "If you worry about falling off the bike, you'd never get on."

This quote reminds me of the times I fell off a bike as a kid while learning to ride. I'd cry and complain to my mother, and she would soothe me, offering to hold the bike while I pedalled. That little act gave me the courage to continue trying. Sometimes you need someone to encourage you, tell you that you can do whatever, you are a true definition of power, and you should never be ashamed of your skin. You are unique, perfect just as you are. I'll be more than happy to encourage you as we continue this journey.

Emotional Courage

Emotional courage has to do with allowing yourself to feel both pleasant and unpleasant emotions without any attachment. There's a secret to outstanding leadership, and I'll let you in on it--Be emotional. Does it sound a bit awkward? Hold on, let me explain.

Most leaders face tremendous challenges. They do not allow themselves to feel; they want to avoid actual vulnerability. But who says letting yourself be emotional makes you weak? Everyone feels, so no one should dictate what you do with your emotions, my dear black queen! You are the pioneer of your life, and you know what's best for you. Open your heart to feel every emotion, but don't let it consume you. That's what makes you stand out, controlling your emotions. Great leaders have emotional courage, a great deal of confidence in themselves, connect with others, and are committed to a greater purpose – all at the same time. Please understand that when I talk about leadership, I'm not only talking about people in large organizations. No. As long as you want to achieve something you care about, you want to move forward, to see yourself grow; you are a leader, so you must allow yourself to feel. The illustration I gave about Zack is also an example of emotional courage. You will let yourself feel the pain, go through it every step of the way, and when you finish crying, you go to the bathroom, wipe your tears and wash your face, put on that makeup, look elegant, and rock that body of yours. Crown it with that heart-stopping smile because there's no way you are going to let what you feel overcome you. It's about having emotional courage--mastering your emotions, remember?

Moral Courage

Moral courage means standing up for what is right. It involves doing the right thing even when it might bring discomfort to you or when the majority does not support it. Martin Luther King, Harriet Tubman, and others who stood up for slaves exhibited great moral courage. My dear black woman, you should stand up for whatever you feel is right. That's how the world can be better.

You probably work at some ministry, and your co-workers cut corners to get extra privileges, and you know what they're doing wouldn't tell well if they get caught. Right now, you're scared of what they would say if you stand up to reprimand them; that's too far even; let's not talk about standing up to them. Not engaging in the act is a massive move in itself!

One Friday morning, you walk up to where they're discussing their spoils and be like,
"I guess you know you're doing the wrong things? It is clearly against our ethics, Ma'ams and Sirs. I think you should stop whatever you're doing, or else I'll make a report to the boss."
Suddenly you hear a loud clap from your audience, followed by the rest doing the same. You have just made a "ridiculously wonderful" speech. All your co-workers make jest of you and

refuse to take you seriously. Instead, they make fun of you and laugh hard. They fail to acknowledge the truth. But deep inside of them, they know it.

But then you go back to your seat and realize that you're not dead, didn't catch a cold, not paralyzed, probably a few heartbeats out of place, but now you're lovely and much better with a burden off your chest. It's that simple! Never forget, one thing about moral courage is that it is very close to the truth.

Do you want to be morally courageous? The truth should always be in your mouth, and you must be ready to burst out when need be.
May I also remind you that being morally courageous is not confined to religion? Yes, remember this always.

Key Points

1.   When people think about courage, they get their minds on physical courage.

2.   Sometimes, you need someone to encourage you and tell you that you can do whatever; you are a true definition of power and should never be ashamed of your skin. You are amazingly perfect, just as you are.

3.   But who says letting yourself feel makes you weak? It doesn't.

4.   When you finish crying, you go to the bathroom, wipe your tears and wash your face, put on that makeup, look elegant, and rock that body of yours. Crown it with that heart-stopping smile because there's no way you are going to let what you feel overcome you.

We have come to the end of the courage chapter! I hope you enjoyed reading it and finding strength in it as much as I did while writing it.

Courage is one of the most extraordinary things you can know. Embrace it wholly and deeply. The next chapter would be all about love and broken hearts. Have you loved before, ever experienced heartbreak? Read on; let's talk about it all!

Chapter Five

Breakups and Broken Hearts

"Cry. Forgive. Learn. Move on. Let your tears water the seeds of your future happiness."
– Steve Maraboli

I'm excited to talk to you about this topic because I have a lot to say about it. Thankfully, you now understand the concepts of negative emotions, self-love, anxiety, and courage. I advise that you read the chapter on Self-Love as many times as you wish because it's a critical factor in mending your broken heart. The others are important, of course.

The concept of love is undeniably quite abstract and very difficult to describe. The fact that love can find expression in many ways makes it even more complicated. But to make this chapter easy to understand, I'd like us to focus on a straightforward definition of love, that is, a deep attachment or affection for another. When we fall in love, our brain embraces 'happy' chemicals, which it makes by itself. But after a breakup or death of a loved one, they stop being produced, and the body suffers from it, leading to a broken heart. A broken heart is a metaphor for the intense emotional stress you feel when experiencing great and deep longing. I know firsthand how difficult and painful it is to deal with a broken heart. I have two experiences to share, and even though they may not be the same with whatever you're facing or faced in the past, I'll share them still. I want you to know that I understand when you say you're heartbroken.

Five years ago happened to be one of the most challenging years I've ever faced. It was the year my grandma died, and I don't know if you'd say she's "just your grandma," but it was different for me, as it is with most people. She had this illness episode, and I travelled home to be by her side. She didn't want to go to a care home, so I took care of her during that period. It was draining, but I loved her with everything in me and was ready to do anything to make sure she was completely okay. I paid a doctor for home-based medical care, making sure he checked on her every day as well. For weeks she was sick until she started recovering, and I would say with all pride that I was the happiest person in this world. You know, there's always this happiness we feel understanding our loved ones are there, and we can see them, we can touch them, these things might look small sometimes, but I've learned not to take it for granted. I had these long talks I used to have with her immediately. She recovered, and we did all the fun stuff we always did. But it was only two days after she recovered, and I was in the living room calling her to come down for breakfast, that she died. It broke me.

I do not know which hurt more, the fact that a week after, my boyfriend of a year plus posted a picture of his new girlfriend on his social media page. Yeah, he left without any explanation. No words, nothing at all. It hurt the most because he was with the type of girl he had always liked. I knew this because he always talked about her. I was too blind to see the signs, and I paid dearly for it. We'll talk more about this, but let's go back to my grandma's death.

I had these episodes of sobbing, rage, and despair. I was at my lowest. I'd stay up all night and think about why my grandma had to die at that time and why my boyfriend left without any explanation. You could call me a glutton, but at that time, I betrayed everything, my food, my sleep, even my hygiene. It was so bad that my broken heart would often cause my body to secrete high-stress hormones, resulting in severe panic attacks. But I didn't care anymore. I even wished for death.

With a broken heart, I went through the five stages of grief: denial, anger, bargaining, depression, and acceptance. It's funny how at first, after my grandma died, I still went up to her room for an entire week, desperately hoping that I would find her awake on her bed like old times. But it was just my mind refusing to accept the fact that she was gone forever. And my boyfriend? I texted him immediately and asked what was going on. But he outright said that I was simply a rebound, a freaking rebound for over a year. It hurt that much, but the pain didn't go away immediately. Nope, I asked to see him, and he declined. After several pleas, he gave in and explained to me that he had made up with his x-months ago. So, he did not only use me, he had been cheating on me, and I couldn't see the signs. It's also funny when I think of it now because then I thought I was foolish to love. But time made me understand that I didn't need to change who I was because of someone who didn't deserve me in the first place.

After he confessed to me about everything, I stopped living in denial. Then, I became furious. I was so pissed at life for taking away someone I loved and pissed at myself for being "foolish," like I said in the previous paragraph. I was angry at him for taking me for a fool, I was mad at everybody, and my social life became a total mess. I wondered what I was doing because I seemed to lose track of time. I was unrecognizable, always angry, self-loathing, and unforgiving. I contemplated begging my ex to take me back. I did it, but it was a waste of time. Then I opted for suicide, although I never carried it out. I never mustered enough courage to carry out my suicide plans. Then I became numb. Fast forward to six weeks later, and I was not in the least better. This time, I had begun to feel, but it was all the negative feelings I didn't wish to handle, and I became the depressed fellow around that people got used to me being like that. You could never see me smile or laugh; I just wore a long face all day.

The day I decided to go for therapy was rather chucklesome. One of my friends walked up to me, slapped me hard across the cheek, and said, "you're not going to die alone and depressed; come with me." And I started seeing a therapist who helped me a great deal. It took me over a year of reorganization and recovery to reduce the intensity of my grief, but it was worth it every day.

Key Points

1.	Love is a deep attachment or affection for another, a parent, child, or friend.

2.	The five stages of grief are denial, anger, bargaining, depression, and acceptance.

3.	When rejection is involved, shame sets in

4.	Continuous, uncontrollable, and distressing intrusive thoughts are often a component of grieving.

Is It a Broken Heart?

Like approaches to heartbreak vary, it looks different on everyone because it is a form of grief. We all grieve differently. If you've lost a partner, my dear black woman, probably due to death or they walked away, or maybe you even had to walk away, I understand the grief that follows. It's so unbearable. Because you're not just grieving over their loss but your dreams for a future that includes that person. This kind of grief can cause emotional and physical pain. Did you know that many heartbreak symptoms overlap with other disorders, especially depression? And trust me, it's far worse for people who have been previously depressed because a heartbreak could trigger an episode.

As a beautiful black woman on a journey to master her emotions, you should know when you've passed the line of sadness and fallen into depression which is a sign of a broken heart. It starts from losing appetites like I once had, nausea, indigestion, overeating, diarrhea, excessive weight gain, or loss. Other signs could be insomnia, bad dreams, lack of energy, restlessness, weakness, body pains, and exhaustion. Never dismiss these as the usual stuff, and it is your body and soul whispering their fatigue and pain.

In relationship breakups, the affected ones usually turn their anger over the rejection toward themselves. Yes, just like I did. I am thankful that this happened to me, so I can relate precisely to all of these as I go on this journey with you. It's beautiful now that I've overcome that phase.

When you can't think about anything else but sit all day and let your ex or dead one run through your mind, it's time to reassess, queen. Self-hate can deepen your depression, beautiful woman, and cause narcissistic wounding. The process of self-attack can range from mild self-doubt to critical self-recrimination or accusation, which is sure to leave a lasting imprint on your self-worth. I beg of you not to let it get to this extent. In this phase, it's eaten deep into you. It is on the verge of taking your self-worth and causing you to doubt your ability to love, personality-efficacy, attachment worthiness, ability to move on, everything, queen, everything.

I've shared a big part of me with you in this chapter. I am glad that I could. Do you think you're in the last phase of self-hate? Let's do a quick assessment test. Do you feel like life isn't worth living without the other person? You feel worthless, right? Possibly, even angry at yourself for some of your decisions? Or mad at life because it took someone you cared about? Alright. Whatever your answer is, write it down on paper; we're heading somewhere. The first step, remember, is knowing the signs. When you find yourself avoiding your friends, my gorgeous black woman, you've got to pause and rethink things. I know how unbelievably difficult it can be to maintain friendships in the wake of a significant breakup. Still, you have to wait for real this time. Please don't take it out on them. Your friends and family are the only ones who'll stand by you when you can't even hold yourself up anymore. So don't push them away. It's okay to explain to them that you do not want company for the time being but don't be out for too long. Talk to them, cry if you're okay with it, and let them offer you comfort. It's part of your healing process.

Finding closure and struggling with boundaries is another sign you shouldn't look past. Oh my, trust me when I say it's damn hard, but you know yourself. You know now that you should love yourself so much, so work, toil all day and try to break past that bad habit of stalking your ex on social media. I understand that pain can make you behave in ways you ordinarily wouldn't, like publishing passive-aggressive posts. That's a red flag, and I want you to be smart enough to notice it. It's only fueling your anger and resentment. You don't also have to block them forever; just let yourself feel, then purge. If you're also thinking of ways to "bump" into them and try to get things working again, you have to stop. Did you break up with them? Think about why you did and remember that you should be courageous and watch how you'd scale through this stage, totally refined. Oh, they broke up with you? It's fine. Their loss and that's on period. You are everything a woman should entail; you are strong and black, so why cry all night and refuse to move on when your ex failed to acknowledge your value. A therapist would tell you this, a good friend would do the same, and I'll let you know the same. It's time, queen, get up.

Last but not least, post-traumatic stress disorder. This disorder is mainly about the inability of a person to recover after experiencing a terrifying event. It may last months or years, with triggers that can bring back memories of the trauma accompanied by intense emotional and physical reactions. Heartbreaks are also known to trigger PTSD. So if you are a PTSD patient, you'd need this book to understand your emotions, master and take care of them. Watch out for the ninety-day plan!

Key Points

1. Heartbreak looks different for everyone because it is a form of grief, and we all grieve differently.

2. When you can't think about anything else but sit all day and let your ex or dead one run through your mind, it's time to reassess.

3. Self-loathe eats deep into you and takes away your self-worth and ability to love.

4. Look for the signs. Are you avoiding friends or struggling in your business?

5. Are you stalking? That's a big no-no.

It's Time To Move On

I wondered how some people moved on so quickly. One of my friends didn't care when his girl broke up with him, which added to my self-doubt. But did you know that everyone has their coping mechanisms? I realized this quite late when I was so depressed that I attended therapy sessions. While many cry all night and wallow in despair and get better, some don't come out of it, and a few repress their feelings, trying not to face the pain. Still, in the end, it eventually leads to panic, anxiety, or depression. Others slip into addiction and rebound relationships to deal with a broken heart. All these are the different ways people deal with broken hearts, but you should deal with a broken heart like a queen for a black woman, and I'll show you how.

I was hoping you could take out the journal I asked you to write on the cause of your pain and how you feel. Now is the time to deal with your emotions, like the strong woman you are. Ready?

The first step is allowing yourself to feel your feelings, and I believe you know what that means from the previous chapters we went through together? With emotional shock, you have to be gentle with yourself and feel your feelings. Don't inflict bodily harm to yourself. Do you think you're at fault? But what if you aren't, and it's just guilt clouding your senses and eating you up? You aren't a robot, and your feelings are there for a reason—they can help you move through difficult experiences, but only if you release them. During this process, validate your feelings by saying things like "I accept I'm experiencing this emotion." or "I'm feeling this way."

Next is cutting off communication with your ex if it's about a breakup. Remember those 'happy' emotions I talked about in an earlier section? I know how much you want to feel them again, how much you crave them, but you'll undoubtedly struggle to move on if you go back to your ex. You broke up with them, so why bend to your craving? They'll eventually dissolve, and you won't even remember them. I advocate for cutting your ex off immediately, but not forever. They still have an atom of humanity in them, or don't they? So if you feel it's okay to check in on them once in a while, it's lovely. Just don't let it become the norm.

Finding a support system is also a step to moving on. And that's why I told you not to push your friends away. I hope you smile as you read this upon realizing that you need people around you. No man is an island, gorgeous one! So pick up that phone and call whoever comes to your mind, no, not your ex, not the one you're getting away from, but those who will fill you with nothing but positivity and warmth. Right now is the time you need people the most. Don't deceive yourself that no one cares about you. Many people love you and want to support you, but how can they when you don't tell them? Who knows, they might have gone through exactly what you're going through and are ready to hold your hand and walk you through every stage. Give it a try.

Hey beautiful black woman, are you still with your journal? We're about to do an exercise. Okay, so you know why you broke up or were broken up with, right? It doesn't matter if you're not sure why they broke up with you. All you're going to do is write a list of your ex's negative aspects, take a deep breath, and look at it. Whenever you feel like going back, flip back to the page and focus on counterbalancing your obsessive thinking with this mental exercise. Avoid thinking that there's something wrong with you. I did just that for weeks, and that's why the healing process was slow. But despite that, don't judge the length of your healing process. I'm different from you, and you're different from me. Stop wondering why you've not gotten over that six months relationship because it all depends on how attached you were to the person.

Take care of yourself, make sure to exercise, eat good food, and breathe. Also, try as much as you can to build a good sleep routine. It helps in fighting your negative emotions. Create new habits, make plans, find all your interests, whether old or new. It's about developing you. Accept that closure is something you may need to find on your own. If your ex did not explain why he left you, you have to create your healthy narrative, but consider seeing a therapist if it doesn't help. If the breakup triggers your PTSD, you must seek outside help. Trust that the pain won't last forever; believe that this too shall pass. Reflect on the positive things. Embrace the excitement of new possibilities and remind yourself of your awesomeness! No matter how difficult it might seem at first, believe me when I say you'd love again and heal. Give yourself time. The healing will come.

Key Points

1.   A few people repress their feelings, trying not to face the pain. Still, in the end, it eventually leads to panic, anxiety, or depression.

2.   Feel, but don't become your feelings.

3.   How would your loved ones know if you don't communicate?
4.   Counterbalance your obsessive thoughts with a list of your ex's opposing sides.

5.   Take care of yourself and find closure with yourself.

My dear black woman, we have reached the end of this chapter! I hope you had a lot of fun in it. Now, come with me; let's explore contentment in the next chapter. It'll be fun, I promise you.

Chapter Six

Contentment

"Fortify yourself with contentment, for this is an impregnable fortress."
--Epictetus

That last chapter was quite the chapter. It stirred a lot of emotions, I know. This chapter is self-explanatory, so it'll be a bit shorter and provide warmth to you. Let's begin. Shall we?

Contentment is being satisfied with what you have. You have a friend who has at least three gowns from all the popular clothing brands, Old Navy. Reuters, House Of Versace, Burberry, Chanel, Gucci, name it! This friend flaunts them all to your face because you have just three gowns from unpopular brands. You don't pay any heed to her, but you rock the outfits you own in all pride and glamor. That's some high level of contentment shit. You're joyful with what you own. It doesn't mean you're not aiming higher. It a just that you're not getting caught up in sadness because of the things you are yet to own.

It takes contentment to be happy with the little thing you possess and not get jealous about the possessions of others. Instead of doing that, please take it as motivation and work hard for self-improvement. I have a friend I tell about my financial progress. I've never seen anyone so genuinely happy for another as much as this friend of mine. Even at his lowest, he would call me to congratulate me on any feat I achieved. It gladdens me so much, not having to feel guilty about my wins or anything.

Some friends can't tell certain things about you, especially your wins, because they'd get jealous, and it always shows even when they try to hide it. From the side comments or mutterings to avoidance, all because you're not happy about the person's growth. As a contented person, you'll be great.

If you are a student and don't have the luxury to live as wealthy as most of your friends, contentment is one key attribute you need to imbibe to scale through college. Contentment keeps you happy and helps you push harder in life. It's not just in college.

As a black woman who is courageous enough to go on this journey with me, I need you to understand that your peace of mind should come first no matter what. Contentment is among the virtues that can offer you that. It would bring positivity and self-love for self-improvement. It allows you to be ambitious and aspire for a better future; it restricts you from greed and gives peace to your present. If you aren't at peace with what you achieved by yourself, how can you be motivated to work toward a better future?

Another reason you should be content is to know what it is to be truly happy. If you're at peace with yourself and your achievements, happiness will find its way into your life with ease. Do not live a sad and monotonous life because you do not own all you desire. You'll regret it if you do. From the things you own, create your kind of life. It dawns on me that humans do not need so much to have a great life every day. No, I'm not trying to make you see reasons why you shouldn't indulge in luxury. I'm only trying to inform you that it is vital that you enjoy life with the little you own while you wait for the big things to come. Also, you need to master the difference between your needs and your wants.

We all have our needs and wants, and I'm sure yours would differ from mine. While I could be desirous of a helicopter of my own, do I need it? Contentment would help me distinguish between my wants and my needs. I need the necessities of life, food, shelter, and clothing to survive in this world. But if I let my greed take over and spend my money every time on mere wants without considering my needs, I may end up begging for food or a roof over my head. You're a pretty woman, and you want to stay pretty, I understand. But first, you have to consider your money at hand. If it'll see you through your needs without you feeling the brunt of it, that's wonderful. You have to cut down on some wants and invite contentment into your heart if it won't. Always fulfil the needs first as they are the necessities. The desires are secondary.

One other importance that you need to remember always is simplicity. We're on a journey through emotional self-care, and what's better than being able to relieve yourself of that thought and take a deep breath in, say to yourself that "you've got this!" Because if you don't, who else would? A content person is a simple person, and that's a fantastic trait. She doesn't have to go around nursing ill feelings because she can't get something she wants at the moment or because of her friends' success. You have to note this beautiful trait because it is critical to self-love and genuine happiness, as simple as it may look. Practice gratitude, assure yourself every day the fact that nothing is permanent and that material things do not often promote long-term happiness.

I watched a short clip some time ago about how satisfying a want would only make you develop another. Mind you, and I'm not asking you not to indulge a desire when you can afford to, not at all. I need you to understand that you shouldn't base your happiness on material things. Happiness should come from within, realizing that you are a perfect creation and that no one can love you better than yourself. Life is not a race or competition. A friend of mine gives me gifts from time to time. I accept them with so much gratitude and sincere happiness, and I'd say to him, "you motivate me to work harder every day." And that's from a place of genuine love. I'm thankful for my present, and I know my future will be better because I'm working towards that with contentment as a weapon.

Key Points

1.   Contentment doesn't stop you from improving.

2.   If you're at peace with yourself and your achievements, happiness will find its way into your life with a lot of ease.

3.   Life is not a race or competition.

Are You Contented?

I know I've been talking about contentment a lot, and you keep saying, "Alright, I've heard what you said contentment is about, but I'm still unsure if I got what it takes." Please read this section well, as it covers a few qualities needed to achieve contentment.

Quick question: Are you satisfied? Satisfaction is a significant attribute of contentment. When you're content, you'll be okay with what you have and happy for others who are progressing. Did you know? Contented people regard the possession of others as entirely usual because they believe it is only a matter of time before they can legally get their own. They never give way for the lust for wealth to affect them negatively.

Get that envy out of your system. To envy is to have negative thoughts over someone else's achievement. On your journey to being contented, my dear queen, many people will celebrate and call you to join in their celebration. Gladly accept their invitation if you have the time to spare and let yourself feel genuine happiness for them. I want to state that feeling envious of someone who got their wealth through illegal means is very wrong. Personally, it doesn't sit well with me. Why would you envy someone you have no idea of what they have been through to reach that level? Focus on your growth. People are different, and so is their growth period. Write out your achievements in your journal when you feel jealous of someone's growth and pat yourself on the back. You're doing great!

When I realize how greedy and desperate some people can be, I shiver in my bones. They can be so desperate to the extent of committing great moral evils, like human trafficking, murder, theft, and the likes. They're never satisfied, always wanting more; that's greed. On your way to being a better version of yourself, you have to take away avarice from yourself. It will help you build trust between you and your colleagues, friends, and family. Contented people have a passionate hatred for greed.

Content people hate corruption. Corruption is any dishonest or fraudulent conduct. Bribery, extortion, fraud, abuse of power, embezzlement, etc., are examples of corrupt practices which people engage in to meet their wants. Yes, wants. Content people are careful to avoid all forms of corruption, and you beautiful black woman should do so too.

The last one I'd talk about is humility. It is the quality of being modest—the liberation from your consciousness and a form of

temperance that does not involve pride or self-deprecation.
Humble people know their self-worth; they understand their
strengths but do not dwell too much on them or announce to
everyone about them.

I love this attribute because it helps one get true friends most of
the time. When people know you're humble and not one to boast,
they'd always want to be around you.

Over the years, I've watched many discontent people reveal their
discontentment, which always harms our society. It's like an ill
wind that blows community no good. Lack of contentment has
served as an ambassador for major moral vices and promoted the
culture of greed, corruption, engagement in criminal acts, the
prevalence of immorality, and so on. We're all working on our
emotions and, in the long run, giving back to society by spreading
good around. Still with your journal? Here's a to-do list for you:

– Count your blessings
– Practice kindness
– Let go of what I can't control
– Listen to my heart
– Be productive yet calm
– Just breathe

It's elementary, and you'd get used to it as you repeat it every
day. You don't have to follow it as it is; feel free to explore your
choices. Good luck being content.

Key Points

1.   Satisfaction is a crucial attribute to contentment.

2.   Get that envy out of your system.

3.   On your way to being a better version of yourself, you have
to take away greed.

4.   Content people hate corruption.

Phew! It's been one hell of a journey. Tell me, love, did you enjoy
this chapter? Did everything I wrote about contentment in this

chapter strike a chord? Have you been a discontented person? It's okay. The good thing is you have the power and knowledge you need to begin your contentment journey at this very moment. I hope you bask in contentment and revel in its goodness. Now, let's start the next chapter! It's all about self-worth.

Chapter Seven

Self-Worth Through a Black Woman's Lenses

Because one believes in oneself, one doesn't try to convince others. Because one is content with oneself, one doesn't need others' approval. Because one accepts oneself, the whole world accepts him or her.
—Lao Tzu.

Self-worth is one virtue that all of us should possess. What is self-worth? It is simply the value you see in yourself. It is that self-pride that glows in you with so much brilliance. Self-worth is what stands you out from the crowd.

For you to stand out in this world, you need a tremendous amount of self-worth. You must know one thing. Your self-worth is a significant determinant of how much people think you are worth. And that plays a vital role in how they would treat you. For this reason, you must wear self-worth like it is your armour. It is one of the most beautiful things you can do for yourself. I learned about self-worth very early in my life, and it helped me immensely. When you fail to define your worth, the world will define it for you. I've never met women who express their worth as much as black women do. Black women do not accept stupidity and poor treatment because they know what they are worth. It would help if you first valued yourself for people to see your value.

I've also met some black women who let people push them around because they do not know what they are worth. When I was in university, I had this gorgeous and intelligent friend named Marilyn. She's one of the most innovative women I've met all my life. The whole class was always in awe of her. Going by this, you'd expect Marilyn to be a girl full of confidence, right? But the reverse was the case with my dear Marilyn. If poor self-worth were human, it would have been Marilyn. She was blind to all the wonders we saw in her. Who wouldn't love such

294

gorgeousness and intelligence in one person? She'd second guess everything and always question if she was worthy of honour. At first, I thought she was just a humble girl. But as time progressed, I found out that she had a very little sense of self-worth.

She'd condone a lot of silly behavior just because she thought she wasn't all that important. I need you to know one thing. The moment people notice that you have minimal self-worth, they'd make it littler by taking you through every shitty thing. My friend, there are lots of Marilyns in this world. People who dazzle yet are unaware of the spark they bear. I am sure that you are curious about what happened to Marilyn. Aren't you? Well, it ended well. She spent quite a lot of time revelling in her poor sense of self-worth. I don't know precisely how or when, but I remember Marilyn suddenly changing from the timid and weak girl into a powerful and bold girl sometime later at school. With Marilyn, I realized something. Black women are at their prettiest when they are aware of themselves and their power. Nothing comes close to the power of a black woman who knows her self-worth. They are the kind of black women that change the world and cause people to marvel. Don't you want to be that kind of strong woman? I know you do.

Many people work hard at making black women see their self-worth through distorted lenses. This class of people is always afraid of the strength of black women. So, they try to make them small by messing with their sense of self-worth. My dear black woman, the truth is, you'd meet a lot of people who would question yourself and all of your abilities. You'd get the good things you deserve and find yourself wondering if you deserve them or not. You'd find yourself in high places and ask yourself if the apex is made for you too. The era when people intimidated black women and made their self-worth into playthings is long gone. In this era, black women wear their self-worth with all the pride in the world. I am more than glad to be born at this time. Tell me, aren't you happy, too?

It would help if you prepared yourself to encounter the people who might make you feel terrible about yourself and your life. Sometimes, preparing yourself for things enables you to respond to them better. You know, people do not learn how to fight on the battlefield. No matter the intimidation such people would try to make you feel, do not give in.

Never stop to ponder on what they would tell you. Instead, pay no mind to all the manipulations they bear by focusing on all the goodness you carry. Yes, I know it is not an easy thing to do. I know how difficult it is not to pay attention to negative people. You know what? I find it crazy that we listen to negativity more than positivity. If we can be so keen on listening to people who say terrible things about us, why can't we do the same when it comes to the good stuff? Well, it is human nature. But, I trust in your abilities to never let what people say or do reduce your self-worth. When I get overwhelmed sometimes, I draw strength from the first line of a quote by Virginia Woolf. It says:

'I feel a thousand capacities spring up in me.'

Whenever I perceive that my self-worth is suffering, I remind myself of all my capacities with this quote. It is one of my favourites. I hope it strengthens you too. Do not give any space for the diminishing of your worth.

Key Points

1. A great sense of your self-worth is one of the best things you can ever have.

2. Nothing has the right to make you feel less of yourself.

3. If you do not define your self-worth, other people will do it for you. They most likely won't describe it the way you want them to.

4. You'd meet people who would try to destroy your self-worth at some point in your life. But, you are more than powerful enough to overpower them.

5. You need a tremendous amount of self-worth to excel in this life.

Walk Away When They Begin To Shrink You

Many people deal with poor self-worth today because they do not know how to walk away. No, I'm not talking about taking pleasant walks in pretty boulevards. I'm talking about walking away from people who make your self-worth a mess, people who make you feel bad about yourself. They are the worst kind of people anyone can call a friend. They do not only make your self-worth terrible, but they also make you conform to things that are beneath you. You won't even realize it until you're fully into poor self-worth.

I've had quite a lot of friends in my life. Now, I have just a few of them. I was that one friend that could go to extreme lengths for anyone I called a friend. I do not mean to brag, but I was an angel. That friend that people always wished they had. Somehow, I attract people to myself effortlessly. Making friends and connecting with people is one thing that has always come easy to me. I like to think that I would have been an expert in my field by now if I had spent the energy I put into making friends on networking. You know, it is no cliché when people say your network is your net worth. But I do not blame myself so much now. I was young; I saw the world in rose-tinted glasses. Just like I've had many friends, I've made a couple of mistakes in friendships. I thought it was cool to keep everyone around me. I never knew the importance of filtering friendship circles. A terrible lesson awakened that need in me. You want to know what it was, don't you? I'll share it with you, my dear. I write this book to empower you, and learning from my experience can do that too.

I metamorphosed from a boisterous youth into an afraid and shy teenager. It amazed my parents a lot. Oh, how reclusive I became. I used to be among those who never believed people could influence them. I can hear my younger self saying, 'no one in this life can influence me. I am strong' as I write this book. I didn't even know when I was under the influence of the friends I swore could never influence me. I think it started with them saying I was too loud and everywhere. They didn't like it that I was as audacious as I was. I tried to please them by shutting away some of my capacities. It took me a long time to know. Knowing was quite tricky for me. People with problems sometimes refuse to see that they have issues. It was that way with me too. I couldn't just believe it nor accept it. I had to do a lot of self-examinations first. Girl, I felt so miserable!

Sometimes, we all make this mistake. We stick with people that diminish our self-worth without even realizing it. We only know it after a lot of damage must have been done. I have experienced it, and I know how it feels perfectly well. This experience made me begin to undertake a personal evaluation at intervals. I think it is something that you would love to adopt, too, for the sake of your personal growth and self-worth. From time to time, take a pause and evaluate yourself and the level of your self-worth. Doing this doesn't only make you a better woman; it also helps you retrace your steps quickly the very moment you begin to stray.

Mistakes are easier to correct with early discovery.
When you discover your mistake, please don't beat yourself up about it too much. Of course, it is perfectly normal to feel wrong about such a thing. Instead of spending a lot of time boasting over it, take your time and study your mistakes. All the places you went wrong. Don't ever deceive yourself by thinking that no one has the power to influence your self-worth. My dear, people are much more potent than they believe they are. Don't permit anyone to make you a mess by ignoring them when they trample on your priceless self-worth.

Do you know one other primary reason why people get afraid when it comes to walking out on people that shrink them? It is friendship and family. You know, the people that will diminish your self-worth are not strangers most of the time. You'd find them among your friends and family members. I have come to learn that humans love to make excuses and tolerate a lot of crazy stuff when it involves their loved ones. I am guilty of it, too. Don't feel bad.

I'll be laconic at this point. My dear black woman, you have to master the art of walking away from people and the things the moment they begin to shrink you. Nothing in this world is worth your self-worth. No matter how good a thing is, you really can't enjoy it with poor self-worth. Walking away may be crazy at first, but it is worth it. Sometimes, you'd feel like you're alone at the end of the world, like all you have is just yourself. In the future, you'll see that walking away from everything that shrinks you and your self-worth is one of the best things you can ever do for yourself.

Key Points

1. Nothing in this world is worth your self-worth.

2. To have the beautiful and sweet life you desire, you have to master the art of walking away from anything that shrinks you.

3. You are powerful enough to walk away. You are much stronger than you know.

4. Forgive yourself for all the times you let people mess with your self-worth.

Embrace Self-Improvement

Sometimes, lack triggers poor self-worth in people. I'm not talking about the lack of material things in the shortage that springs from the inside. For example, staying in a room full of intellectuals and having nothing meaningful to say during discussions is one great kind of lack. You'd most likely feel less of yourself. You might begin to weep and hate those people simply because you do not measure up to their standards. That would be one hell of an adverse reaction. Instead of reacting negatively to the situation, how about trying something different?

When feelings of inadequacy trigger your self-worth, the first thing you should do is identify. Sit your ass down and go through a self-valuation. Try as much as possible to remember every single thing that reduces your self-worth. Knowing the problem always makes it easier and faster to get a solution. I know you're curious now. After identification, what comes next? Or, is that where it all ends? Certainly not. When you finish identifying the things that make you feel less important, embrace self-improvement. Self-improvement comes in different forms. When it comes to feelings of inadequacies like not having enough skill, poor growth, and the likes, don't waste your time by wallowing in self-pity and crying about the situation. Stand up and improve yourself. Take courses, learn from mentors, do research, and share your ideas. These things might seem easy to do now, but they are not. They require a lot of dedication, time, and most importantly, the zeal and willingness to improve yourself. You'd be amazed at how much your self-worth would shoot up by the time you improve yourself. Not only does it make your voice bolder, but it also makes you open to better opportunities.

Sometimes, our poor self-worth arises from things we have no control over. It could be the way we look, speak, the family we come from, scars, race, and many others. I had a classmate who talked with a lisp back in the day. Almost everyone in the class always laughed whenever this particular student spoke. We were kids who didn't fully realize the damage those giggles, peals of laughter, and side talks caused. The student was brilliant, but she was quick to recoil into her shell because of our laughter. Writing about this now, I feel terrible for what other classmates and I did to that girl. We never give her space to shine. Also, we never got to learn from her because we were too busy. We only had time to make fun of her unique accent. As I grew older, I learned to embrace people more. It also dawned on me that the differences we share give the world its beauty. Nothing creates beauty more than variety.

If you're like this classmate I used to have, I need you to know that it is perfectly normal to feel wrong about these things. But what isn't okay is allowing the things you have no control over control your own life. You have to master acceptance. Acceptance, in this case, is serious self-improvement. You might need to do some work on your self-worth by standing up for yourself and refusing to allow anyone to silence you for any reason. It is not an easy thing to do, but the very moment you step out of silence is the moment you teach people not to ridicule you.

Take your time and improve yourself in the areas needed. Then, accept yourself for the things that you cannot undo. Never fail to remind yourself that you are lovely in all your elements.

Key Points

Embrace self-improvement and see how your self-worth would improve significantly. Start with a tiny step at a time. A lot of small steps make the significant steps. Remember this every day. Find the critical points for this section below.

1. Embrace self-improvement with all that you are.
2. It is okay to feel inadequate. What is not okay is wallowing in it.
3. Self-improvement makes your voice bolder and louder.
4. Do not gloat over your inadequacies. Focus on working on yourself instead.
5. Self-improvement increases self-worth.

My dear black woman, we have come to the end of this chapter. I hope you get enough value from it. The next chapter will be all about depression and its elements. Let's dig in!

Chapter Eight

Depression And Its Elements

I found that with depression, one of the most important things you could realize is that you're not alone.
—Dwayne Johnson

Depression is one illness that many people do not like to talk about despite affecting a considerable percentage of humanity. Before I go on with this topic, I would first talk about the meaning of depression.

So, what is depression? A lot of people begin to think about grief and sadness. No, depression is deeper than that. Although, grief and sadness are elements of depression. Do you know the difference? I'll explain to the best of my ability with a concise story.

Losing people and things I hold close to my heart is one thing that scares me to my bones in this life. We all want people to be with us forever—such beautiful wishful thinking. People will always come and go like the seasons. One of the most challenging phases of my life came when I was twenty years old. I feel teary writing about it now. Somehow, the grief never really goes away. It just hides somewhere and comes out on days you least expect. So, I lost my boyfriend to death in a car accident when I was twenty. It felt like a wild dream. My brain and body went numb with shock and deep sadness. For days, I'd lock myself in and weep until I lost all my strength. It felt like it was the end of the world for me. I'd look through the pictures we took together, relive the magical kisses, sniff his shirts, and cry. On some days, I wished to go back in time to hug him tighter and love him harder. But time travel happens only in science fiction, right?

My boyfriend's death affected me for quite a long time, and I began to think I was depressed. After I had healed from the loss, I realized I mistook my grief and sadness for depression. It is normal to grieve when bad things happen to us. It is our sorrow finding expression. But depression doesn't work like this. It just hits you like a tornado. Depression can come to you for no reason. It can envelop you and hold you intensely even if you are not grieving about anything. Do you get the difference between depression and sadness now? I hope you do.

Depression comes in varying degrees. Sometimes, a whiff of it hits you for a short time, and you bounce back quickly. Other times, it rents a room inside you and refuses to go. Either short or long time, depression is still depression. Do you know the signs of depression? The commonest of them all is the sudden and absolute loss of interest in things that used to set your heart on fire. You have to note that this is different from taking a break. I'll use myself as an example. I am a writer who thrives in writing. But I take a break from writing sometimes. It gets overwhelming. I accept these breaks to keep my head above water and observe everything around me more keenly. Not only does this increase my creativity, but it also keeps me from losing touch with my environment.
In the case of depression, I'd dislike writing and lose interest in it. It'll no longer intrigue me like it used to. Do you get the drift now? Depression involves a total loss of interest.

It would interest you to know that almost everyone goes through depression at some point in a lifetime. What does this mean? It means depression is an illness, just like any other. But the crazy thing is that people shy away from talking about depression and supporting people that suffer it. There are a lot of misconceptions and wrong knowledge about depression in our society. Some people hold the belief that depression is the work of some demon. Some believe that depression is the fate of evil people. These things make me shake my head and laugh in sorrow. There is so much to unlearn about depression in society. If you're among the group of people who have wrong ideas of depression, I hope this book helps you unlearn. It is a gradual process, but you can go through it if you set your heart to it. Remember, there is nothing that you cannot do if you're determined. As you unlearn, do not hesitate to educate the people around you. Depressed people would get more help and support the more people become enlightened. You want that to happen, don't you? I know you do! So, make it all easier by doing your bit.

Key Points

Depression is one illness that a lot of people demonize so much. I am thrilled to talk to you about depression in this book. Find the critical points for this session below.

1. Depression is not taboo, do not be ashamed if you are depressed.

2. Depression, grief, and sadness are very different things. Knowing the difference between them would help you so much.

3. Depression is not the punishment one gets for being evil; neither is it the work of some demon. It is a mental illness that can happen to the best of us.

4. Depression is not the end of your life.

There Is No Shame In Seeking Help

Many depressed people die in silence every day because they think getting depressed is a weakness. So they become 'strong' by bottling up their woes and keeping mum until depression finally becomes their end. My dear black woman, I do not want this to be your lot. I need you to know that getting help is not a weakness in any form. Yes, it takes a lot of courage to open up to anyone about their problem. What if they judge me? What if they don't understand me? What if I'm going crazy? These and many more are the questions that pop up in your heart from time to time. It is perfectly normal to have these fears. But don't let them dictate your life. You are in charge of your life; act like it. There's one great line in 'Summer Day,' a poem by Mary Oliver which reads, 'So, what is it you want to do with your one wild and precious life?'

I am asking you this question too. What do you want to do with your one wild and precious life? Are you going to spend it depressed? I hope you do not want to spend your life in depression.

Until you open up, you'd not realize that there are thousands and millions of people battling depression too. You are not alone. Depression makes you feel like you're the only one in this life. Like nobody loves you nor cares about you. That's one great lie that you should never believe. You are greatly loved and cherished. Your friends and loved ones do not love to see you wallowing in depression. I have learned that people with depression are perfect at masking it and acting like everything is normal. You wonder how I know this, right? I've had my bouts of depression in the past. I've once lost every will to live too. I am glad I did not let go of life. During that time of my life, I locked everyone out and cried about how it was just me. I find it funny and ironic now. Depression made me lock people out and still lament how alone I was. Sad stuff. People only see what you show them. Most of my folks didn't even realize I was depressed because I hid it so well. You know, people do not have eyes that can bore through your brain to see what goes on there. I beg of you, my dear black woman, to speak up.

You could talk to your family members or trusted friends. What if you do not understand people around you who would listen to you talk about your depression?

Speak to a professional. No one can help you deal with your depression better than a therapist. Some people shy away from speaking to a therapist about their depression because they fear being ridiculed or judged. Most of these fears exist only in your head. Do you know why I hold this belief? Therapists are adept at helping you deal with your mental health problems. They'd understand you more than you can ever imagine.

When I was diagnosed with clinical depression years ago, my doctor had recommended that I see a therapist. I didn't buy the idea at all. I couldn't even stand the thought of opening up to anyone about my demons. I stayed by myself, self-destructing and fading away. I later saw the need for a therapist when my condition became severe. My therapist was excellent. I owe a lot of my healing to him. My dear, I am not dismissing the possibility of encountering a lousy therapist. It happens. But don't allow the prospect of that to keep you from the healing you need. Go to the therapist with an open mind. If it doesn't work, go to another one. To avoid the stress that comes with going from therapist to therapist, you could have a doctor recommend one for you. Doctors seem to know the best therapists for different kinds of people.

There's one mistake that people make when getting help for depression. People would rather talk to their friends or people who are not in the best positions to help them. Your friend could be kind and understanding, but that doesn't make your friend a therapist. Remember this as often as you can. You know, a good player won't always make a great coach. It is like this with therapy too. Every reasonable person isn't a therapist.

So, my dear woman, I urge you never to be ashamed to reach out for help when depression knocks at your door. You are greatly loved and unique, and you have everything you need to heal from your depression.

Key Points

There is nothing shameful about depression; I beg you to remember this always. People may not always see that you're depressed if you do not say it. Don't be afraid nor ashamed. Get help. I believe that you'll heal. I know you will.

1. It is not your fault that you are depressed. Please do not feel bad about it.

2. You have all you need to heal from depression.

3. Depression is not a death sentence.

4. Over 80% of people who suffer from depression heal eventually. You, too, will heal.

Recovering From Depression Is a Gradual Process

The fastest way to get caught up in your depression is by setting a timer for your healing. 'I must be healed completely by the end of January.' You know, I've met people like this who love to fix specific time frames for their healings. It's one excellent idea, but it never works like that. Hurrying through recovery will only end in hurting just you.

You must understand that healing is a gradual process on your healing journey, especially when it involves mental health issues. You know one thing I've learned about this mental health thing? I've learned that mental illnesses always take longer to heal than physical conditions or injuries. Diseases are easiest to treat when they have a name. For instance, a person gets bitten by a snake. The snake slithers away swiftly after the bite. The victim goes to the doctor. The doctor would need some time to find out the exact time of the snake bite. Of course, treatment would commence immediately to save the victim's life. But, most of the treatments given to the victim would be wild guesses until the exact snake is known.

It is not like this with physical illnesses because of the ease of identifying the condition.

There would be times you would get frustrated working on healing. You might even desire to give up and continue living with depression. But that is the point where you need to fight the most. No, not fistfights and hair-pulling. This type requires you to not give up on your healing, no matter how distant it might seem. Also, never let other people's experience with recovery make your own experience into a lot of frustration.

Some people heal faster than others. Some heal very slowly as well. Sometimes, you may feel incapable of healing because of the incredible amount of time you put into it. You could even become more depressed by trying to heal as other people do.

For this reason, I always advise black women to heal by themselves. Begin by studying and understanding your healing process. If you know it fully, you'll stop trying to heal like another person. My dear black woman, heal the way you desire to. Take your time. But while at it, do not introduce toxicity into it. Do you get what I mean? I'll talk about it more in the next section.

Key Points

Many people give up on overcoming depression because they feel incapable of healing. Every one of us can heal from depression. But not all of us understand our healing processes. Understanding your healing process will keep you safe from a lot of troubles. Find the critical points for this section below.

1. Healing takes time; it is not magic.

2. Study and understand your healing process. It'll help you manage your emotions and deal with your depression better.

3. Do not allow any space for toxicity in your healing process.
4. Different people heal differently. Don't make anyone's healing process your process. You'll end up frustrated.

Incorporating Toxicity In Your Healing Process

Does this topic sound strange to you? Well, it doesn't seem to me. In a bid to heal from trauma as quickly as possible, people sometimes incorporate toxicity into their healing processes. Is it still confusing now? I'll explain it more lucidly.

So, a girl is depressed. She doesn't want to come to terms with that she's depressed and needs help. She tries to get past it all by herself. She tries to elicit some catharsis by listening to depressing music and reading sad books. She does this intending to overwhelm herself with her depression. You know, when we feel emotions like depression very violently, we might 'cry' it out. And that could help with healing. You wonder how I know this. Don't you? Well, I used to incorporate toxicity a lot into my healing processes. She is getting a new partner just after the previous one ended things with me in a bid to make the previous one jealous and angry. I find it hilarious and stupid now because I'm the one that gets hurt in the end.

Incorporating toxicity into your healing process is one of the most harmful things you could ever do to yourself. The truth is, a few people do it and come out fine. Many others don't. They'd only succeed at getting deeper into depression.

Some even become suicidal. No matter how much time your healing takes, I beg you not to become toxic in your quest for healing.

Remember what I told you in the earlier section? Healing is a very gradual process. It doesn't happen all at once. It would be best if you were patient with yourself. It would help if you were kind to yourself.

Sometimes, you might begin to incorporate toxicity into your healing process without knowing it. You'd only notice after a considerable amount happens. I know a good way to avoid this. You could start with journaling everything you do concerning your healing. Then you go back to check them at calculated intervals. Doing this can help you retrace any wrong steps early enough. You could also try speaking with a confidant from time to time about all the things that your healing makes you do. I prefer the first method. I feel like myself the most when I use it.

Key Points

In your quest for healing, you have to be deliberate and careful not to incorporate toxic processes into your recovery. Find the critical points for this section below.

1. Toxicity and healing are like fire and water; they do not mix.
2. Be intentional about your recovery.
3. Journaling your healing process can help you retrace wrong steps quickly.
4. Be patient with yourself.

Healing Begins The Moment You Say Yes To It

I've been going on and on about healing. So, I'm dedicating the whole of this section to answering the question. How does healing come? It is a straightforward answer. Healing begins the very moment you say yes to it. Sometimes, I see healing as a groom proposing to a bride. You know the part where the groom asks will you marry me right? That's what healing does too. In this case, you are the bride. Healing is the groom. No matter how deep you are, the very moment you say yes to healing, it will begin to disappear bit by bit like the moon disappears at the onset of the morning.

A lot of things in life come with choices and choosing. But depression is not one of those things, though. It doesn't take permission from you before it visits as it comes like an unexpected period. And you'd have to deal with it until you gather enough strength to eliminate it. I know you got curious here. Like, is it possible to eliminate depression? Yes, my love. It is very much possible. People have been getting over depression since a long time ago, and that won't change at all. Some people argue that depression doesn't go away. They say it hides inside a person and comes out when triggered. Before I go on, I will leave you with a few sentences about depression triggers for better understanding.
Your triggers are simply those things that make you depressed. They trigger you. Different things trigger different people. Depression triggers in another person. Aye, people are differently wired even in something like this.

Now, I have been able to establish the fact that depression is very much curable. If you are among the misinformed people who hold a contrary belief, the hour of your unlearning has come. I understand that with certain levels of depression, healing might seem like an impossible thing. But be constantly reminded that it is not. Are you confused? Don't you know how to go about this healing thing anymore? Do you feel like you'll be depressed all your life? I've felt these feelings too. You are not alone at all.

Believe me. Start your recovery from depression by saying yes to healing. Deciding to heal from depression is one of those decisions no one can make for you but yourself. So, woman up and say yes to recovery. You'll be amazed at how much progress you'll make.

A lot of things change when you make a decision. You begin to heal from depression when you make that one decision to heal. I urge you to make that one decision today, my dear black woman. Will you?

1. Your healing begins the very moment you decide to heal.

2. You have all it takes to recover from depression.

3. Depression is very much curable.

4. No matter how deep you are in depression, it all begins to change when you decide.

Support Groups; You Are Not Alone

These days, there are a lot of support groups available for people who once battled depression and those who still fight it. Fighting depression is exhausting. Depression makes you feel like you're all by yourself, right? Like you are that one unlucky person. It is all a lie. First, you're not alone. Second, you're not unlucky.

Joining a support group for depression is an effective way to deal with it. Somehow, support groups have a way of reminding you that you're not alone over and over again. Instead of recoiling into your shell and trying to fight by yourself, how about joining a support group? It isn't easy at all, I know. But it is worth it. Sometimes, the things you'd find about depression online are not applicable in real life. Nothing comes close to meeting with people who have wined and dined with depression. With them, you'd always find a reason to keep on living. To keep on fighting. They have an excellent way of motivating you to keep up with your antidepressants and therapies.

Also, people who suffer from depression find it very challenging to build and sustain relationships the way other people do.

Support groups will help you break through that barrier. Do you know why? You'd have to socialize with people there. You'll hear people share their depression stories and how they overcame it. You'll hear people talk about their relapses. You'll hear people talk about therapists that they do not like and laugh at. At some point, you'll share your own stories too.

Joining a support group is not a weakness, my love. It would help if you mustered the courage to try it. I hope you get to join the perfect support group for you, I hope you like it there, and I also hope you fight depression and win. I know that you will win. Do you not remember that you come from a generation of women who wear strength and survival-like crowns?

Key Points

At first, a support group might seem like a bad idea to you. But believe me when I say it is not. It embodies a lot of good things that you'd certainly love to explore. Find the critical points for this section below.

1. Support groups can help you fight your depression better.
2. You are not alone.
3. It would be best if you had as much support as you could get.
4. Support groups can help you make your social skills better.

My dear black woman, we have come to the end of this chapter. If you noticed, this chapter is way longer than the other ones. It is a deliberate action. I put a lot of attention and soul into writing this chapter just for you. You know, depression is the number one mental illness that black women face. It is only fitting that I do enough justice to it. I hope this chapter helps you greatly as you fight depression.

The next chapter will be all about body positivity; let's explore! I've got so much in store for you.

Chapter Nine

I can't think of any better representation of beauty than someone unafraid to be herself.
—Emma Stone.

Body Positivity and The Black Woman

Do not think about cute photographs and social media posts when I talk about body positivity. Instead, look inside you and answer this one question. Do you genuinely love and accept your body? I need you to be honest with me here, my dear black woman. But most importantly, be open to yourself. Everyone seems to know a lot about body positivity. But the irony of the whole thing is this; people get body shamed more now than ever. What do we know about the #bodypositivity, which has become very dominant in our everyday language?

What does body positivity mean? It simply refers to the social movement that focuses on the total acceptance of all body types, gender, skin tone, abilities, etc. The keywords that you should note here are 'total acceptance.' With body positivity, there are no exclusions. It is common knowledge that many black women get bullied in various ways because they are black women. It sounds crazy. But it is the truth. Black women get maltreatment for daring to be so rich in melanin. For daring to own a forest of afro on their heads. For simply being black. I used to wonder why black women get bullied for being themselves. It took me quite a while to know that people try to destroy what they envy or can't be.

Every day, the media is agog with body positivity pros. But it isn't precisely so in real life. No, I'm not saying everyone that preaches the gospel of body positivity in the media is fake. I'm simply making you realize that not everyone that talks about body positivity practices it. Some of them do it to go with the crowd. Some do it to get favors, even. But don't you ever let them

314

discourage you from wearing your body with pride as you should.
Tell me, if you do not carry yourself with dignity, who will do it
for you? Nobody. A good number of black women are yet to know
this. People give your body the same treatment you give to it. If
you carry your body like a piece of shit, trust people to double the
energy for you. But I believe that that's not what you want for
yourself. So, carry your body with pride and treat it like a queen.
You'd see that people would treat your body as such too. The
most beautiful women can master the singular art of carrying
themselves well.

I love my body so much that I can't help taking gorgeous
photographs of myself all the time to admire all the beauty in me.
I don't remember exactly how I began to love my body the way I
do now. I do not even have a single memory of me hating my
body and wishing to change a thing about me. I love my face with
the hormonal acne that comes at intervals. I love my thighs with
stretch marks on them. When I hear people say they detest
stretch marks, it makes me wonder. How could anyone not love
such gorgeous stripes? But then, I understand that taste differs.
What I would kill for could irritate you. You know, beauty is
relative. It comes in different forms and styles. Everyone mustn't
fit into your idea of beauty. People should be free to be beautiful
like themselves. Yes, I am beautiful like myself. You are beautiful
like you. Isn't that fascinating?

My parents played a significant role in making me love my body
right from childhood. They gave me the best compliments. They
gave me the freedom to wear my body with as much pride as I
wanted. I grew up thinking I was a princess. But I didn't live in a
castle or have many maids like the Disney princesses. I was my
parents' princess. My parents never failed to remind me that I
was the most beautiful child they had ever seen. Their words
always got into my head. I'd stand before my bedroom mirror
and smile at myself. My mother said. I grinned like an angel.
Thinking of it now, I wonder how my mother got to know how
angels smile.

I understand that not everyone grew up in a loving home and had a beautiful childhood as I did. Body positivity might be a challenging thing for such people. But it is not impossible, and that's the good thing. That's one wonderful thing I love in this life. I love how things begin to change when we make up our minds about things. Body positivity begins to take meaning in your own life the moment you permit it to do so. Of course, you'd encounter people and things that would make you feel like you're not enough. The most beautiful people meet them too. Do not pay them a mind. Your opinion about you is superior to anyone else's. When I do something that makes me happy, and someone else tries to ruin it, I remind myself boldly that my opinion is the most important. Nothing else matters.

Body positivity is not a one-time thing. You know that don't get positive today and become negative tomorrow. It doesn't work like that because you'd have to pick a stand. I'd advise you to choose body positivity, though. Nothing compares to its excellence!

Suppose you're used to not being a body positivity kind of woman; switching all of a sudden would most likely be very difficult for you. That is why I advise you to take it little by little—one step at a time. The first step you should begin with is self-acceptance. You'll read more of it in the next section of this chapter.

Key Points

Different people see body positivity through different lenses. For some, it's just one of those things people say. For others, it is the very core of existence. Body positivity is one of the best things that has ever happened to humanity. Yes, that's how I see it! Find the critical points for this section below.

1. The first step you need to take in your body positivity journey is self-acceptance.

2. Body positivity is way beyond social media posts and hashtags. It encompasses the whole beauty of human existence.

3. You are most beautiful when you accept your body with all of its perfections and flaws.

4. People's opinion of your body doesn't matter at all. Could you not treat them like they do?

Self-Acceptance and Body Positivity

I said self-acceptance is the first step to your body positivity journey in the previous section. Without self-acceptance, body positivity wouldn't even exist. If you look deeper, you'll see that people who are genuinely into body positivity are people who have accepted themselves wholly.

What is self-acceptance? In simple words, it is embracing everything that makes you who you are. A lot of things come together to create a person. Some people are lucky enough to have more good experiences than bad experiences. Others are not as lucky. Some people have known more terrible experiences than they have known good ones. That's the way life swings sometimes. For the former, self-acceptance might not be a tricky thing. A good number of them wouldn't even hesitate to share their life stories with you.

Body positivity might seem like a farce for the second group of people who have known more tears than laughter. You know, people do not love to share sorrowful tales about themselves. People like this may have trouble accepting themselves. Some of them have lives that do not make them happy. Asking such people to be optimistic about their bodies and selves, in general, is like asking them to flaunt their traumas.

This set of people would have to do some unlearning. Life becomes much easier when people do not throw away the experiences that shaped them. I once read this book about a fire accident survivor. In the book, the survivor told her story. She said after her wounds healed, she became suicidal. She couldn't just bear to see the scars every day of her life. She also locked everyone out of her life because the spots made her begin to hate herself. Somehow, she got professional help. Her life came alive again when she stopped hiding her scars. She started to call them her trophies. Do you know why she called them trophies? They showed that she wrestled with fire and won. I smile anytime I remember this.

I shared this story with you because it is one beautiful way to look at life. Not only does it help you heal from past hurts, but it also strengthens you. There's no need to beat yourself up and lament every day about the things that have happened to you. Bring out those scars and stop hiding away. It is not great to hide trophies.

Now, I'm back to talking about accepting your body just the way it is. There's one thing that you must know. If all women eat the same food and do the same exercises, they still have different body types. Body types do not arise by just exercise, diets, and waist trainers. It is more than that. Genetics and environmental factors all have their roles to play. I think genetics plays the most prominent role in determining body types. Every other thing comes secondary. Your body cannot be like the one of every girl you admire on the gram. You have your unique body. Your body stands out from the crowd. That body that you loathe so much is someone else's dream body. Crazy, right? But that doesn't stop it from being true. Be proud of your cellulite, your jutting collarbone, your small breasts, your full breasts, your small eyes, your big eyes. Be proud of all your features. You are beautiful in every part. I was hoping you could do something for me right now.

Please go to the mirror closest to you and peer into it. Now, smile at the angel that looks back at you from the mirror. Don't you love what you see? You are the angel in the mirror. How wonderful!

To embrace your body better and love it better, take your time to study it. You know, different body types have different needs. Study your body type and find out what your body needs, From Diet type, wardrobe type, and so on. Doing this will help you greatly in caring for your body and carrying it with pride. You could check out the styles of people whose body types are similar to yours. Trust me; you'll be glad that you did. But, you are under no compulsion to do this. My black women are creative geniuses. I believe in your unique ability to create excellent styles for yourself. Your body is like a flower. The more your nurture it, the prettier it gets. So, my dear woman never quit nurturing that gorgeous body of yours. The world is thousand times more colourful and stunning because your beauty dwells in it. You know this, don't you?

Key Points

1. You are beautiful and perfect just the way you are. It would help if you had no one's validation to stay beautiful too.

2. If all women did the same things simultaneously, they would still have different body types.

3. Your body is perfect and full of beauty.

4. Your scars are trophies. Never be ashamed of them.

5. Self-acceptance is the first step you need to take in your body positivity journey.

What Is The Definition of True Beauty?

A lot of people have tried over and over again to define beauty. But the truth they fail to realize is that beauty has no definition. Why will anyone try to put something as broad and endlessly attractive as beauty in a box by defining it?

A lot of people try to give beauty a label by defining it. It makes me wonder. I wouldn't say I like tags. In the words of the famous poet Walt Whitman, I contain multitudes. Yes, I include too many things to limit myself by labels and definitions. Black women have a lot of excellencies too. Please don't limit yourself by tags and others' intentions who do not even explore beauty in all forms.

Every day, different people come up with varying definitions of beauty. It is the trend now. It has become so common that the moment you ask people about beauty, you'd get almost the same answers from everyone. They'd mention a specific eye category and particular hair color and tell you it is the most beautiful thing in the world. I find the whole thing sad, but it also makes me realize that many would gladly accept that they are not beautiful because they do not meet a certain standard. Well, I do not blame them so much. I blame society. I blame some modelling agencies more. Talking about modelling agencies, I remember something that happened at high school.

It happened to one of my seniors and friend. We called her Maggie. Maggie was passionate about modelling and walking on the biggest runways while rocking the best brands. Her passion for modelling was so beautiful to see. I've never met anyone passionate about modelling the way Maggie was. She put the whole of herself into it. We were overjoyed when Maggie got invited for an interview by one big modelling agency at the time. We were already looking forward to Maggie becoming a star already. We were more than convinced that she would breeze through the interview. I mean, asking Maggie about modelling is asking her about her life. Who would fail to answer questions about their own lives well?

All our joy and enthusiasm died when Maggie told us how the interview went. Of course, she did very well in the question and answer part of the interview. You are curious as to where Maggie failed. She wasn't tall enough. Yes, that was the reason. It hurt me so much to see Maggie crying. The helplessness of the situation made it sadder. It was so unfair. Not like people made themselves or something. If people had the power to create themselves, there would have been a lot of gorgeousness in this life. You know, it would be a competition of beauty, poise, and class.

The thing with most modeling agencies is that they are very unrealistic. If you follow them as closely as I do, you will notice that they seem to follow a particular pattern. Has it ever occurred to you why almost all the top models are slender and tall? That is what they define beauty to be. But I am glad that many agencies have also included different body types in their walks. It makes it all more realistic. I love it when fashion is natural. That's the issue I have with some TV commercials too. You'd see the girls some sanitary pad brands to advertise, and you'd think periods are all sweet and rosy when it's not even anywhere close to that in real life.

My dear black woman, I beg you not to let yourself get so caught up in the stereotypical and crazy definitions of beauty that you begin to lose yourself. Take your time and admire all of your features whenever that starts to happen. Spend time loving those parts that excite you the most. Remind yourself about the graciousness of your body. It's not easy having a perfect body like your own. Carry that body with pride. It's okay if you feel better in your body by enhancing it. Yes, it happens. Don't be sad about feeling this way. A little more ass would make your body as perfect as you want it, right? Small boobs will make you proud of your body. Go for the body that you love. Things you want can happen with consistent workout sessions and better diets. You might need surgery for others too. Whichever ones you choose, I urge you to get them the right way. Many women die in the course of going through beauty processes the wrong way. I do not want you to add to the numbers. I know you do not want that for yourself too. So, love, take your time and get your dream body the right way.

Remember, your definition of beauty is valid. You do not have to bend to any beauty standard. You are beautiful all by yourself.

Key Points

1. Beauty has no one definition.

2. You are perfect, so is your body.

3. You can get your dream body through workouts and surgeries. Don't let anyone make you feel guilty for going for the kind of body you desire.

Chapter Ten

The Black Woman and Failure

Success is stumbling from failure to failure with no loss of enthusiasm.

--Winston S. Churchill

I'm guessing by the title above that your mind already diverted to an incident or two where you had an objective in mind but couldn't meet it along the line. Or you did, but the outcome wasn't what you desired. Did you sink yourself into the hole of depression and self-loathe? Or did you let yourself feel the emotions that come with failing for a brief moment, and shake it off, saying to yourself that you are strong and you've got all it takes to succeed?

Everyone comes across failure at some point in their lives. Even that big-time reality star you drool about and think their life is a bed of roses has experienced loss. Not once, not twice. The billionaires, social media personalities, your favorite artists, and other thriving characters that you look up to have all experienced to fail. Most have come out to tell tales of their pasts and how they got to the top, while some sit back and act as if everything has always been excellent, whereas it's a sham. My dear black woman, do not allow these to deceive you that you'll begin to access yourself negatively, letting room for anxiety, depression, and even envy.

When we talk about failure, most people say it is one's inability to reach a particular goal or do something that you must or wish to do. Even babies fail. Yes, my black queen. When they try to start walking, only to fall back down, that's failing. And the teenager who's continuously in a battle with his books in preparation for a math test only to end up failing the test. He'd cry out and even go as far as hating that subject. But that is not always the case. Some people take up their failure as a challenge to do better, and I have a personal story to share concerning this.

When I was a teenager, I was conflicted between choosing the sciences or arts many years ago. My parents were very supportive and said they would offer their support no matter my choice. So I decided I was going to study medicine to be a doctor. I had always heard the most impressive and fascinating tales of doctors; how they contributed to the growth and saving of humanity. Take, for instance, Ben Carson, who made the separation of conjoined twins possible. It served as a trigger, and I wanted to badly do something worth being in the Guinness book of records. Despite this, there was a doubt looming within me about my decision.

I wanted to be a thoracic surgeon and make a remarkable impact in the medical world. Still, there was an irony, black Queen, and do you know what it was? I didn't have what it took. You know, becoming a surgeon involves putting your fears asides and going all in, but I do not like to see blood at all. The mere sight of it makes my hair stand on edge. I also knew my academic strengths and weaknesses, and I was more robust in the arts. Still, because I wanted to be a surgeon, I tried to get over the feeling and went as far as taking the exams for the course. Well, you can guess what happened. I failed woefully.

No, I'm not dumb. The thing is, people don't seem to understand the concept of failing. Many think failing at something means you're not good enough. But it was not so for me. I already knew my strengths and had my parents support me in whatever I chose. My mom advised me earlier to go for the art courses, but I was pig-headed. I told her my desire, and she agreed to give it a shot. But with my failure in that shot, I realized one thing. I was forcing things.

Deep down, I knew I would end up in the arts, but I also wanted to have the experience of being a surgeon because of the story I had read about Ben Carson. I failed at it, I agreed that I would be better off in the arts, and it's been a fantastic ride. Of course, I sulked and cried for days; let myself feel the negative emotions that come with failing. But I did not let them consume me. I had to get up and try something better because failure isn't final.

Some people fail and refuse to try something else. They keep on repeating the same thing over and over again. If you know something isn't working for you, there are many alternatives to try out. Indeed, something out there must interest you. You'll find that one thing that'd set your heart on fire if you look deeper. That you failed at being an artist doesn't mean you'll fail at being an actor or actress. You have to understand that some things are not just for you. Failing at them is the universe's way of letting you know because the worst that would happen is that the goal may haunt you when you eventually achieve it. Yes, my beautiful black queen, it happens. Many people today would have been living their lives in the most peaceful ways on earth. But they were so focused on getting something that they failed at repeatedly; they delved into illegal things, which eventually devoured them.

Key Points

Many people have had more than one experience of what it is to fail. Some see it as a prerequisite to a truly successful life; others believe you don't have to die to be successful. Whatever you choose to think, I want you to understand that failure isn't a death sentence but a step to self-realization. The critical points for this section are below:

1. It's okay to fail; no one should judge you for failing.

2. If you fail, you can always try again, or it's the universe's way of telling you, "this isn't it."

3. Experiencing failure exposes you to your strengths and weaknesses and helps your personal growth.

4. It's okay to feel the negative emotions of failing, but you shouldn't let it define you.

Redefining The Concept of Failure

Earlier, I stated that most people believe failure entails not reaching their desired goals. But it is more than that. Failure is a thing of the mind, like when you do well in a test, scoring as high as 80% in your grades. Still, you consider your performance a failure because you set your mind to 90%. Let's go deeper.

Do you know that some people look up to you, and even the smallest of your actions is a big deal to them, and they're like, "Wow, this lady is amazing!" Yes, my beautiful black woman, some people think you're doing just right, that when you tell them you got a job with good pay, instead of the one you wished for, they'll laugh and walk you through how far you've come. A promotion from a measly paying job to a better one, which, however, isn't what you desire, is not failure. The thing is, we become so focused on the wrong side and choose to forget that there were even good times. Writing this makes me emotional as I remember an incident some years back. I want to share it with you because I want you to understand what I'm saying entirely.

Everyone says you shouldn't focus too much on the wrong side but on how far you've come, and it took me quite a while to realize this; to truly understand and abide by it.

I used to be the type of person who gets anxious and irritable whenever I'm low on cash, and it happened to be a big issue for me. During such times, I would take out my anger and frustration on my family and friends, setting me apart from most of them. I pushed them away. I considered myself a failure to achieve what I had planned to until a particular day. One of my friends told me some things that I still remember vividly. He asked me to check my pictures from the previous year and what I noticed. The first thing I noticed was my phone. I was no longer using the phone I used the last year because I had bought a better one without even selling the previous one.

I also noticed I had gained a few pounds and many other things I would not want to bore you with by listing. The summary is that the comparison I made of myself in the previous year and myself the following year was an eye-opener. It showed me that my inability to achieve some goals did not mean I was a failure. You don't have to pressure yourself so much that you refuse to believe there's any progress in your life. Take the saying of Oprah Winfrey that "If you look at what you have in life, you'll always have more. If you look at what you don't have in life, you'll never have enough," and put it to heart.

In our quest to redefine failure, I'll discuss what can help you understand the concept of failure and see it as more than your inability to attain that desired goal. The first is being a novice at something.

When you're new to something, there's every tendency that you won't get it right the first time. I mean, how can you be perfect at what you just started? Perfection is all about flawlessness, the highest degree of skill. You can't just wake up one morning and do something you've not done flawlessly. It's not magic. The baby who just began toddling is bound to fall a few dozen times, or the cyclist who has no initial experience of cycling will have a few scratches from falling. It's always like that. So why beat yourself up for something you just started doing? Yes, it's been months; you're a fast learner, so why is it taking so much time? I know. All these questions are pricking hard at your mind, and all you do all day is sigh and shake your head in weariness. Listen to me, my beautiful black queen; you don't need any of that unnecessary stress and overthinking. Everything will move at its own pace. Access yourself, where you were before you started and where you are now, and you'll see that you're making some progress. But if you think you're not, then it's a hint that you're not doing a few things, or you're not doing things the right way.

Another thing to note and ask yourself is if you're a perfectionist. I can not outrightly say that being a perfectionist is a bad thing. I do not believe that it is terrible because it has its perks. However, I'm not too fond of the excessive stress that comes with it. In trying to attain perfection, you're faced with constant anxiety and worry about if you're doing or looking alright. You say inwardly to yourself, "I have to get this right without a flaw," and ask yourself specific questions as a result of self-doubt like, "am I still on course?" and the "what ifs?"

Being a perfectionist is working hard to put things in order, even if it takes your time and energy, and you wouldn't mind finishing late. I have a perfectionist friend, and I can say most times that people are the way they are because of their upbringing. Some people are so scared of experiencing failure because the society where they grew up shamed loss and extolled success. They made loss seem taboo, which is more impactful on a child when it comes from the parents. Imagine having a parent who scolds you repeatedly when you get a grade less than an A and goes as far as comparing you to your peers who happen to do better. It's disturbing and even more problematic that parents still engage in this act. So you can correctly guess how such a child from these parents would be, endlessly questioning their actions and assessing themselves to do better, at times being reclusive or unhappy.

A perfectionist does not like to align with failure, and that's the issue here. They believe that since they are putting in much more effort than their peers, the outcome should indeed be better, and when life does its thing with bias, they get into a hell hole of depression. If you are a perfectionist, you should relate. You have incredibly high standards, and sometimes you're scared that they're too high, and you end up procrastinating because you're afraid of failure. No, my beautiful black queen, you have to understand that failure is a part of life and helps you grow. Rather than beat yourself up when you know you tried your absolute best, why not focus on what was missing instead of sulking all day and telling yourself that you're not enough.

I used to criticize my perfectionist friend a lot, and we would even fall out occasionally because, let's say, we didn't align well at that time. I was the carefree type, and she was the ever anxious one. She was always so bothered about me, and I watched her laugh over how worried she could be. You only live once. I would always say, so don't be afraid to do what you've intended to do. If you're a perfectionist and the opposing sides are eating you up, you have to seek help and also try to tone it down a little. Believe in yourself, try your best, and take solace in the fact that you put in your all. If it still doesn't work out, you have to get up and try again.

In redefining failure, you might agree that it's not about not being able to achieve a goal, so you've decided to try, but you still end up failing. Then, it could be that there's a systemic bias against you, my black woman. In a situation where you put your all to work assigned to you, it's even clear to everyone in the company that you're doing great. Still, a high-ranking officer comes at you and talks down on your work because of their bias against your color. My beautiful black woman, I do not wish you to beat yourself up because someone is prejudiced against you. You don't have to go on with the sleepless nights in an attempt to "satisfy" such people because the truth is that they'll never be satisfied.

If you cannot leave them, you'll have to think of ways to work with them. Arm yourself with all the qualities we've discussed. Have the courage to speak your mind in the face of oppression, and if you're able to do this, you won't have to feel you're failing when really, you aren't.

Key Points

Many people believe failure is all about being unable to attain your desired goal, but I think it goes past this. Sometimes, things are hindering your progress that you fail to check, so failure reminds you to take note and sets you on the right course, that is, if you let it, of course. Let's go through the points in this section:

1. That you didn't achieve your aim doesn't mean you failed. You need to stop and assess yourself.

2. Think of what's missing or why you think you failed, and try again.

3. If you're a novice at something, you cannot achieve perfection immediately in redefining failure. You'll fall at certain times. But, rise!

4. Sometimes, failure isn't your fault, so you shouldn't be too hard on yourself.

5. You could be doing great, but someone biased towards you would always fail to acknowledge it. Don't let that define your progress.

Starting Again After a Failure

No one likes to fail, and successful people dread failure even more because they've tasted success and failing is barely an option to them. Have you ever watched your house burn down from scratch? I have, and that very day broke me to pieces. It was shattering because I built the house with my sweat, time, and money, sustained a couple of injuries and went broke a few hundred times to make sure the house got finished. Only to watch it get razed to the ground by a raging fire and unable to do anything tangible. I sulked for weeks and barely gave myself any attention because one of my fears happened. One day, I stumbled across the story of J.K Rowling, Harry Potter's author, on the net. Rowling's story was that she was a single mom living off welfare and suicidal when she had the idea of the story on her way from Manchester to London on a train. Rowling's original pitch for the Harry Potter series was called the bluff by the first twelve places she sent it to, but she persisted. Today, she has about 400 million books sold, and it all hit deeply. Then, I was at my lowest, so I understood what it was to fail, and at the same time, I knew what it was to succeed. I made up my mind; I had to start again.

The first thing I did in starting again was to accept responsibility for my failure. I know I said sometimes you're not the one at fault, and that's fine. But when you're confident you are, like I was, you have to set your ego aside and own up to your actions. How was I at fault that my house was razed to the ground by fire? Good question you might have. To finish the construction, I cut corners and used substandard materials for the roofing and wiring. The day it caught fire, it rained cats and dogs, and I was away at work. In summary, before anyone could do anything, the fire had already grown too big.

At first, I was reluctant to accept that I was at fault. I blamed the companies that manufactured the materials; I inwardly blamed my neighbors, who I assumed didn't want to do anything about the fire. Still, with time, I realized it was entirely my fault. I didn't go for quality building materials. And blaming my neighbors for my misfortune was altogether unfair and immature because they weren't at the scene on time, neither were they trained firefighters. Suppose there's something you failed at, maybe a project work or did not get a promotion as you anticipated. In that case, the first thing you have to do is check yourself and if you're at fault, be humble enough to accept it.

The next step to starting again is to pick up the pieces of your life again. My strong black woman, hurting doesn't make you weak, you're allowed to sulk all day and sob over that failure, but as I've always said, when you finish, you have to get up and keep going. You can always set things right. If there are people that say bad things about you, trust that there'll also be good people to repair that image, but you must first apologize if you're in the wrong. Or did you get kicked out of work? There are always different opportunities out there for you. Explore all of them.

The third step is to remind yourself of your past successes constantly. Did you bag that degree? That's a success. Did you graduate from college? It's a success. Got a job? Got married? Started something you always wanted to? Attended an occasion you had always wished to attend? They're all successes. Success doesn't have to be significant. That workout you completed is a success. Whatever you constantly desire to do is your success. When you're feeling down because you failed, take out a pen and write out ten things you did successfully. You'll see that there's even more. Don't think you're worthless just because of a failure. No black queen, you are a conqueror, and you have all it takes to succeed. If this isn't your first time failing, take a quick look back at your past failures and successes. Everyone makes mistakes that can lead to losses, but just as you recover from that previous failure, comfort yourself with the belief that you'll also recover from your present failure. It will make the process faster for you and spur you to your next step - making a decision.

When you finish thinking deeply about your mistake or failure, accepting your faults, and reminding yourself of your successes, make a decision. And I do not mean that you do nothing, for it is in itself a decision. But it is a negative one capable of impeding your progress and, worse still, causing damage to your life. You know what you want, beautiful black woman, and it is only proper that you decide to get it. If it requires you to take a course on it, reading intensively, communicating with people around, and seeking advice from those knowledgeable in that field, do it. You're on a self-development journey, and failure is part of it. What is the reason you failed? Can you try again on your own? If not, then you need to decide to talk to someone, probably a therapist, friend, or confidant.

Now you're done deciding, the final step is to forget about your past and focus on your vision. It may seem hard, but thinking about it would only make it harder. It's your past, and you can't change your history, can you? So why bother so much, queen? You have only the present guaranteed, and the best you can do is make good use of it. If you're going to continue on that journey, do it. If you wish to start something else, by all means, begin.

Key Points

Failure should teach us, not overcome us. It's not a death sentence but an eye-opener. It should show you what you were doing wrong, not make you feel worthless. You're in charge of what failure can make you think, and let it spur you on to the next success story, my black woman. Here are the key points:

1. No one likes to fail, but they tend to forget that failure is part of what you must experience to succeed.

2. Accepting responsibility for your mistakes is a crucial step to overcoming failure.

3. Rather than soak yourself up in your loss, you should make a list of all your achievements and go over them.

4. You're not worthless because of a mistake. Everyone makes mistakes.

5. Talking to someone would aid your recovery from failure a lot faster, as well as taking that course you always wanted.

We've finally come to the end of this chapter, my dear black woman! It's been an incredible ride with you all the way, and I'm excited to talk to you about what's in the next chapter. Let's go!

Chapter Eleven

On Pedestals and Living For Other People

When you become famous, people can have a powerful yet illusory idea of who you are. You want to live your life, but still, you don't want to let anyone down. I know Ed Vedder, Kurt Cobain, Jerry Cantrell, all those guys felt it. They're smart, real, and all of a sudden, they're put on a pedestal.

---Ann Wilson

Before we begin fully into this chapter, let's clear the air about what it means to be put on a pedestal. When I say someone placed me on a pedestal, it simply means someone thinks of me as a perfect person with no flaws at all. Quite funny, but that is the case where followers or fans put celebrities on pedestals, even when they didn't ask for it, expecting only a particular type of behavior from them. Lovers also put each other on pedestals, with one of them usually the male putting the female on a pedestal. Or it could be anyone; anyone with some distinct feature can be placed on a pedestal by another.

I don't know if you get the point already, my dear black woman. I always laugh whenever I encounter this phrase because I've been in that situation and put someone on a pedestal. Yes, I have first-hand experience with this topic, at least on the relationship level. The one based on popularity is a story about my friend. Don't worry; I'll try to share it all.

Do you remember what we discussed about self-worth in chapter seven? How do some people let others push them around because they believe they're better than themselves and that they're not good enough? That's usually the case when we talk about putting others on pedestals. My black woman, like it or not, you may have or might come across someone or people who would place you on a pedestal, and I want you to get ready for it. It often takes a whole lot from an individual. It narrows your life to only the line the person wants you to thread with them, forgetting that you have a life to live; I hope you understand?

I dated one person who had placed me on a pedestal, and he had himself living for me. The thing is, I didn't intend to make him live only for me, but something just happened, and before I could blink, he was already exhibiting the signs. My ex never faulted me because he admired me so much; he firmly believed I was incapable of doing any wrong. However, with my experiences, I can say that's possible - being obsessed about someone so much that you choose to forget the red flags and live in an illusion. I would have him try to talk things with me regarding a particular negative behavior I could put up with all week, but he'd never be straightforward. I'd make it clear to him that I needed him to speak up, but he just couldn't.

He had placed me above himself from the onset, and although he wanted to communicate with me, he couldn't. I mean, how can you relate well with someone on a higher level than you? That's the idea. I didn't even ask to be there, just like how the person I put on a pedestal did not ask for it. I think, by all means, it is unhealthy to be the one on the pedestal and the one doing the pedestal-placing. No one sees it as a fun thing to be perceived as a god or robot. Sure, it's an ego-booster, but this is by someone constantly looking up to you as a perfect human incapable of errors. It's a big shock to them when you eventually fall short of their expectations. Haha. It's funny because I've been through it even though it was not a fun ride then. When someone places you on a pedestal, as my ex did, they have many questions about their self-worth popping up in their head. Questions like, "how is it you have your life together, and they do not?" or statements like, "everything you are, they're not," and "everyone loves you but not them."

It is not envy per se. Suppose you look at it from a different angle. In that case, it's just a conscious or an intense unconscious admiration that grows into low self-esteem. You know, dear queen, social media is a crazy place. You have people portraying all kinds of genuine and fake lifestyles that you barely know,

335

whether real or not. When you focus entirely on someone more successful than you are, it leaves room for self-doubt and anxiety, and that's no way one should live.

I have a friend called Brandon. He's into music, specifically the electronic dance genre. Brandon once told me that he did not wish to go into hip hop because, to him, it didn't allow you much freedom of getting your privacy, so he stuck to EDM. But even with that, Brandon was perceived by his social media fans as collected, intelligent, and gentlemanly. He wasn't far from what they saw him be, but the truth was that the fans didn't care to know what his interests were or what he indeed was. All they saw was a peaceful, contented artist worth emulating.

One day, Brandon came crying to me that he was in a sex scandal plotted by his foe. Brandon explained he had been going through a lot and was drinking all night in a bar when two girls approached him and led him on. With all evidence against him, most of his so-called fans revolted and called him all sorts of debasing names that left him dazed. That's what being there feels like; You face constant pressure from people who want you to live up to the hype. If you're a popular personality like my friend and perhaps a perfectionist, you'll find yourself striving towards it. Most perfectionists don't like to disappoint their loved ones, so when they realize these loved ones are looking up to them, they try everything to live up to the hype and not hurt them, but most times, it doesn't end well. For some people, they do not want to be on a pedestal, and while the feeling may be nice for a while, in the end, they'll ask you for some form of closure; that is for you to know their truth and understand them. Others are entirely okay with it. Which are you, my dear black woman?

Key Points

While being admired dramatically by someone may feel good, it can pose a problem when they begin to idolize you and expect nothing less from you. These people sometimes forget that you're human too and make mistakes. However, it's up to you, dear black woman, to decide if you want to be on a pedestal or not. The key points are listed below:

1. It's okay to admire someone, but it can become a problem when it gets too much.

2. It would help if you stopped allowing someone to make you doubt your self-worth is an unhealthy practice.

3. If you can't cope with being on a pedestal, you're going to have to let them know eventually.

4. Don't try to be what you aren't to live up to the hype. Being you is the best form of self-care.

5. Before you consciously place someone on a pedestal, ask yourself if you're going to be comfortable if it were you.

Dangers of Being Placed On a Pedestal

There are many side effects of being placed on a pedestal that you might want to avoid at all costs. For emphasis, if you can handle the pressure, no one's stopping you, but otherwise, you have to get out. I don't advise that you allow someone to limit your life by putting you on a pedestal because then you're living the life they're not courageous to live. Remember, I talked about low self-esteem as one factor that leads people to pedestal-placing. For one to rank you above themselves, it means they've concluded that you're better than them and are now watching you achieve a whole chunk of what they wish to. They expect a lot from you, and allowing yourself to this pressure means you are allowing them to tell you how to live your life.

I've seen a lot of mothers place their kids on pedestals. Things they could not achieve as kids tend to impose on the little ones and try to pattern their lives in a certain way favorable to them, but usually not the child. Dear black woman, I need you to veer away from this course and treat your children with all the love they deserve, not idolize them or force them into things they do not like. Even in your marital or relationship life, placing your partner way above you because you feel they're doing you a favor by loving you is wrong. You deserve all the love you can get, and no one should make you feel less, not even yourself. He brought you from grass to grace, that's wonderful and very kind, but it should never be a reason for you to worship him or feel inferior, dear black woman. I do hope you're getting what I'm trying to nail. The essence of this is that it will help your relationship better. With that pedestal out of the way, you can be able to effectively communicate with your partner or child, get to know them, and improve your relationship with them.

Allowing people to put you on a pedestal can ultimately damage you if you're not careful, my beautiful black woman. As I said earlier, you shouldn't dictate what that child should be because it's what you've always wished for, and so also should you not allow anyone to dictate who you are. It's you we're talking about here, no one else but you, and that's all you've got. So you have to take care of yourself and carry yourself with pride. When I was put on a pedestal by my ex, we seemed happy because he didn't want to fault me. You know, he always let me call the shots, and we even rushed into a significant relationship milestone under five months of dating. Everything was all sunshine and roses, but he was dying on the inside. He struggled to know me, but it was all in vain because he had set me up high above him, like going up ahead and putting banana peels on your way. That was what it felt like, and in the end, he blamed me. While my other ex, whom I placed on a pedestal, had me question my abilities as he walked all over me, and the crazy thing was, I let him. He made plans that often didn't involve me, and when I realized, I'd feel like my world had come crashing because, at the time, I was very dependent on him. It's a relationship that stirs negative feelings anytime I remember it, to show the extent of the damage this could cause.

Being placed on a pedestal to the extent that you're living someone else's life has to be the worst kind of punishment to yourself. It fills you with irritation and envy when you see others living their desired lives. You're not; you can't find happiness at your workplace or whatever your pedestal placers want you to do. You're sad or infuriated by someone else's enthusiasm because you don't feel the same way about it pedestal. The only things that inspire you are your reputation, money, and the people's praise, and you sit back and watch life pass you by without actually living. It's sad in the least to say, even more, shameful if you allow it for fame and money.

But again, I repeat, if you enjoy being put on a pedestal and can handle the pressure, by all means, have it your way. But if you don't, you must agree with me that it's detrimental to your growth when you let a partner or society at large dictate how you should live your life.

Key Points

It's heartbreaking seeing people in their workplace moving about with their minds far away because they do not wish to be there. It's not encouraging to see someone being downtrodden by their partner, and they do nothing because they've placed their partner above them. This section has briefly highlighted the dangers of being placed on a pedestal. The key points are listed thus:

1. You allow people to live your life for you when they deliberately impose their wishes on you.

2. Placing people on pedestals because they've been generous to you isn't the right thing to do.

3. It would help if you didn't dictate another person's life.

4. You're all you've got, so you shouldn't let someone damage you.

5. It's not proper to live someone else's life, especially for fame or money.

How To Stop Living for Other People

My dear black woman, we've come this far in identifying what being on a pedestal and living for other people are about, as well as the dangers attached. I do hope you've accessed yourself if you'd like to be on a pedestal or not. This section is for those who wouldn't want to and how to stop living for other people. There are many ways to stop being placed on a pedestal and living for other people. Also, I'll share tips on how to stop putting people on pedestals. It's going to be a general discussion.

Defining your relationship is crucial to avoid being placed on a pedestal. When you let your partner know that they should see and treat you equally, there'll be less room for assumptions, and they will act accordingly. If I say, "Alright, here are my conditions. I don't want anyone see me as a god; I want us to be able to communicate effectively," she would understand that I don't want to be on a pedestal and act accordingly. You can also apply this method with your fans. Let your fans repeatedly know that you're human, and they shouldn't have high expectations from you more than they should from themselves. People tend to do that a lot, and it's not cool; telling people how to handle their life when they've not even attempted to run theirs. So communicating and laying boundaries is a significant step and being open to your partner about your insecurities.

If you're currently living someone else's life, there's a high chance that you're unhappy, and if that's your case, my beautiful black woman, you need to act. It might be not very easy, I do not know, but you really shouldn't let go of life without at least achieving most of your goals. You have the right to do whatever makes you happy, and every other thing should be next. Let the words of Steve Jobs guide you; "Your time is limited, so don't waste it living someone else's life. Don't be trapped by dogma — living with the results of other people's thinking. Don't let the noise of others' opinions drown out your inner voice. And most importantly, dare to follow your heart and intuition."

If you're used to putting people on pedestals, you also have to stop it. You may think it's hard, but I guarantee it will help you; you'll be on your way to increasing your self-esteem in no time. Firstly, you have to look inside of yourself. Black queen, I'm going to restate this because I need you to understand; there's only you in this game, and you can't afford to lose yourself to others. Are you getting married to that person because he's got all you've always wished for yourself? Why can't you get it? What's stopping you? You have to free yourself and soar high else. You might end up regretting it. Or you're envious of that girl because of her perfect figure? Then focus on it and stay committed to the gym and healthy diets. Most of these things you envy in people require you to be committed to them, so you must imbibe the virtue of commitment.

Key Points

I understand that being placed on a pedestal can be discomforting, so there's no justification for you to put another on it. Work on yourself instead and begin to own your life. The key points are listed below:

1. If you're not comfortable being placed on a pedestal, you must communicate.

2. Achieve most of your goals now that you have the time.

3. Increasing your self-worth and self-love is a significant step to stop putting people on pedestals.

4. Who says you can't be whatever you want to be?

The Ninety Day Plan

Finally, we've come to the last part of this book—the ninety-day plan for managing emotions. I am writing this plan in the simplest way I know how to. I want you to have fun going through the schedule for each day, so I made them very concise and straight to the point. It takes between 21-66 days to build habits, so I am hoping, and I believe that by the time we come to the end of this ninety-day plan, you would have gained a lot of control over your emotions. You'll be needing a notebook to write down certain things. Let's dig in already, shall we?

Week One: Managing Anger

Day One — Breathe In

Some situations cause you to be so angry, and all you want to do is yell at someone or punch someone in the face, but you shouldn't let your anger consume you. Everyone knows that life is not fair, but it is not defined by what happens, instead of by your response to situations. Imagine a situation where someone angers you and retaliates by throwing a punch at the person. You might be unaware of the person's health status, and that one punch could send the person to the other side, with you eventually being sent to jail. So before you take any action in anger, you have to stop, black Queen, and breath in.

Tips for Day One

• Accept that not everyone aligns with you, and some may annoy you.

• Get that life is not a bed of roses and some days are harsh.

- Overall, remind yourself to take a deep breath and think about the consequences of that action you want to take out of anger. You might not like it.

Day Two — Focus On The Bright Side

Now my dear black woman, how did you feel after breathing in again? I imagine you were still angry, but the singular fact that you could stop for a second to live is an outstanding achievement. Some people become so blinded by rage that they completely forget they're supposed to stop taking a deep breath, but remember, this is a journey to control your emotions. I need you to remember always to breathe in, and then you'll be able to see the silver lining. If it's a problem bugging you, you'll be able to stop fussing and eventually find a solution to it and trust me, that's good progress.

Tips for Day Two

- When you can take a deep breath in, you'll find the light at the end of the tunnel.

- Remind yourself that it's just a problem, and there's no problem without a solution.

- Worrying and getting angry have never held positive solutions.

Day Three — Forgive and Let Go

Maybe the breathing technique didn't help in soothing your anger. Can I ask, are you holding a grudge? If yes, the task of this day in particular for you. Holding a grudge is only detrimental to oneself, no matter how you see it. You may wish to punish the person by doing so, but it's a sham. The person may even be unaware of your grudge while you're dying on the inside.

Beautiful black woman, let go of that grudge and experience how light your heart can feel without resentment sitting on it. Task yourself today, text that person you've been angry with, ask how they are. It's okay if you don't want to seek closure because of whatever they might have done to you, but forgive them and stop thinking about that hurt because, trust me, it's not worth your stress.

Tips for Day Three

- Holding a grudge only weighs your heart down and affects your happiness.

- Decide to forgive that person today. You'll feel a lot better.

- It's okay if you can't forget the hurt they caused, but you have to forgive and move on.

Day Four — Exercise

Research has proven that exercise helps to deal with anger. Whatever type you're comfortable with, I want you to do. If it's cycling, jogging, stretching, aerobic, boxing and don't forget our very own dancing. Yes, dancing. It's my best way to exercise, and it helps me feel good, just syncing with the music and allowing it to cleanse my heart. Jogging is also great because I embrace the fresh air and see people around. Please do your research and whatever is good for you, do it.

Tips for Day Four

- Don't procrastinate exercising. Just as it helps you stay fit, it also boosts your mood and helps to soothe your angry mind.

- You can exercise daily, but if it's not convenient for you, list out the days you'd be chanced and enjoy yourself.

- I understand if you say you can't exercise in your moment of anger, but have you tried a mental exercise while in a clear state of mind? It helps a whole lot.

Day Five — Get a Stress Ball

I found out there's a medical explanation for carrying a stress ball around from my research.

Scientists say that the limbic part of the brain is where our emotions are, and stress balls stimulate nerves in the hand that connects to these limbic parts. In simpler terms, when you press a stress ball in anger, it helps you feel better, especially for small amounts of fury, high-stress levels, and anxiety. It worked a lot for one of my friends and what was even more astounding was the fact that she could carry a stress ball anywhere.

Tips for Day Five

• I think you should add a stress ball to your shopping list and give it a try.

• Stress balls help us cope with anger. It teaches us discipline because we're careful not to lash out at anyone but pour out wrath by pressing the stress ball.
• The stress ball is a great friend for people coping with anger; it doesn't complain but understands and supports you in this fight. I do too.

Day Six: Find People To Vent To.

Dear black woman, have you heard of anger support groups? It's a great way to check on your anger because you can identify with people who are going through similar anger issues with you. You meet and talk about your anger and its causes and solutions. I did this personally when the stress ball didn't seem to help me.

Tips for Day Six

• Stress balls may not work for you if your level of anger is at a high rate, so you might need to find other ways.

• Talking about your anger helps way more than you know it. It's a whole lot better way than keeping it in and letting it swallow you up.

• During my anger support group, I realized my anger issues were nothing compared to some people's own.

Day Seven - Go Over Everything

I require only one thing from you on this day, my black queen; that you go over everything we've done since day one. Did you breathe in during your fit of anger? Did it help you see the bright side of things? Have you forgiven and let go? How's your exercise coming? I hope you found the perfect one for you? Did you get that stress ball or opt for the support group? Don't tell me you did none; it would be unfair to me and my hard work writing this plan. Or did you do everything? Kudos, my beautiful black woman! Kudos! How's it been so far?

Tips For Day Seven

- Reflection is one of the significant tools for assessing oneself

- After consideration, even if you did not do everything thoroughly and ideally, don't be so hard and disappointed in yourself. Go again, and harder!

Week Two: Drain That Jealousy Out Of Your System

Day Eight - Acknowledge The Impact Of Jealousy

Many ladies fail to understand that it's natural to get jealous, but it doesn't mean it's a good thing. However, rather than accept that they're jealous and seek possible solutions out of its firm grip, they choose to deny the fact, thereby prolonging its effects. Accept you're jealous and accept the impact you've felt from jealousy.

Tips for Day Eight

• Many people are dying inside because they'd rather not admit to being jealous.
• The first step to getting rid of that jealousy is accepting that you are jealous.
• Are you with your pen? Can you write out a list of the effects of that jealousy? Can you see it's not helping you?

Day Nine- Find The Root

Once you finish accepting your jealousy and its impact, you have to begin clipping its grip out from your body, and the next step is to find the root cause of your jealousy. What's its trigger? Is it your friend's promotion? Your younger brother's marriage? Is your partner away on a business trip with another female? Whatever it is, you've got to figure it out.

Tips For Day Nine

• Once you finish accepting your jealousy, you have to find the cause.

- Take the whole day to look around you and make your observations.
- At your convenient time, whip out your pen and write down the cause of your jealousy. Look over it for a while and take a deep breath.

Day Ten - Let Your Voice Out

You can go through this step by talking to your partner or a third party. Let's say your partner is doing something to trigger jealousy in you rather than get angry at them; why don't you communicate. They might even be unaware. And if it's not something you can talk to a partner about, talking to a third party is always great. However, only do this with someone you trust.

Tips For Day Ten

- Set out an appropriate and convenient time for you and your partner to communicate and let them know how you feel.
- If the trigger for your jealousy isn't your partner and you can't talk about it with the person, you can always talk to any trusted friend.

Day Eleven: What Are Your Insecurities?

To master your emotions, you need to be truthful to yourself. Take your time to think about what your insecurities could be. Perhaps there are some underlying ones you might not know. This exercise is a step to knowing yourself better and would help deal with these insecurities you now know.

Tips For Day Eleven

- Please write down your insecurities and go over them.
- Some insecurities take a lot of self-confidence to go away.

- That insecurity could be the source of your jealousy.

Day Twelve - Begin Jealousy-Reducing Practices

These include practising gratitude for what you have. It also helps to reduce stress when you're grateful and content with your achievements. Realizing you're not where you were yesterday is a great spur to being thankful. Remind yourself of your self-worth and have it at the back of your mind that someone out there may be envious of your life, which should help boost your self-confidence. Lastly, practice coping techniques to help you at the moment. If you're overwhelmed with jealousy, you can try taking a walk, taking your time to do something calming, listening to music, writing your emotions down, and so on.

Tips For Day Twelve

- The activities for this day are quite a while lot. Split your time and begin each of them.

- I hope you're still with your notepad? List out ten amazing things about you.

- If you desire, get a notebook to write down your emotions.

Day Thirteen - Give it time

So far, you've come a long way in tackling jealousy. The practices you did the previous day are guaranteed to help you fight jealousy, and all you need is to give it time. So day thirteen, grab a cup of coffee, sip it in the most gentle and lady-like manner, and flip through the pages of your notepad. See how far you've come!

Tips For Day Thirteen

- Today doesn't require much from you other than relaxing and going through the previous tasks.

- Have fun today, and don't forget your daily exercise!

Day Fourteen: Talk to a therapist.

Here comes the final stage for mastering your jealousy, my dear black woman. If it's working positively for you, that's awesome, and I applaud your ability to master and bend it to your will. But if it still isn't despite all we've talked about, then it's a sign you have to see a therapist. Please don't be scared. It's not a bumpy ride.

Tips For Day Fourteen

● Everyone is different, and while what I've written for this second week might have helped you become better, for others, it hasn't.

● My next piece of advice is that you see a therapist who'll walk with you till you've overcome.

Week Three: Coping With Loneliness

Day Fifteen - Find a Hobby

Whatever may be the cause of your loneliness, probably a breakup, retirement, or loss of your loved one, it's understandable to grieve for weeks. But it would be best if you didn't let that loneliness lead to depression. Begin the fight against loneliness by doing the things you've always wanted to do. Stop procrastinating!

Tips For Day Fifteen
● Everyone has what they love to do. Find yours.
● If you've been using your busy schedule as an excuse not to do your hobby, you might as well start and get your mind occupied whenever you feel lonely.

Day Sixteen - Decide To Volunteer
Being a volunteer in a charity organization or any good organization not only fights loneliness but boosts your happiness. You get out of your house and meet new people while doing something good. It's a lovely feeling.

Tips For Day Sixteen

• It's a great idea to search for organizations around you to act as a volunteer.

• Doing service work to people can help get your mind off that thought for a while.

Day Seventeen - Rebuild Old Relationships

There have been some relationships you might have ignored for too long. My dear black woman, don't you think it's time you revive them? I'm talking about the ones that used to give you so much joy you never wanted to be anywhere if not with them. It's not too late to start rebuilding. If you're losing how to begin, I suggest you go through a mutual friend. Things would be a lot easier.

Tips For Day Seventeen

• Sometimes, we spend so much time on something or someone we forget the ones who used to bring us joy.

• In fighting loneliness, socializing is key, and what better way to start other than talking with old friends?

Day Eighteen: Get That Pet You've Always Wanted.

Getting a pet helps in many ways. First of all, they're great companions and true lovers, especially a dog which stays with you through thick and thin. Also, taking your dog out for a walk helps you meet new people and fellow dog-walkers. It also encourages you to exercise.

Tips For Day Eighteen

• Most people get a pet for companionship.

• When I was going through a heartbreak, I got myself a dog, and trust me; my dog helped keep me in the company that I shed tears the day she died.

Day Nineteen - Why Not Sports?

I ask this question again, why not sports? There are many benefits linked with engaging in sports; physical, emotional, social benefits. Engaging in team sports helps you meet new people and even make friends while fighting your loneliness.

Tips For Day Nineteen

• Participating in sports will serve as a health booster and help meet new people.

• You can also make friends and business partners through sports.

Day Twenty - Books And Socializing

Books and Socializing go together because of book clubs. Book lovers are usually interested in either being a part of a book club or setting up their own. People interested in books gather at a specific time to discuss books. It opens your mind to different people's thoughts and helps develop you mentally.

Tips For Day Twenty

• Book clubs are usually fun for book lovers.

• Take a walk out of your home and find a good book club around you.

Day Twenty-One - Find Online Support

Sometimes, you may be unable to associate with people, but trying online can be more accessible. If your loved ones are far away, chatting with them via social media platforms and video calling via Skype is a great way to combat loneliness. On the other hand, if you're looking for friendship online, it's great too, but you have to be extra careful to avoid scammers.

Tips For Day Twenty-One

• You can set up a social media account to connect with your loved ones far away.

• It would help if you trod with care while talking to strangers online; some are harbingers of evil.

Week Four: Stop Feeding That Guilt

Day Twenty-Two - Spell Out Your Guilt

Let's begin by stating your guilt. I hope you're with your notebook and pen. Whatever that's eating up your mind poorly, I need you to write down. This exercise is as easy as it can be and challenging because of the emotions that could overwhelm you, but I need you to be strong and do this. When you finish stating your guilt, think about what the source could be.

Tips For Day Twenty-Two

• Trying to suppress your guilt doesn't help matters. You have to admit and accept it.

• Guilt doesn't always have to be about what you've done. It can be a result of an experience, maybe surviving an accident.

• People can guilt-trip you when you're not wrong.

Day Twenty-Three - Say That Apology And Make Amends

Apologies always have to come before amendments. It requires you to apologize to whoever you've hurt and apologized to yourself. Oh yes, sometimes you deserve an apology when you cling to that guilt and blame yourself constantly. So if you've been beating yourself up as a form of punishment, I advise you to apologize to your beautiful self and make amends.

Tips For Day Twenty-Three

• Asking for forgiveness doesn't necessarily mean the person you've hurt would forgive you immediately or at all, but it helps you heal faster.

• Sometimes you need to tell yourself it isn't your fault and get over some things.

• To decide to make amends means you've decided to change, and that's a massive step to mastering your emotions.

Day Twenty-Four - Letting Your Guilt Teach You

How did day twenty-three go? Did you ask that person for forgiveness? What did they say? As I said earlier, some people may not forgive you because of how hurt they are, but you don't have to slide into depression, my black queen. Take solace in the fact that you're genuinely repentant and choose to move on. Work on that habit that marred your relationship; stop it if it's a bad one. Now you're going to need your notepad again. I need you to write out the lessons you've learned. What do you regret doing? What would you not want to do anymore?

Tips For Day Twenty-Four

- Identify the behavior behind your guilt and work on it. It might take a while to find it, but once you do, be assured you've solved half of your problem.

- Understand that you can't change your past, but you can work on the present.

Day Twenty-Five - Be Grateful For That Guilt

I know this is concise work, but let me share this story with you. We can't work every day and not have some fun, not so? A few weeks back, I was to go on a date with a lady, but I fell under the weather. Rather than be honest and go straight to the point, I told her I would make it, but I didn't, and to date, she sees me as a liar and untrustworthy person. It's funny if you look at it from an abstract perspective, but then again, it taught me never to lie. And up to date, I'm meticulous in telling the truth because I know the consequences can be grave at times. So be grateful for that guilt you're feeling; it helps you feel human. While being grateful, use it to your advantage rather than let it destroy you.

Tips For Day Twenty-Five

- Most negative emotions can be used to our advantage rather than breed more negative ones.

- Let your guilt guide you to become a better person.

Day Twenty-Six - Take It Easy On Yourself

I am hammering on what I said initially on day twenty-three. Forgive Yourself. It's your fault, I understand. But how long can you continue to wallow in depression and self-inflicted pain? If someone keeps guilt-tripping you, you've got to walk away from that person and take it easy on yourself. Allow yourself to heal, my dear black woman.

Tips For Day Twenty-Six

- Most people set stumbling blocks to their growth and happiness by refusing to forgive themselves

- It's okay to feel remorseful, but don't let that shame eat you up.

Day Twenty-Seven - Begin To Work On Your Self-Esteem

I understand that guilt and shame come hand in hand and feeling ashamed downthrows on your self-esteem. You're on a journey to becoming a much better you, and how can you do that without your self-esteem in place? Once you've forgiven yourself, begin to work on your self-esteem by declaring only positive words about yourself.

Tips For Day Twenty-Seven

- Learning to forgive yourself helps you overcome your shame

- If you want to boost your self-esteem, show compassion to yourself. Remember what we talked about self-love?

Day Twenty-Eight - Meet With Your Therapist

It's day twenty-eight already, my beautiful black woman. How far have you dealt with that guilt? Do you still feel so guilty? Then I may not understand how bad it is, so please talk to your therapist. Therapists know how best to handle things, and trust me, you'll feel better in no time.

Tips For Day Twenty-Eight

- An excellent step to showing yourself love is asking for help when you're unable to help yourself.

- There's no shame in telling someone you need help.

Week Five: Getting Over Disappointments

Day Twenty-Nine: Be Human; Feel.

When disappointed, please do not push it deep inside. It would only worsen matters because you'll still feel those emotions at unexpected times. It's not a death sentence to be disappointed. Maybe you hoped in someone or something or went the extra mile, and the results were the opposite of what you wished for, it happens sometimes, and that's okay. Trust me on this. So accept that disappointment, but DO NOT dwell in it for too long.

Tips For Day Twenty-Nine

• Don't hide your disappointment with a big smile, pretending everything is okay.

• Pretense kills faster than acceptance.

Day Thirty- Say To Yourself - You're Not A Disappointment

It's day thirty and the second day of this week. We just started on this journey, my beautiful black queen. I sincerely hope you're not tired. Now that you've accepted that disappointment and felt it, can you let me tell you that you're not a disappointment and you'd believe it? Do yourself the favor of going through the things you wrote about yourself and let yourself know that you're not a disappointment.

Tips For Day Thirty

• That you had a setback doesn't mean you're a failure.

• Because you were disappointed or disappointed in someone doesn't mean it can happen another time.
• If you step out of your comfort zone, disappointments are sure to occur at certain times.

Day Thirty-One - You're Not A god That Can Control Everything

As far as you cannot control everything in this life, my beautiful black woman has to be prepared for disappointments. People disappoint, and you are people, so sometimes it can happen to you. It's a natural phenomenon, so why exactly do you have to beat yourself up or it?

Tips For Day Thirty-One

• Setbacks are a sign that you're trying to grow, so it's alright.

• If you had no control over a situation, you should not feel guilty for what happened.

Day Thirty-Two - Constantly Seeking Perfection Can Be Unhealthy

If you're the type that always expects the actions of others to be perfect, sorry to burst your bubbles, but you're going to get disappointed more often than not. Do you remember what we discussed in Chapter Nine about perfection? So you should know the strains constantly seeking perfection may cause to you.

Tips For Day Thirty-Two

• It's only proper that you adjust your expectations from people and not expect too much.

• If you're a perfectionist, you might procrastinate a lot due to fear of your work not being perfect.

• Constantly expecting perfection from people can cause a strain on your relationship with them.

Day Thirty-Three: Learn from it.

When you stop wallowing in the sorrow that comes with disappointment, you'll be able to see your mistakes clearly and learn your lessons.

Tips For Day Thirty-Three

• Ask yourself what it is you can do differently next time.

• Also, think about the one thing you can learn from this experience.
Day Thirty-Four: Create Time For A Break.

Sometimes all you need is a break from everything. Instead of going back right in after a disappointment and overworking yourself, I suggest you take a break. Starting work again in a hazy state of mind is not advisable to create time from your busy schedule to recharge, and then you can begin.

Tips For Day Thirty-Four

• Don't rush your healing process. You're allowed to take your time.

• Another disappointment might crush you if you jump back in with no rest or plan.

Day Thirty-Five - Stop The Comparisons

My dear black woman, it's day thirty-five and the last day of this week. I hope you've understood that you're not supposed to wallow so much in your disappointments and that they're natural. A significant step to improving your self-esteem is to stop comparing yourself with others. Your achievements and their achievements are not the same because you're not the same person and everyone has a different time for their success story. Focus on yourself and start again with baby steps.

Tips For Day Thirty-Five

• There'll always be people ahead of you, but don't forget it's your race, and only yours.

• Rather than compare yourself with other people, why don't you compare yourself to your present self to your former self instead of comparing yourself with other people?

• Focusing on yourself is a helpful habit in building your self-esteem.

Week Six: Coping With Apathy

Day Thirty-Six - Identifying The Root Cause

It may be hard to find the cause of your apathy, especially when you don't take note of your emotions. Keeping a mental or physical record of your feelings can help you know why you're feeling indifferent. Be careful not to judge your feelings and try to understand yourself.

Tips For Day Thirty-Six

• Think back and check if any recent happening negatively impacted you.

• Check your daily routine if it's wearing you out, and change it.

Day Thirty-Seven - Begin That Old Hobby Again

Being in a numb state can be a whole lot as you slowly watch yourself losing a grip of all the things that once got you excited and gave you joy. My dear black woman, I need you to pause and think about what you loved doing and give them a try.

Tips For Day Thirty-Seven

• Was it singing that gave you joy? Try doing it again.

• Do you enjoy hanging out with friends? Or simply reading a book? Do whatever brings you joy.

Day Thirty-Eight - Open Your Mind To Only Positive Thoughts

Thoughts have the capacity of influencing how we feel, negative and positive thoughts alike. More often than not, negative reviews are bound to come in to unsettle you, but you have to stop them and declare positivity into your life.

Tips For Day Thirty-Eight

• Write out positive words in your notepad to declare over your life.

• Some positive words to say to yourself are, "I open my mind to positive ideas that will change my beliefs. I agree to change my life intentionally."

Day Thirty-Nine: Step Out Of Your Comfort Zone.

Endorphins are great mood boosters, and exercise helps in their release. So if you're feeling indifferent, it's best that you step out of your comfort zone and socialize with people and try activities. Anything but sit at home idling about.

Tips For Day Thirty-Nine

• You don't have to swim a thousand miles before you decide to exercise. Just taking a few steps for ten minutes will do great to boost your mood.

• The little steps can sometimes reverse even the most extreme apathy we take daily.

Day Forty - Meditate Daily

Meditation has been known since the onset to be a great mood booster. It helps you relax and experience ultimate tranquility, allowing your mind to be calm. Sometimes stress can be a factor of apathy, and all you need to do is meditate.

Tips For Day Forty

• Meditation helps to slow our minds and allow us to breathe correctly.

• You can always google ways to meditate if you're unsure where to start.

Day Forty-One - Celebrate Every Win

If your apathy results from your work, you're probably tired. I want you to look on the bright side and realize that you're still winning. Don't ignore the small wins, and make sure to take yourself on a date once in a while because you deserve to be spoilt.

Tips For Day Forty-One

• You can celebrate yourself by giving yourself gifts whenever you achieve something. It doesn't necessarily have to be significant.

• Have you worked all year long, and you're weary? Take a break and go on that vacation.

Day Forty-Two - Change Your Scenery

Your apathy could result from your environment, my beautiful black woman. As said in the tips for Day Forty-One, I think you deserve that vacation or even move out entirely. I know it sounds like running away when I talk about leaving your current environment altogether, but it isn't. See it as the motivation you may need to be interested in things again.

Tips For Day Forty-Two

• Even a weekend away from your place can do magic in boosting your mood.

• If your financial situation or work cannot allow that vacation, that's fine. You can still explore your neighborhood or even go hiking!

Week Seven: Putting Your Abusiveness In Check

Day Forty-Three – Admittance

First of all, I need you to get something straight. Abuse is not only about physical abuse. So while we walk together this week, I need you to have emotional, verbal, and physical abuse in mind. As a lady, physical abuse may not be as prevalent in you as in a man, but what about emotional and verbal abuse? You might see the signs of abuse in your relationship, but you might not find out in time that you're the abuser. The first step to getting rid of your abusive behavior is accepting that you're the problem and admitting it.

Tips For Day Forty-Three

• When you pause to think about your actions, you might find out you're the one at fault.

• That you're the abuser in your relationship doesn't mean you're a devil, but it isn't a good thing either, so you're going to have to work on it.

Day Forty-Four - Make A Commitment To Change

How did your reflection go yesterday? Did you find that you're at fault or not? If you are, I'm glad you've accepted. Today, we're going to do a little exercise. I want you to think about your actions to your partner, and if you want your relationship to get better, then you're going to have to commit to change. I understand that it's not going to be an easy process. Still, it's a habit you have to get rid of, so you can bookmark this page and look back at it every day for the rest of your journey and work towards it. You also have to change for your own sake and not just keep that relationship with your partner. This part is essential.

Tips For Day Forty-Four

• Sticking to old habits is a lot easier than changing, but you have to choose to be a better version of yourself.

• Have it in mind that change is never easy. Then think about the worthiness of this cause and make a decision.

Motivate yourself daily to work towards that change.

Day Forty-Five – Apologize

Many abusers don't deem it fit to listen to their partners and know how they feel. This step is crucial, and I suggest you do this carefully. Have a conversation with your partner and let them tell you how they think about some of your actions, and when you finish with that, do this - Apologize. No, don't explain yourself. Apologize.

Tips For Day Forty-Five
• Communication is crucial, but most people seem to ignore it. To know what you're doing to hurt your partner, you need to talk to them.

• Try to put yourself in their shoes and understand them. No one likes to suffer abuse, so you as the abuser should understand and ask for their forgiveness.

• If you're no longer with that partner, you can still go ahead with this task to give you an idea of what to do and what not to do in your next relationship.

Day Forty-Six - Don't Give Excuses.

While you communicate with the person you're abusing or have abused, you might want to get defensive. I understand that abusive persons are not necessarily sadistic people but people in deep suffering. This deep suffering affects their self-esteem and makes them insecure and vulnerable, bringing others down in their sorry state. So if this is your case, giving excuses or justifying your actions will not help. Only let them understand what you're going through and ask for help or opt-out to go through it yourself without hurting anyone.

Tips For Day Forty-Six

• People you abuse would not listen to your justification after you've abused them.

• Let your partner know what you're going through and find ways to become a better you.

Day Forty-Seven - Forgive Yourself

I know it's a whole lot realizing that you're an abuser, but it's not a death sentence. It's what you've done, but it shouldn't define who you are. Everyone is capable of good within them. You can start forgiving yourself by taking responsibility for your actions rather than blaming others. This way, you can stop hurting other people and easily forgive yourself.

Tips For Day Forty-Seven

●   Everyone can change, and forgiveness is a significant step to change.

●   Abuse is something people do, but it isn't who they are. Don't let guilt eat you up poorly. Ask for forgiveness, forgive yourself and decide to change.

Day Forty-Eight - Don't Expect Too Much.

At times you can expect too much from your partner, probably because you're better than them in something or you're a perfectionist. You tend to get irritated when they don't match your expectations-thereby abusing them and blaming them for not meeting your expectations. You need to chill out and give them a break. No one is like you, so you shouldn't expect too much from anyone. Also, don't expect your partner to forgive you because you apologize. Some wounds may be too deep that they for you to ignore, but take solace in the fact that you've admitted to your flaws and chosen to be a better you.

Tips For Day Forty-Eight

●   Lowering your expectations of people sets you and them free from unnecessary patterns.

●   Please don't blame your partner because he failed to meet your expectations.

- Focus on forgiving yourself without expecting forgiveness from others.

Day Forty-Nine - See A Therapist

Sometimes abuse doesn't always stem from the pain we feel but can include mental health conditions. I implore you, my beautiful black woman, to set aside a day to meet with a counselor or therapist and pour out your heart to them.

Tips For Day Forty-Nine

- Some people stop behaviors faster when they're seeing a therapist. You can give it a try if self-help isn't working for you.

- You may not know that you have a mental disorder causing your abuse; always seek professional help before things get out of hand.

Week Eight: Working On Your Passive-Aggressive Tendencies

Day Fifty - Recognizing Your Passive-Aggressive Behavior

To be passively aggressive means to show your anger in indirect ways like pouting, stubbornness, sulking, and so on. Have you thought about what your own is?

Tips For Day Fifty

- Observe yourself and know what your passive-aggressive behavior is.
- These behaviors don't develop in one day and will take time to change.

Day Fifty-One - Observe Other People

Another person may be exhibiting as much passive-aggressive behavior as you are showing in response to yours. Look out for them. Also, did you stop to wonder if you're overreacting?

Tips For Day Fifty-One

• Communication is more than talking and listening openly and directly. You also have to read the signs and unspoken messages.

Day Fifty-Two - Stop Being Sarcastic

Most passive-aggressive people resort to sarcasm in heated situations, but this only fuels fire.

Tips For Day Fifty-Two

• Some sarcastic words are, "yeah, right." "Whatever." "Good for you." Try to avoid them when in a quarrel.

Day Fifty-Three - Stop The Temporary Compliance

It happens when you accept a job and submit the task late, usually because of procrastination. If you feel unappreciated or underpaid, this could be a cause. Realize the effects of your behavior and work on the grounds of your temporary compliance.

Tips For Day Fifty-Three

• If you feel unappreciated, try to express your feelings rather than keep them.

• It's good to support your partner in doing the chores to quell passive aggression from building up in them.

Day Fifty-Four - Stop Intentionally Being Inefficient

If you're an employee, stop being hostile or stop giving less than required energy at work and then playing the victim card. You know how detrimental it can be to you and your organization, so you need to stop.

Tips For Day Fifty-Four

- If you're holding grudges with anyone, it's best to tell them.

- Inefficiency can manifest in taking a long time to wash the dishes because you're unhappy with doing the chore.

Day Fifty-Five - Face That Problem

Now it's time to stop your habit of passive aggression. Stop avoiding that problem and face it before it escalates into something big.

Tips For Day Fifty-Five

- Stop procrastinating or stalling at work or home because you don't want to face a problem.

- Avoiding problems and exhibiting passive aggression can cause people to become angry with you.

Day Fifty-Six - Avoid The Desire To Revenge Or Self-Deprecate

Stop spreading rumors about that person who upset you. Stop causing setbacks in that project because you're offended because you'd still be affected either way. Also, stop harming yourself because you're trying to get back at someone who might be unaware that they hurt you.

Tips For Day Fifty-Six

- Sabotaging someone or something is an act of wickedness you should avoid.

- Talk things through and let go of that judge.

Week Nine: Managing Stress and Anxiety

Day Fifty-Seven - Take A Break
If you're feeling stressed out, it's a sign that your body needs a break. Step back to relax.

Tips For Day Fifty-Seven

- Listen to music, dance, do whatever helps relieve your stress.

Day Fifty-Eight - Get Enough Sleep

You might be anxious and stressed because you're not getting enough sleep.

Day Fifty-Nine - Eat Healthy

Do not skip meals and always eat balanced diets.

Tips For Day Fifty-Nine

- Get a reminder to always eat on time.

- Do not stress-eat.

- Always carry healthy snacks around.

Day Sixty - Exercise Daily

Exercise as it boosts your self-esteem and reduces anxiety.

Tips For Day Sixty

- Taking deep breaths is a form of fitness.

- Count to ten slowly. You could exceed this number.

Day Sixty-One - Allow Yourself To Humour

Laughter, they say, is good medicine. So whenever you're stressed, listening to or watching comedies is an excellent way to relieve off your stress and anxiety.

Tips For Day Sixty-One

- Hanging out with friends can also bring you happiness.

- Allow yourself to find humor in most situations.

Day Sixty-Two - Know Your Triggers

Write out what's triggering your stress and anxiety in your notepad and look for ways to reduce these triggers.

Tips For Day Sixty-Two

- If work is stressing you, you should probably take a break.
- Going on a vacation away from that trigger is a great way to manage stress.

Day Sixty-Three - Talk To Someone

If you're still feeling anxious or stressed, you should probably see a therapist, counselor, or doctor.

Tips For Day Sixty-Three

- It's okay to tell your friends you're overwhelmed and need your private time.

Week Ten - Dealing With Embarrassments

Day Sixty-Four - It's In The Past

You need to understand that wallowing in the past will not help matters because you can't change your history. Embarrassments are bound to happen, and all you can do is move on.

Tips for Day Sixty-Four

- I know it can be hard to move on at times, but dwelling in your past won't help as well.

Day Sixty-Five - There's No Need To Apologize

It's a natural phenomenon to feel embarrassed, but you're not guilty of anything, so you don't have to apologize.

Tips for Day Sixty-Five

- You shouldn't apologize because you trip in front of people. These things happen.

Day Sixty-Six - Laugh It Out

As you know, embarrassment is in the past so do well to laugh at the incident as a means of letting go.

Tips for Day Sixty-Six

- It'll be easier to laugh at the situation when you can look at things from the proper perspective.

Day Sixty-Seven - Tell Someone Else

If you're not sure how to stop feeling embarrassed, you should tell your trusted friends about it. Who knows, they could even laugh about it with you, and you'd feel a whole lot better.

Tips for Day Sixty-Seven

- It's great to have a support system that makes you feel a whole lot better.

- Meeting with someone who wouldn't judge you and has gone through this experience is a blessing.

Day Sixty-Eight - It's Okay To Be Afraid

I understand that you're afraid to go to that place or try out that thing or see that person because of the embarrassment you faced. But you have to overcome that fear if you're going to be able to conquer it.

Tips for Day Sixty-Eight

- Don't hinder your growth because of fear.

- Believe that others also have things pricking their mind and that you're strong enough to overcome.

Day Sixty-Nine - Focus On The Present

Once you're able to deal with the embarrassments from your past, it's time, my beautiful black woman, to focus on the present.

Tips for Day Sixty-Nine

- Focusing on the present helps you to stop dwelling in the past.

- What do you intend to do now? Where are you now? Do you feel better? Ask these questions.

Day Seventy - Try Again

It's time to face your fears and try again. Have you avoided meeting that crush since the day you slipped in front of everyone, including him? You've got to stop hiding and try again.

Tips for Day Seventy

- Heal from that embarrassment and start being productive.

- Understand that sometimes, things can go wrong, and that's fine.

Week Eleven - Steps To Stop Feeling Self-Conscious

Day Seventy-One - Stop Thinking Negatively

An excellent step to stop feeling self-conscious is to accept that you think negatively and decide to stop it.

Tips for Day Seventy-One

If you're at the club and think someone is staring at you and mocking you inwardly, most times, it's not even true.

Day Seventy-Two - Stop Putting People On Pedestals

Stop believing everyone else is better than you because you have what it takes even to be better.

Tips for Day Seventy-Two

•   We often feel insecure because we place others on pedestals who don't deserve such glorification.

•   Remember that no one is perfect, and everyone has their bad moments.

Day Seventy-Three - Be Your Motivation

If your friend was in your situation, I'm guessing you would motivate them to feel better, so do the same for yourself.

Tips for Day Seventy-Three

•   Think of what you'd tell your self-conscious friend to help them stop worrying.

- Read ego-boosting words to yourself.

- Have pep talks and show yourself excess love.

Day Seventy-Four - Love Yourself

Loving yourself entails accepting every part of you wholeheartedly, including that flaw. Know your strengths and work on them to boost your self-confidence.

Tips for Day Seventy-Four

- Focus on yourself and revel in your glory.

- Despite your flaws, remember that you have something to bring to the table that'll leave people wanting more.

Day Seventy-Five - You're Probably Overthinking Things

While you're worried about others, do you know that these people are jumbled up with thoughts?

Tips for Day Seventy-Five

- Most times, when we get out of the spotlight, we realize no one was looking, and it's all just in our heads.

- Did you stop to check if you're overthinking things?

Day Seventy-Six - Give It Your All

Rather than shrink back, it would be best to give your everything. If you're dancing before a crowd, go all in. That way, people will be excited to watch you, and they wouldn't even see through your Insecurities.

Tips for Day Seventy-Six

- Watching someone with enthusiasm helps them relax in their environment and allows zero room for anyone to judge them.

Day Seventy-Seven - Start From The Root Cause

Being self-conscious is unlikely to go away if you don't find the cause and deal with it quickly. Whatever is making you feel anxious, you have to face it bravely.

Tips for Day Seventy-Seven

• Remember our talk on courage? You'll need it to face the causes of your self-consciousness.

• Build your confidence by taking positive actions and celebrating those positive results.

Week Twelve- Handling Resentment

Day Seventy-Eight: Accept and feel your emotions. Don't ignore those feelings. Accept them.

Tips for Day Seventy-Eight

• Saying out loud what you feel helps you accept them

• Allowing those feelings to build inside of you will cause harm to you.

Day Seventy-Nine - What's Behind Your Resentment

Think about what made you feel this way. It could also be a person.

Tips for Day Seventy-Nine

• You can task yourself with remembering when these feelings started

• Your resentment could be because you feel unappreciated or overwhelmed.

Day Eighty - Stop Allowing Room For Those Negative Thoughts

It's normal to remember the past and feel terrible, but you have to stop those negative thoughts.

Tips for Day Eighty

• When you notice those negative thoughts will overwhelm you, distract yourself by doing an activity.

• Choosing to call a friend is a great distraction.

Day Eighty-one - Keep Track Of Your Feelings With A Journal

When you can not talk to someone about your emotions, venting out your resentment in your journal is another excellent option.

Tips for Day Eighty-one

• Writing allows you room to assess the situation from a different perspective and show you what is and what isn't.

Day Eighty-two - Talk To That Person

If you're having resentment against a person, it's best to talk to them about it.

Tips for Day Eighty-two

• Be assertive when you're stating what you do not like.
• If they refuse to change after you've talked to them, then you might have to let go.

Day Eighty-three - Don't Expect Too Much.

I think I've hammered on this enough that no one is perfect, so you shouldn't let yourself feel the disappointment of expecting too much.

Tips for Day Eighty-three

• If they fail to do something you wish they'd do, you can talk to them about it or take solace in the fact that they genuinely care.

• If at all they'll change, it'll take time, so be patient.

Day Eighty-four - See A Therapist

Harboring resentment can be detrimental to your health and cause depression to you. It can even affect your relationships with other people. Therefore, you should see a therapist or counselor to talk to them about your feelings.

Tips for Day Eighty-Four

• Therapists can help you through the stages of getting past resentment and provides techniques to help you cope.

Week Thirteen - Stopping The Habit Of Being Judgemental

Day Eighty-five - Know When You're Judging Someone

Be conscious of your thoughts and nip that judgmental thought in the bud by questioning the importance of those thoughts.

Tips for Day Eighty-Five

• If you think someone needs to lose weight, ask yourself how that's any of your business and opt for a compliment instead.
• If those thoughts do not benefit you, they shouldn't even be there in the first place.

Day Eighty-six - Take A Deep Breath

The frontal lobe of your brain helps you to be calm. Taking a deep breath activates it more.

Tips for Day Eighty-six

• Take deep breaths often so that it becomes a habit. It's helpful.

Day Eighty-seven - Be In Charge Of Your Thoughts And Feelings

Allowing disgust to control you makes you a slave to it. Be in charge of your emotions.

Tips for Day Eighty-Seven

• You're not entitled to feel disgusted. Don't convince yourself otherwise.

Day Eighty-Eight - Put Yourself In Their Shoes

You have to accept that you're not other people and that they have the right to their decisions. You have no control over them so try to understand their perspective instead of judging them.

Tips for Day Eighty-Eight

• It's unfair to judge someone without first hearing their story. Could you get to know them first?
• That person you're considering might be who he is because of his upbringing, but you're too blind to see it.

Day Eighty-Nine - Show Gratitude

As two fingers are not the same, you're not on the same level with certain persons. Express gratitude for where you are and to everyone who has helped you grow.

Tips for Day Eighty-Nine

• Remember to take a deep breath and wish them good whenever you feel tempted to judge someone or say something that would hurt them.

Day Ninety - Cultivate Compassion

My beautiful black woman, here we are. The last day! Go over everything we've talked about and cultivate the virtue of compassion in you. You won't judge anyone with it because you're moved to empathize with them.

Tips for Day Ninety

- A compassionate person is a happy person.

- To be human, you have to get rid of that negative thought about someone.

Conclusion

I had quite a lot of fun writing this book for you, my dear black woman. Every chapter was done to fill you with love, strength, motivation, and energy. They were also noted to spur you to action. To become a much better version of yourself who is full of potential and so much greatness.

I started this book with 'how to deal with negative emotions because I understood perfectly the turbulence of emotions. It is not an easy one to manage at all. I hope the tips in this book help you immensely. But, you have to be patient with yourself as well. The Italians would say poco a poco—little by little.

I explored self-love to understand what it means to love oneself truly. My dear, self-love is the most excellent romance ever. Love yourself wholly and proudly. It is the best thing you can do for yourself. I also explored courage. To do great things, even loving yourself, you would need a lot of courage. That is why I poured so much of myself into writing that chapter for you.

Did you enjoy the anxiety and self-worth chapters? I hope you did. Anxiety and self-worth issues are among the most significant problems black women usually face. I hope this book helps you deal with and manage them better. I also had great fun writing about beauty and body positivity. It is one topic I love so much. I hope you never let the world fill your head with so many ideas about beauty that you forget the wonderful that you are. In one of the chapters, beauty has no single definition. So, dare to be beautiful as you are and define it your way.

I hope the mental health part of this book awakens great zeal in you to care for your mental health with all the tenderness in the world. It is essential. Also, how did you enjoy the chapters about failures and pedestals? My dear woman, I urge you not to be afraid of failure. Live audaciously; it is okay to fall. What matters the most is rising again. But, never forget to learn lessons from every fall. Also, love your life on your terms. Pedestals are limiting. Don't walk through your life without the thrill you desire.

The ninety-day plan will be of immense help to you if you allow it to. Go through each day with love, dedication, and intent. You would be amazed at how well you would manage your emotions.

It is where we say goodbye, my dear black woman; it was beautiful telling my stories to you in this book and guiding you. Go on and be badass from this moment on. I love you dearly.

Thank You

You could have picked from dozens of other books, but you picked our book **Emotional Self Care for Black Women.**

So, THANK YOU for getting this book and for making it all the way to the end.

Could you please consider posting a review on Amazon?

Posting a positive review is the best and easiest way to support the work of independent authors like me.

Your feedback will help me to keep writing the kind of books that will help you get the results you want.

It can be something short and simple ☺

Thank you so much